VIOLENCE, TRANSFORMATION, AND THE SACRED

VIOLENCE,

TRANSFORMATION,

AND THE SACRED

"They Shall Be Called Children of God"

Margaret R. Pfeil and Tobias L. Winright,
Editors

THE ANNUAL PUBLICATION
OF THE COLLEGE THEOLOGY SOCIETY
2011
VOLUME 57

ORBIS BOOKS
Maryknoll, New York 10545

Founded in 1970, Orbis Books endeavors to publish works that enlighten the mind, nourish the spirit, and challenge the conscience. The publishing arm of the Maryknoll Fathers and Brothers, Orbis seeks to explore the global dimensions of the Christian faith and mission, to invite dialogue with diverse cultures and religious traditions, and to serve the cause of reconciliation and peace. The books published reflect the views of their authors and do not represent the official position of the Maryknoll Society. To learn more about Maryknoll and Orbis Books, please visit our website at www.maryknollsociety.org.

Library of Congress Cataloging-in-Publication Data

Violence, transformation, and the sacred : "they shall be called children of God" / Margaret R. Pfeil and Tobias L. Winright, editors.
    p. cm.—(The annual publication of the College Theology Society ; v. 57
    Includes bibliographical references.
    ISBN 978-1-57075-969-7; eISBN 978-1-60833-131-4
    1. Violence—Religious aspects—Christianity. I. Pfeil, Margaret R. II. Winright, Tobias L.
    BT736.15.V497 2011
    261.8'3—dc23
                                                            2011045705

Contents

Introduction

Margaret R. Pfeil and Tobias L. Winright

"In the field of theology, as in political science, there is extraordinary confusion about both terms of our subject, religion and violence. Few words in our common vocabulary have been subject to greater abuse or misuse."[1]

In the immediate aftermath of the horrific attacks on September 11, 2001, people in the United States asked: Who is to blame for such violence? Why did it happen? Where is God in all this? How should we respond? Because the nineteen hijackers were Saudi Arabian, Egyptian, United Arab Emirati, and Lebanese, the citizens and government of the United States responded in the subsequent weeks in a number of ways. One particularly tragic reaction at the outset was the killing, by a handful of independently acting citizens, of several persons because they looked Middle Eastern, including Balbir Singh Sodhi, a Sikh, who was gunned down on September 15 outside his gas station in Mesa, Arizona. A few weeks later, after identifying al-Qaeda and Osama bin Laden as responsible for this atrocity, the United States and the United Kingdom pursued another response by launching a "war on terrorism," beginning with Operation Enduring Freedom in Afghanistan on October 7, 2001.[2]

A more hopeful response over the ensuing years was the desire of many Americans to learn more about Islam and religious extremism, with a spate of scholarship from respected experts, such as John L. Esposito's *Unholy War: Terror in the Name of Islam,*[3] quickly reaching the hands of readers in coffee shops as well as in classrooms. At the same time, other bestselling books, such as Stephen Prothero's *Religious Literacy: What Every American*

Needs to Know—and Doesn't,[4] continued to lament Americans' lack of understanding of religion (including Christianity, let alone Islam), or such as New Atheist Christopher Hitchens's *God Is Not Great: How Religion Poisons Everything*,[5] blamed religion itself for the world's violence. Indeed, as we write this a decade later, questions still abound about violence, religion, and the prospects for hope and peace on our planet.

Although the number of wars has declined worldwide since 1999, the number of organized violent campaigns against civilians has increased.[6] From the civil war in Libya to the drug-related murders along the Mexico-U.S. border, from the Palestinian-Israeli conflict to the enmity in Burma, the examples of ongoing civilian casualties due to what we think of as forms of direct, overt, and organized violence—such as war and genocide—continue like the ticker at the bottom of our television screens. Undeniably, religion often appears as a variable in the equation of much—not all—of this violence, but why and how so? To even begin to answer these questions, it is imperative that we come to grips with these terms "religion" and "violence," about which Robert McAfee Brown has noted "there is extraordinary confusion. . . ."

When we were initially invited to serve as editors of this annual volume, the board of the College Theology Society expressed interest in a theme along the lines of "Violence and the Sacred," which of course immediately brought to mind the literary critic turned anthropologist René Girard and his groundbreaking book, *Violence and the Sacred*.[7] In 1997, in *My Hope for the Church: Critical Encouragement for the Twenty-First Century*, which was the last of over ninety books he authored, Father Bernard Häring devoted a chapter to "Today's Burning Issues," where he observed, "René Girard, Raymund Schwager, and many others have pointed to the centrality of violence and nonviolence in the total picture of human history, especially in our time."[8] While we wished to retain this focus on violence and the sacred, we also wanted to broaden the scope to include other perspectives on these questions, as well as to consider other manifestations of violence. Moreover, as Häring pointed out, nonviolence belongs in the picture, which is why we chose to call attention to hopeful signs of, or prospects for, *transformation*, as well as the possible role of theology—and theologians—on that score.[9]

Monika Hellwig once wrote, "As the world becomes smaller through technology and communications, and as the power of destruction becomes larger, the need for such reflection and for self-critical awareness becomes more and more urgent."[10] At the 2011 annual convention, members of the College Theology Society took time to do just that. The theme for the convention came to be "They Shall Be Called Children of God: Violence, Transformation, and the Sacred." The conference included four plenary assemblies with five presenters, and fifty-seven sectional meetings, with several joint sessions with members of The National Association of Baptist Professors of Religion. The papers considered a host of topics related to the theme. In addition to the papers from the plenary sessions, forty papers were submitted to us for possible publication in this annual volume, making our decisions—informed by the helpful feedback of scores of reviewers—challenging, to say the least. The essays included in this volume, we think, correlate in fresh and interesting ways with the theme of the convention, its Girardian undercurrents, and the vocation of theologians in the transformation of violence (hence the subtitle gleaned from Matthew 5:9, "Blessed are the peacemakers, for they shall be called children of God.").

Manifestations of Violence Viewed through a Theological Lens

In her plenary address, Shawn Copeland offered a trenchant examination of violence evidenced in "bruised human creation and bruised created nature." Interpretations of Judeo-Christian scripture in ecclesial tradition have yielded accounts of the notions of nature and matter that lend themselves to patriarchal, white supremacist, sexist, classist, and anthropocentric systemic violence visited most egregiously upon both human and other members of God's creation deemed inferior and expendable. Vocationally, she urged, the theologian must witness through passionate agapic love to God's abiding, endless love for all of God's creation in its interrelatedness, an ethical, moral, and religious task.

In response to Copeland, James Logan affirmed her insight that "what happens to people and what happens to the land [and the whole of the natural world] is the same thing." U.S. history reveals multivalent violence inflicted upon one particular manifestation of God's beautiful creation, the bodies of black persons, through the Middle Passage, enslavement, lynching, Jim and Jane Crow legislation, mass incarceration, and systemic sexual assault and harassment of the black female body specifically. "Wherever there is a struggle for the dignity of the Black body and its holistic presence in opposition to multiple strands of White Supremacy, there we have an environmentalist cause." If the College Theology Society is to strive toward the transformation of violence, Logan suggested, it will need to confront, in persevering love, its own practices and structures of white supremacy.

Elisabeth Vasko is the first of several authors in this volume to engage directly René Girard's theory of mimetic violence. In particular, she explores the correlation of his concept of surrogate victimage through scapegoating to cases of lesbian, gay, bisexual, and transgender (LGBT) bullying, attending to the ways in which sexualization of an already marginalized person systemically reinforces existing power differentials in favor of socially acceptable interpretations of masculinity and heterosexuality in both secular and sacred spaces.

As Brian Robinette notes, human beings are neurologically wired for imitation, and theologically, Girard's theory holds hope for the possibility of good mimesis, finding ultimate expression in Jesus Christ, who invited his followers to cultivate desire for God as part of Christian discipleship. While the potential for conflict between subjects over a contested object of desire is very real, the triangularity of desire also presents an opportunity to uphold the dignity of "the other" through empathy and to direct human desire toward contemplative practices of transformation of violence.

Secular and Sacred: Theoretical Considerations

William Clark writes of some of his students' reaction to Osama bin Laden's killing as a "dramatic demonstration of what must be called 'sacred violence.'" Some of them noticed a tension between their perceived patriotic and faith commitments in a broader national U.S. context that readily sacralized bin Laden's death. The "social cohesion" resulting from the mass scapegoating of bin Laden took root in violence and, uninterrupted, would lead to further unrest, both interiorly and exteriorly.

Daniel Horan, evoking Copeland's perceptive comments about the cooptation of the notion of nature for violent ends of domination, writes of the vehement reaction to his blog after bin Laden's death. He critiqued what philosopher Jamie Smith has called the secular liturgy of American nationalism in which violence is perceived as part of "the nature of the world." In John Caputo's Christian engagement with deconstruction, he finds an important resource for a Christian reclamation of the vision of the "kingdom of God" in Christian worship over against its antithesis, the concept of kingdom at stake in the secular liturgy of American nationalism.

Do terms such as "sacralized violence" and "liturgies of American nationalism" imply a necessary connection between religion and violence? When nationalism, once so closely held that it seems to constitute a sort of civil religion, leads to violence, is that violence considered secular or religious in nature? In his plenary address, William Cavanaugh invited the audience to explore the "myth of religious violence" by way of addressing such questions. Creation of the categories of "religious" and "secular" in Western parlance, he argued, has paved the way for a dichotomy between the supposedly secular, rational peacemakers of the West and their foil, characterized as irrational, religious fanatics of the Muslim world. The very category of "the religious" thus becomes defined as violent, divisive, and irrational, thereby justifying use of violence as a "rational response" on the part of "the secular." He advised closer attention to the problem of violence, however it is justified.

To counter the logic of the world that justifies violence, Horan highlights Caputo's appeal to the illogical, poetic qualities of God's promised reign, the possibility of the impossible seen in Jesus' embodiment of forgiveness and invitation to *metanoia* in the face of violence: The stranger becomes neighbor, the sinners receive preference over the righteous, and the last are first. Each of these contrasts posits a relationship. The last are so designated only in necessary connection with the first; the self needs the other to establish a particular identity.

This intersubjective relationality, as Copeland indicated, ultimately finds grounding in God. In Georges Rouault's work, Gael Mooney sees a fine example of celebrating divine beauty through the face of the other, encountered not as mimetic rival but rather as gift and invitation to mutuality. This artist's depictions consistently relate Jesus Christ's passion to the suffering of those on the societal and global margins, cutting across boundaries of social class as well as divisions between the sacred and profane. Particularly through his portrayal of clowns, often employing a mirroring technique, Rouault sought to encourage empathetic identification with them, highlighting the way in which all humans navigate the tension between surface representation and the interior life. Mooney's treatment of Rouault's artistic method invites correlation with Girard's understanding of good mimesis.

Transformation of Violence

Girard's concept of "good mimesis" also finds application in early Christian monastic practice, as Robinette notes. Cassian and Evagrius offer models of the quotidian asceticism that shapes the virtuous imitation of Jesus. John Kruse's careful treatment of Clare of Assisi's *askesis* of absolute poverty as integral to her practice of nonviolence represents a similar example of the good mimesis of Christian discipleship. Following Jesus' practice, she let go of all possessions in order to become ever more fully available to, and possessed by, God's love.

This volume's authors, in distinct but complementary ways, highlight a few ascetic practices useful in the process of transforming violence. First, St. Clare, like the desert fathers and mothers, understood the inextricable relationship between interior and exterior transformation. The inner temptations toward violent thoughts, dispositions, and behavior, including disordered love of material goods, represent the necessary starting place of transformation for every person desiring to work for peace in the interpersonal and societal contexts. In his essay, J. Milburn Thompson highlights Franciscan ascetic practice as a key component of developing a creation-centered consciousness as part of peacebuilding.

Daniel Scheid's essay implicitly reflects the implications of Thompson's suggestion and reinforces Copeland's analysis of contemporary manifestations of violence seen from the standpoint of history's marginalized. He appeals to another representative of Franciscan spirituality, Leonardo Boff, to contribute to the discussion of just peacemaking in the field of Christian ethics, offering a corrective: The theory of just peacemaking ought to consider a focus on dignified subsistence rather than sustainable development, given that practices of global economic development are often at odds with sustainable use of natural resources. Sharing Boff's contemplative focus on the world's poor, he encourages the promotion of ecological subsidiarity, in which the dignified well-being of local communities and their interrelationship with particular ecosystems would serve as a counterweight to the dominant, globalized approach to development.

Second, hospitality to the other through contemplative attention and awareness emerges as a thread woven through the essays of Copeland, Mooney, Robinette, Clark, and Thompson. Scott MacDougall also takes up the issue from the angle of intellectual hospitality, raising the meta-question of the ethics of doing scholarship as he examines the coherence between John Milbank's theoretical framework of radical orthodoxy and his practical engagement of interlocutors.

Third and related, Robinette refers to the beatitude, "Blessed are the pure of heart, for they shall see God." Deepening contemplation as a spiritual practice and orienting the heart to desire as Jesus desires provide the essential wellspring for transformation of personal and structural violence. This represents a fundamental goal of Christian prayer, Clark observes, and he finds a similar emphasis on contemplation in James Alison's interpretation of Girard's "good mimesis."

Fourth, Kevin Ahern, using a Thomistic lens, invites consideration of the transformative value of cultivating the virtues of magnanimity and humility in a sociopolitical context, particularly in the face of vulnerability, such as in the attacks of September 11, 2001 or the inexorable manifestations of climate change. Taken together, he suggests, these virtues may help the practitioner disarm the fear in which violence takes root, steering a course "between the sins of prideful self-interest and destructive self-emptying."

From another perspective, Elizabeth Gandolfo's insightful treatment of the women's peace movement in Liberia provides fruitful ground for interrogating gender essentialism in official Catholic teaching texts, in which humility and other putatively "feminine qualities" have been used to suggest the ideal of passive receptivity for women as they consider their roles within ecclesial life, family, and society. The recently named Nobel Peace Prize laureates, Leymah Gbowee and Liberian President Ellen Johnson Sirleaf, together with thousands of Liberian women, "strategically subverted" gender-based stereotypes to direct their life's generative energies toward the active, socio-political task of ending the bloody, fourteen-year civil war in their country.

For Thompson, virtuous practice leads in the direction of communal living as a key element in treating nature nonviolently. As Clark's negotiation of the academic labyrinth of proposing and teaching a course on Christian prayer illustrates, community serves as a primary location of ascetical purification as part of growth along the journey of becoming a peacemaker.

Finally, Copeland and Logan used their plenary to model the method of dialogical group discernment with the participants. Dialogical process represents a highly counter-cultural ascetic practice of peacemaking in contemporary U.S. society, as well as in some ecclesial settings and academic communities. As Clark's essay shows, today's students, immersed in an extremely polarized model of public discourse, find it challenging to develop the ear of the heart as part of a contemplative approach to issues of violence, and their professors are hard-pressed to model it, hampered by personal frailty and institutional limitations.

Scheid's suggestion of participative decision-making according to "ecosystem belonging" rather than arbitrarily defined political borders would extend the ascetical practice of listening to include not just other human interlocutors but also other living, interdependent manifestations of God's creation within one's local ecosystem. Taken together, the dialogical method of discernment modeled at this year's conference and suggested in these essays offers the means of transforming violence by redressing the violent effects of disparities of power among human beings and in relationship with the rest of creation.

The Vocation of the Theologian in the Transformation of Violence

In his plenary address, Todd David Whitmore drew upon his extensive fieldwork in Uganda and southern Sudan (now the Republic of South Sudan) to explore the concept of anthropological theology. Foregrounding the particular cultural context of first-century Palestine permits a historical-critical understanding of Jesus the Nazarene that highlights his mission to both the poor and the wicked. Using the ethnographic lens of anthropology, he suggested, will allow theologians to deepen their account of Jesus' mission in relation to contemporary concerns. In his work with the Acholi people of Uganda, he has become aware of cosmological presuppositions that seem consonant with those of first-century Palestinian culture. In this respect, the Acholi context represents a "bridge culture" that may deepen theological interpretation of the contemporary significance of Jesus' mission.

By implication, Whitmore's essay supports the insight that cultivation of anthropological sensibilities to the cultural context as part of theological method may open new horizons for theological understanding of how violence might be transformed. Whitmore pointed to Ugandan Archbishop Odama as a moral exemplar of taking up Jesus' mission to both the poor and the wicked, nourished by a profoundly sacramental and contemplative dwelling in God's forgiving love extended to all.

Whitmore's understanding of anthropological theology might also find application in the theologian's cultural context of academia. Clark's pedagogical account of teaching a course on Christian prayer in the shadow of bin Laden's killing invites consideration of what it might mean to meet the violence of the world, and even of the academy, from an interior space of surrender to God's love, the heart of Girard's understanding of the "good mimesis" of Christian discipleship. He desired to introduce his students to the concept of a relationship with Christ "as a potential seedbed for the intellectual openness, courage, passion, and *com*passion" so central to the Catholic and Jesuit educational tradition.

Thompson highlights the multivalent role of the theological vocation in service of the academy, the church, and the public. Working with traditional teaching on the environment, he pushes the developmental edges of official texts to include the relationship between environmental issues and peace by exploring what it might mean to "treat nature nonviolently," while also providing tools for the broader peace movement to give greater attention to the environmental dimensions of the task of peacemaking. Echoing the call for humility issued by Ahern and Kruse, he contributes to a growing theological trend away from an anthropocentric conception and toward a creation-centered view of nature that would emphasize the fact of interdependence among all members of God's creation, as Copeland advised.

* * *

The planning and production of this volume involved the efforts and support of many persons, to whom we are very grateful. We wish to thank the officers and the board of directors who entrusted us with the great honor of editing this year's annual volume and the responsibility of choosing the plenary speakers for the convention. Executive Director David Gentry-Akin provided invaluable guidance and assistance to us throughout the process. It was wonderful to see how the planning that we began to do while walking around the scenic campus of the University of Portland during the annual convention in 2010 came to fruition a year later at Iona College.

For all her supererogatory efforts and hospitality as the local coordinator for the convention at Iona College, Elena Procario-Foley deserves heartfelt thanks from all of us. We are also deeply grateful to the plenary speakers—William T. Cavanaugh, M. Shawn Copeland, James Logan, and Todd David Whitmore—for their stimulating presentations. We are, of course, indebted to the section conveners who reviewed proposals, organized topic sessions, convened, and kept an eye out for promising papers to include in the volume. Nearly eighty members and friends of the College Theology Society volunteered as reviewers of papers submitted for publication in this volume, offering helpful feedback to authors of essays in the fine spirit of the enduring collegial charism of the Society. We are humbly grateful for all of their work, knowing that our requests for their discerning, scholarly collaboration came amid busy summer schedules and cherished, unstructured time set aside for their own writing projects.

Also, Laurie Cassidy and Maureen H. O'Connell, the editors of last year's volume, generously offered assistance to us, so that we did not have to reinvent the proverbial wheel. Last but certainly not least, Susan Perry, senior editor at Orbis Books, has for many years now turned her keen editorial eye and theological acuity to the tightly timed production of the annual volume, a task made all the more formidable by the current challenges facing publishing houses. We extend our deepest gratitude to her and to Orbis Books for their steadfast fidelity to the College Theology Society.

Notes

[1]Robert McAfee Brown, *Religion and Violence*, 2nd ed. (Philadelphia: The Westminster Press, 1987), 1.

[2]Osama bin Laden did not take immediate responsibility for the 9/11 attacks. By October 7, 2001 bin Laden still had not taken credit for the 9/11 attacks even though he praised them. He finally claimed that responsibility in a television address on October 29, 2004, after the U.S. had invaded Iraq so that he could attempt to argue that Muslims were acting in self-defense against American aggression. See Alia Brahimi, *Jihad and Just War in the War on Terror* (Oxford: Oxford University Press, 2010), 193, 271, n. 10.

[3]John L. Esposito, *Unholy War: Terror in the Name of Islam* (Oxford: Oxford University Press, 2002).

[4]Stephen Prothero, *Religious Literacy: What Every American Needs to Know—And Doesn't* (New York: HarperOne, 2008).

[5]Christopher Hitchens, *God Is Not Great: How Religion Poisons Everything* (New York: Twelve, 2007).

[6]See Lotta Harbom and Peter Wallensteen, "Patterns of Major Armed Conflicts, 1990-2005," in Stockholm International Peace Research Institute (SIPRI), *Yearbook 2006: Armaments, Disarmaments, and International Security* (Oxford: Oxford University Press, 2006).

[7]René Girard, *Violence and the Sacred* (Baltimore: Johns Hopkins University Press, 1979).

[8]Bernard Häring, C.Ss.R., *My Hope for the Church: Critical Encouragement for the Twenty-First Century* (Liguori, MO: Liguori/Triumph, 1999; originally published as *Meine Hoffnung für die Kirche: Kritische Ermutigungen* [Verlag Herder, 1997]), 62. Raymund Schwager was a Swiss Roman Catholic theologian and a co-founder of the Colloquium on Violence & Religion (1991), its first president (1991–1995), and an honorary member of its advisory board from 1999 until his death on February 27, 2004.

[9]We chose this word "transformation" in connection with the recent shift in peace research from conflict resolution to conflict *transformation*. See, for example, John Paul Lederach, *Preparing for Peace: Conflict Transformation across Cultures* (Syracuse, NY: Syracuse University Press, 1995). In addition, one of us (Margie) served as co-organizer with Sr. Ann Astell of the 2010 annual meeting of the international Colloquium on Violence and Religion on the theme, "Transforming Violence: Cult, Culture, and Acculturation" (University of Notre Dame, July 1-3, 2010), which provided a conceptual springboard for the 2011 CTS conference theme.

[10]Monika K. Hellwig, *A Case for Peace in Reason and Faith* (Collegeville, MN: Michael Glazier/The Liturgical Press, 1992), 11.

PART I

MANIFESTATIONS OF VIOLENCE
VIEWED THROUGH
A THEOLOGICAL LENS

God among the Ruins

Companion and Co-Sufferer

M. Shawn Copeland

I am no environmentalist, although I begin to understand that I must become one. My personal geographic experience is urban. I was born in the city of Detroit and grew up there when it was a bustling industrial and cultural center, quite unlike the skeletal ruin to which it has been reduced. Because of Detroit and New York and Boston, for me cities signify energy, vitality, motion, and culture—architecture, libraries, concert halls, museums, restaurants, coffee bars, taxis, trains, and traffic.

As a graduate student at Boston College, I hiked with friends in the White Mountains of New Hampshire and along trails in the Maine woods; but I was happy always to head home to the city to a good meal and wine. The three miles of white sandy beach in Ogunquit, Maine, that border the Atlantic Ocean are precious to me; that ocean always commands my respect and more than once I have ritually mourned the thousands of Africans whose battered bodies were thrown into its waters.

Still, the urban experience shapes me and shapes my theology. My care and scholarship is committed to the flourishing of God's human creatures—especially those who are materially poor, despised, and marginalized in the cultural and social (including the political, economic, technological) order that some of us have constructed and too many of us sustain. As I said before, although I am no environmentalist, I begin to understand that I must become one. Chickasaw writer Linda Hogan teaches us that we need not choose between broken humanity and broken Earth: "What happens to people and what happens to the land is the same thing."[1]

In this reflection, I bring together concerns about nature, matter, environmental degradation, and persons in all their splendid and damaged particularities of gender, race, and class.

Nature, Matter, and the Christian Imaginary

The terms "matter" and "nature" represent key notions in the construction of the Christian "imaginary"—the way ordinary Christians imagine their religious lives as mediated through images, experiences, stories of the sacred, and evoke shared and complementary understandings that make possible common practices, shared religious and spiritual sensibilities, as well as a sense of fittingness in worship.[2] The mythologist Joseph Campbell describes the biblical tradition as a "socially oriented mythology" of a nomadic people in contrast to a nature-oriented mythology of an agrarian people.[3]

The Genesis narrative of the expulsion of the first earth-creatures from the garden discloses disruption in the created matter that Elohim made and saw as "good" (Gen 1:12, 18, 21, 25, 31).[4] But the earth-creatures yield to temptation, thus bringing about dramatic change in the ecology of Eden. In the evening breeze, with the approach of Elohim, the primal couple hide themselves among the trees in fear, shame, and guilt; they have grasped in muddled fashion the impending disruption of what had been an ideal order. The man blames the woman; the woman accuses the serpent, which the Lord God condemns. Because of their grievous blunder, the human condition is altered radically, yet, as Christian teaching maintains, not absolutely. Still, the pain of childbirth is intensified, the exercise of human labor toughened, relationships between human creatures troubled, and the very earth cursed (Gen 3:8-19). Eden comes to ruin for human creatures, yet they—and we—are wounded with a longing for it and for the God who brought all into existence. "In the Bible," Campbell declares, "nature is corrupt, nature has fallen."[5]

We Christians hold an ambiguous, even contradictory, view of matter. The apostle Paul faced squarely the demands of the material, the corporeal (1 Cor 6:13b-7:40), and embraced the body as a central metaphor through which to explicate what being in "Christ Jesus" means (1 Cor 12:12-27). Four centuries later, striving to come to terms with Neo-Platonism, Manichaeism, and Christianity, Augustine of Hippo wrestled long and hard with those same demands. He did not declare as did Tertullian that women are "the devil's gateway [who] crushed the image of God, the man Adam."[6] In Augustine's account, the primal man lost control of his will, his body, especially his genitalia; thereafter, humans were mired in concupiscence. Augustine's solution lay in word and sacrament and in the mastery of passion, of the body (of matter), of sexuality in order to live a life pleasing to God. Paul framed the Christian response to the existential, cultural, and social conditions of the body in relation to the return of the Lord; remain as you are until he comes. Augustine re-framed this response and pressed it into a morality that reinforced compartmentalization in pursuit of sanctity.[7]

Through certain interpretations of Pauline letters and the writings of Augustine, in particular, the Christian imaginary has marshaled negative judgments against matter, against the body, rendering it complicit with a dynamics of domination. These dynamics stem from a "logic" driven by a dualistic evaluation and an oppressive hierarchy in which females and non-whites were identified with (fallen, corrupt) nature and thus marked as inferior, while (white) males were identified with the "human," possessing reason and culture and deemed superior. Certain aspects of the European Enlightenment project coincided with that dynamics of domination and contribute to the ways in which various (Western) social imaginaries construe women and people of color as substantively "other" and nature a "thing" to be mastered.

More than three decades ago, essayist and feminist critic Susan Griffin culled and compiled from a range of sources, ancient and modern, contemporary and esoteric, the underpinnings of the nexus between matter, nature, female, and dark bodies, on the one side, and power and control, on the other. The following statements taken from her *Woman and Nature* sample the historical contempt in which matter, nature, women, and people of color have been held.[8]

- Matter is only a potential for form or a potential for movement. It is decided that the nature of woman is passive, that she is a vessel waiting to be filled.[9]

- It is observed that women are closer to the earth [to nature].[10]

- Slavery is said to be a condition of every higher civilization.[11]

These assertions embarrass, startle, and shock. Griffin details the use and abuse patriarchy and white racist supremacy have made of nature, matter, women, the poor, and people of color. Captured, tamed, trimmed, domesticated, guarded, and controlled, each is re-made in the pornographic gaze of patriarchy and white racist supremacy. Griffin pushes us to probe for new possibilities, deeper connections, and transformation, to reclaim the sacredness of our own humanness, of matter, of woman, of man, of Earth.

The Bible offers another account that upholds the goodness of matter, of the body and the significance of nature. The closing dialogue in the Book of Job presents a set of questions that parallel the creation narrative: "Where were you," the Lord God asks, "when I laid the foundation of the earth?" "Or who shut in the sea with doors when it burst out from the womb" (38:4, 8)? Job replies: "I am of small account; what shall I answer you? I lay my hand on my mouth" (40:3-4).

For more than twenty years, naturalist Bill McKibben has been trying to help us understand that we *are* of small account and ought not to "judge everything from *our* point of view—that all nature is *not ours* to subdue."[12] But we *have judged* everything from our point of view and, in his thinking, this has brought about the "end of nature as we have known it."[13] What might the "end of nature" mean? Bluntly, McKibben argues that nature, "the independent force that has surrounded us since our earliest days, cannot coexist with our numbers and our habits."[14] If twenty years ago we did not understand the "sensitivity of the Earth's physical systems to small shifts in temperature,"[15] we do now.

Consider, then, that the environmental degradation of the planet may be understood as the successive breakdowns in a world process of certain recurrent schemes, series of schemes, and their correlative defensive circles. The build-up of increasing quantities of industrial offal, complex gases (carbon dioxide, nitrous oxide, and methane), and synthetic chemicals has disrupted those defensive schemes that regulate atmospheric gases and protect the ozone layer in the stratosphere. This breakdown, in turn, impairs other schemes—including the circulation of the water over the surface of the planet, the nitrogen cycle, the process of photosynthesis, and the routines of animal life. The by-products of these inter-related breakdowns of schemes yield acid rain, dead lakes, soil erosion, choked trees, the loss of terrestrial photosynthesis, the loss of animal and plant species, and the radical diminishment of organic and, therefore, intellectual development in human beings. And that diminishment, our diminishment, can only augment and prolong disruption and breakdown. We are responsible for the end of nature in a physical sense.

We are also responsible for the end of nature in a moral and ethical sense through the biotechnology of genetic engineering. McKibben tracks the path we have taken since the discovery of the double helix in 1953: the stitching together of unrelated organisms to make new forms of life as, for example, through the fabrication of new and different genetic strains of mice, pigs, rabbits, fish, trees, and foods.[16] Regarding the 1980 Supreme Court decision "that a man-made micro-organism was patentable under current statutes," McKibben concludes, "not only could [humans] make life; [humans] could make money."[17] Not for the first time, but certainly, definitively, has life been rendered a commodity, a thing, although now not only something to be bought and sold, but something to be fabricated and manufactured.

Desire and Commodities, Power and Control

Perhaps Augustine has captured better than any other Christian writer the dynamism of desire, of human want, of love—*dilectio*—to direct us toward or away from our Final Good, which is God. Tell me, he asks in *The City of God*, what a human being loves and I will tell you that human being's end or *telos*.[18] Discover what a people or society loves and you will be able to form a judgment about the character of that people or society. If a people or society is oriented toward or loves the good, then that society is good; but, if what a society prizes or loves is not good, then neither is that society. On this scale, the earthly city, its objects of desire and choice, its claims and allegiances are judged.[19]

The market tantalizes and seduces, offers and withholds the very commodities it coaxes us to want, even as it controls our desire.

Commodities are the objects of our desire; we want things and more of them. More than a century ago, Karl Marx commented on the peculiar and stimulating character of commodities: "A commodity appears, at first sight, a very trivial thing, and easily understood. Its analysis shows that it is, in reality, a very queer thing, abounding in metaphysical subtleties and theological niceties."[20] No longer does nature set the ground of human valuing, but rather it is efficiency, effortlessness, disposability. No longer does the transcendent hold us; instead, commodities displace mystery and usurp the power of the sacred. We humans flirt relentlessly and stupidly with idolatry, surrendering ourselves to the power and control of commodities. We define our being as having; not to have, not to possess is not to be. We have become dominated by the making of money, and acquisition has become the ultimate purpose of life.

We humans define ourselves by having and making money, by exerting our will-to-power through sexism, racism, the exploitation of human labor, and mastery of the Earth. We control and exclude; we manipulate and exploit desire. As theologian Jung Mo Sung points out, to be excluded from the market does not result in exclusion from society. Rather, market exclusion spawns "a tragic situation [in which] the poor (young and adult) are stimulated to desire the consumption of sophisticated and superfluous goods while being denied the possibility of access to the satisfaction of their basic needs for a dignified survival."[21]

We in the United States need a wide global, and even better, planetary perspective; yet the poor and despised, blacks, Latinos, "troublesome" women, prisoners, and "unwanted" migrants and refugees also strive daily for survival and dignity in our country. Consider the following:

- The wealthiest 20 percent of U. S. households have slightly more than half of the nation's total income. The poorest 20 percent have 3.4 percent of total income.[22]

- Since 1990, the United States has held the record for the highest rate of incarceration in the world, imprisoning 765 people out every 100,000; including pre-trial detainees, the prison population totals roughly 2.3 million. The U. S. has

4 percent of the world's population and 25 percent of the world's prison population.[23]

- More than nine million people (9,222,000) in the United States are estimated to live in neighborhoods within 3 kilometers of the nation's 413 commercial hazardous waste facilities. Over 5.1 million people of color, including 2.5 million Hispanics or Latinos, 1.8 million African Americans, 616,000 Asians/Pacific Islanders, and 62,000 Native Americans live in neighborhoods with one or more commercial hazardous waste facility.[24] Since the United States lacks any national reporting system, the precise number of farmworkers sickened each year by pesticides is unknown. However the Farmworker Justice website publishes the EPA estimate that 10,000 to 20,000 workers are poisoned each year.[25]

"What happens to people and what happens to the land is the same thing."[26] Our commodity fetish is what happens to the Earth, to all who are poor, and to people of color. All these, "in a consumer society," Bryan Massingale charges, "are, at best, irrelevant; at worst, they are a burden. In any case, they are a matter of indifference provided they are quiet, docile, and non-disruptive."[27] We have damaged a creation "charged with the grandeur of God,"[28] leaving living organisms mutilated, the soil barren, the air and oceans fouled, humanity desecrated—all smudged by our reckless voraciousness.

God among the Ruins: The Ground and Possibility of Love

Once again God walks among ruins, searching for us, yearning for our companionship. Once again, God weeps at the divine image distorted by desire gone awry in rampant greed and waste. If McKibben is right, then we shall need to learn to live differently, "lightly, carefully, gracefully" on the "tough new planet" he spells *Eaarth*. McKibben's point is that the ecological order of the "planet on which our civilization evolved no longer exists."[29] In other words, we humans have fundamentally altered the functioning of the planet, endangering all creation.[30]

Such living will not be achieved easily. The principal capitalist countries (the G-8) have intentionally reshaped the global economy by disengaging the primary-products economy from the industrial economy, and the industrial economy from employment while replacing trade with the movement of capital.[31] Further, they have disregarded protracted and structural unemployment, wresting power and resources from local communities, and transferring these to transnational elites, while eliminating crucial export markets of small countries at will (this under the guise of fair, open trade).[32]

These coercive tactics compromise the fecundity of Earth and put humanity at risk. Far too frequently they trigger the complex conditions for fetal malnutrition and early childhood nutritional deprivation—damaging, sometimes profoundly, cellular potential for the sensitive and systemic integrations of the chemical, biological, and neural processes critical to normal human growth and development. When such growth is obstructed or stunted, normal brain development is jeopardized and this, in turn, renders human capacity for moral decision and action uncertain. To obstruct or stunt such vital growth interferes with God's human creation and frustrates the probabilities of practical and intelligent stewardship of the Earth.

Just as significantly, the despoiling of the Earth defies the intention seeded in the order God has for our planet.[33] We need, as postcolonial theorist Gayatri Spivak suggests, to "imagine ourselves as planetary subjects rather than global agents, planetary creatures rather than global entities."[34] To understand ourselves in this way is to grasp ourselves as an integral rather than superior part of God's creation.

In what follows, I draw on the work of Sri Lankan theologian Tissa Balasuriya and Brazilian theologian Ivone Gebara in order to propose witness as a task for us as theologians. If the notion of planetarity sounds innovative, recall that nearly three decades ago Balasuriya worked out a planetary theology that emphasized a holistic analysis of the multiple interrelationships, sectors, and events that affect the whole Earth as well as humans and that read the person and example of Jesus in a fresh way.[35] Although he did not write explicitly from the paradigm of ecotheology, given our present grim conditions, his work is suggestive and prescient.

A praxial commitment to the liberation of the masses of poor and excluded children, women, and men as well as regard for the sacredness of the Earth constitute the point of departure for the ecofeminist theology of Brazilian theologian Ivone Gebara. Her reflection on the various implications of "primordial relatedness" help to clarify what it means to be a planetary subject, a planetary creature. Gebara explicates relatedness as a human condition, an ethical reality, and a religious experience.[36]

As theologians, our vocation requires us to attend intellectually to the deteriorating condition of God's creation. The pressing ecological and social assaults (such as degradation of the planet, racism, sexism, and exploitation of human labor) endured by the Earth's people hurt young children, the poor, excluded, and vulnerable most of all. These problems signal what Lonergan named the longer cycle of decline. They stem from alienations of intelligence or bias—that is, the more or less conscious and intentional refusal to ask further questions, to admit new insights, to fail to take intelligent, responsible action.[37] The problems we face are so pervasive and so entrenched that without the exercise of practical intelligent cooperation even the most minimal conditions for their reversal verge on the improbable. Without the gift of grace, those conditions are impossible. Working within the most fundamental domain—"the cosmic breadth of a simultaneous context of nature, history, and grace"[38]—we theologians are called to be witnesses of God's transcendent presence and care, of God's willingness to abide with us, suffer with us, suffer for us. Let me suggest five dimensions of our collaborative witness:

1. We are called to witness to the *interrelatedness of God's creation.* "To enter the omnicentric unfolding universe," astrophysicist Brian Swimme tells us, "is to taste the joy of radical relational mutuality."[39] Interrelatedness constitutes a distinctive and integral viewpoint that respects and supports "the intrinsic value of nonhuman nature alongside human nature."[40] All creatures—human and nonhuman—take their intrinsic and ontological value from their distinctive and essential relationships with God. Indeed, Roman Catholic teaching insists that creation is a sacrament, disclosing God's very presence.

Human insistence on the superiority of the human brain focuses not on interrelatedness, but on the relative value of all creation to human desire, which long ago trumped human need. The notion of interrelatedness entails intentional and conscientious awareness, understanding, judgment, decision, and responsible action. We must begin and we must help others to live in such a way that we understand that planet Earth is a living organism, not merely one object among others or an object of manipulation.

2. We are called to witness to *interrelatedness as a human condition*. As a human condition, interrelatedness recalls basic human interdependence. Human beings are relational, and being human is to be in relation. Interrelatedness intimates multiplicity, plurality, differentiation, yet finitude and limitation as well. Further, it suggests need, cooperation, collaboration, even communion.

Relational being or interrelatedness challenges us human creatures to relinquish dominative hierarchical control in living in the created order. Through racism, sexism, the exploitation of human labor, and abuse of the Earth for profit and accumulation, the logic of domination injures the basic condition of interrelatedness, reinforcing arbitrary socially constructed hierarchies, privileging a few humans to the disadvantage of all the rest of us—human and nonhuman creatures alike. By understanding, reverencing, and valuing differentiation and plurality in creation, not only do we renounce oppressive relations among human creatures, we also shed our aggressive anthropocentrism toward nonhuman creatures.

3. We are called to witness to *interrelatedness as an ethical and moral condition*.[41] Sexism, silence in confrontation with white supremacy, commercialization of desire, and despoiling the environment pose contemporary instances of the primal breach of cosmic harmony. Taken together these are grievous sins against the interrelatedness of creation.

Authentic recognition and acceptance of interrelatedness call us to repentance and to compassionate, practically intelligent solidarity not only with bruised human creation, but also with bruised created nature. Critical attention to the interrelatedness of human creation uncovers just how sexism and racism are not problems *already-out-there* now to be solved, but problems that suffuse our consciousness and are expressed in sexist and racist actions and behaviors. Many of us are immersed in and enjoy racial privilege and entitlements. Cultured indifference to indigenous people, blacks, Asians, and Latinos allows some of us to disregard an uneasy conscience, to overlook the ways in which historically constructed racial and gender privilege disadvantage these women and men and their children. Such cultured indifference allows us to deny, belittle, and reject whoever and whatever questions our putatively "inherited" status.

Most of us have been taught and have learned to override the intersubjective spontaneity that characterizes being human: parents, relatives, and other agents of socialization told us with whom we should not play or whom we ought not to befriend, whom we should suspect or whom we might affirm. We must unlearn these lessons, turn the hermeneutics of suspicion on ourselves: admit and name our prejudices; identify and critique our assumptions, values, decisions, and actions; acknowledge our complicity in a social order built on thoroughgoing inequality; face up to our inner conflicts; unmask our illusions. We may have taken down the signs "white" and "colored," but walls still stand, doors are still closed to keep out indigenous people, blacks, Asians, Latinos, women, immigrants, and refugees. We must chip away at those walls: take small steps—cultivate curiosity, study the histories and cultures our teachers failed to teach us, accord respect, join in common causes and common work, walk into friendships, and, perhaps authentic experiences of intimacy. We must break through those walls and doors barred against all those made poor and excluded by our privilege; if they are unwelcome, then we must stand outside with them and God.

As an ethical and moral condition, interrelatedness concerns the Earth.[42] We must approach the Earth with reverence as a living being. We must accept the responsibility to know, to care for, and to love the Earth. Compassionate, practically intelligent solidarity resolutely enacts a rigorous analysis of consumer culture. Our rapacious consumer culture appraises everything, human and nonhuman, from the perspective of the market; everything, human and nonhuman, is for sale. The only antidote to our consumer culture is less—less energy consumption, less waste, less things, less demand, less supply. The only counter to the market worthy of the Earth is our sacrifice and simplicity. And, in the face of the intransigence of the so-called "American way of life," these will require humility and courage, self-control and perseverance.

4. We are called to witness to *interrelatedness as religious*

experience. To witness interrelatedness as religious experience means to live consciously and intentionally in relation to and in the presence of God, of Transcendent Being, and to live in openness and love with the whole of creation.

Spirituality is another way of speaking about such conscious and intentional response to the divine invitation to transforming relation, to communion, to prayer. Thus, a prayer-rooted, lived response becomes a mode of being; we become beings-in-love with God, whose love reorients us and all that we are. This love opens, attunes, sensitizes, and unites as creation—human and nonhuman.

Moreover, for us as theologians, such love makes possible both the offer and gift of "a profound, radical theological hope" for ourselves, for all humanity, for all creation. Carmelite theologian Constance FitzGerald encourages our "witness to this [hope] in [our] lives, [our] work, [our] scholarship; even in betrayal and suffering."[43]

5. *We are called to witness love.* Jesus of Nazareth came preaching and healing and teaching that God is love. He taught all who would and will listen that "the way" to God is through love. Love grounds interrelatedness. In the words of John of the Cross, love helps us to value "the entire universe as a sea of love in which [we are] engulfed, for conscious of the living point or center of love within [ourselves, we are] unable to catch sight of the boundaries of this love."[44] Love privileges intimacy and passion over instrumentality and violence, solidarity and generativity over self-regarding self-determination and predation.

In *The Christian Imagination: Theology and the Origin of Race*, Willie James Jennings poignantly critiques the failure of Christianity to live up to its original thrust of intimacy and its surrender to the realities of "oppression, violence, and death, if not of bodies, then most certainly of ways of life, forms of language, and visions of the world. What happened," he asks, "to the original trajectory of intimacy?"[45] What happened to love? What "thwarts the deepest reality of Christian social imagination"?[46] The collusion and complicity of Christianity, indeed, Christian theology in conquest and enslavement, land expropriation and exploitation, colonialism and neo-colonialism fly in the face of love.

But, only Divine Love can save us—all of us, human *and* nonhuman. God is Love and as Love God generates the ground and possibility of all loving. We humans need to learn to *love*. We need to learn *agapic* love. *Agape* has nothing to do with sentimental attachment or fleeting emotion, but rather grasps the interrelatedness of all creation (Rom 5:5). We humans need to learn to love matter, to love nature, to love the Earth. We need to learn to love other humans—simply, honestly, openly, fearlessly. Love is selfless and self-transcendent, other-centered and uncompromising, active and committed.[47] Love is radical: it defies death with fidelity and refutes defeat with constancy. Love reverences and delights in the other, it seeks union. Still, only Divine Love can save us, only Divine Love knows how.

Once again God yearns to walk with us, to offer us the choice of life—delight in the differentiation of all creation, refreshing work, joy, friendship, peace. Here is the question: Will we "remain God's creatures" or yield again to the awful temptation "of making ourselves gods?"[48] The choice is ours.

Notes

[1]Linda Hogan, *Dwellings: A Spiritual History of the Living World* (New York: W. W. Norton & Company, 1995), 89.

[2]I borrow the term "imaginary" from Canadian philosopher Charles Taylor, *Modern Social Imaginaries* (Durham, NC: Duke University Press, 2004), 23.

[3]Joseph Campbell, *The Power of Myth* (1988; repr., New York: Anchor Books, 1991), 29.

[4]New Revised Standard Version used throughout.

[5]Campbell, *The Power of Myth*, 30.

[6]Tertullian, "On the Dress of Women," in *Women in the Early Church*, ed. Elizabeth A. Clark (Collegeville, MN: The Liturgical Press, 1983), 1.1.2.

[7]See Augustine, "On Marriage and Concupiscence," 1.3, 5, 7, 16–18. Available online at http://www.fordham.edu/halsall/source/aug-marr.html, accessed September 29, 2011.

[8]Susan Griffin, *Woman and Nature: The Roaring inside Her* (New York: Harper & Row, 1978).

[9]Ibid., 5.

[10]Ibid., 7.

[11]Ibid., 32.

[12]Bill McKibben, *The End of Nature* (1989; repr., New York: Random House, 2006), 65, italics mine.

[13]Ibid., 66.

[14]Ibid., 144.

[15]Ibid., xiv.

[16]Ibid., 138-39.

[17]Ibid., 138.

[18]Augustine, *Concerning the City of God against the Pagans*, trans. Henry Bettenson (London: Penguin Books, 1972). A contemporary writer of great skill in delineating desire is Benedictine monk and theologian Sebastian Moore; see his *The Fire and the Rose Are One* (New York: Seabury Press, 1980) and *Jesus Liberator of Desire* (New York: Crossroad Books, 1989).

[19]Augustine, *Concerning the City of God against the Pagans*, 14.28.

[20]Karl Marx, *Capital*, vol. 1, 1.4 (first published 1887). Available online at http://www.marxists.org/, accessed September 29, 2011.

[21]Jung Mo Sung, *Desire, Market and Religion* (London: SCM Press, 2007), 66.

[22]Kristen Lewis and Sarah Burd-Sharps, *The Measure of America 2010–2011: Mapping Risks and Resilience* (New York: New York University Press, 2010), 6.

[23]Roy Walmsley, *World Prison Population List*, 8th ed. (London: International Centre for Prison Studies, 2009). Available online at http://www.kcl.ac.uk/, accessed September 29, 2011. See also Michelle Alexander, *The New Jim Crow: Mass Incarceration in the Age of Colorblindness* (New York: The New Press, 2010).

[24]Robert D. Bullard et al., *Toxic Wastes and Race at Twenty, 1987–2007: A Report Prepared for the United Church of Christ, Justice and Witness Ministries* (Cleveland: United Church of Christ, 2007), 1. Available online at http://www.ejrc.cau.edu/, accessed September 29, 2011.

[25]Farmworker Justice, "The Dangers of Pesticides for Farmworkers," n.d. Available online at http://www.farmworkerjustice.org/pesticide-safety, accessed September 29, 2011.

[26]Hogan, *Dwellings*, 89.

[27]Bryan N. Massingale, "'Cultured Indifference' and the Option for the Poor Post-Katrina," *Journal of Religion & Society*, Supplement Series 4 (2008): 58-59.

[28]Gerard Manley Hopkins, "God's Grandeur," in *The Major Works*, ed. Catherine Phillips (New York: Oxford University Press, 2002).

[29]McKibben, *Eaarth: Making a Life on a Tough New Planet* (New York: St. Martin's Press, 2011), 27.

[30]Ibid., 10.

[31]Peter F. Drucker, "The Changed World Economy," *Foreign Affairs* 64, 4 (1986): 768-91.

[32]The IMF required "structural adjustment" of Jamaica's domestic economy stands as one example. Anna Kasafi Perkins offers a theological ethical analysis of the condition of the region in *Justice as Equality: Michael Manley's Caribbean Vision of Justice* (New York: Peter Lang, 2010); see also *Life + Debt*, directed by Stephanie Black (2001; New York: New Yorker Video, 2003), DVD.

[33]Hyun-Chul Cho, "Interconnectedness and Intrinsic Value as Ecological Principles: An Appropriation of Karl Rahner's Evolutionary Christology," *Theological Studies* 70, 3 (2009): 636.

[34]Gayatri C. Spivak, *Death of a Discipline* (New York: Columbia University Press, 2003), 73.

[35]Tissa Balasuriya, *Planetary Theology* (Maryknoll, NY: Orbis Books, 1984), 15-16. Available online at http://tissabalasuriya.wordpress.com/, accessed September 29, 2011. There is ample evidence that ecology has been moving to the fore in theological conversation: See John B. Cobb, *Is It Too Late? A Theology of Ecology* (Beverly Hills, CA: Bruce, 1972); Sallie McFague, *Models of God: A Theology for a Nuclear Age* (Philadelphia: Fortress, 1987); idem, *The Body of God* (Minneapolis: Fortress, 1993); idem, *Super, Natural Christians: How We Should Love Nature* (Minneapolis: Fortress, 1997); Rosemary Radford Ruether, *Gaia and God* (San Francisco: HarperSanFrancisco, 1992); Elizabeth A. Johnson, *Woman, Earth, and Creator Spirit* (New York: Paulist Press, 1993); idem, *Quest for the Living God: Mapping Frontiers in the Theology of God* (New York: Continuum, 2008), 181-201; Larry L. Rasmussen, *Earth Community, Earth Ethics* (Maryknoll, NY: Orbis Books, 1996); Denis Edwards, *Ecology at the Heart of Faith* (Maryknoll, NY: Orbis Books, 2006); idem, *Breath of Life: A Theology of the Creator Spirit* (Maryknoll, NY: Orbis Books, 2004).

[36]Ivone Gebara, *Longing for Running Water: Ecofeminism and Liberation* (Minneapolis: Fortress, 1999), 84-85.

[37]Bernard Lonergan, *The Collected Works of Bernard Lonergan*, vol. 3, *Insight: A Study of Human Understanding*, 5th ed., rev. and aug. (Toronto: University of Toronto Press, 1988), 214, 244-61.

[38]Bernard Lonergan, *The Collected Works of Bernard Lonergan*, vol. 4, "Finality, Love, Marriage," in *Collection*, 2nd ed., rev. and aug., ed. Frederick E. Crowe and Robert M. Doran (Toronto: University of Toronto Press, 1998), 19.

[39]Brian Swimme, *The Hidden Heart of the Cosmos: Humanity and the New Story* (Maryknoll, NY: Orbis Books, 1996), 111.

[40]Cho, "Interconnectedness and Intrinsic Value as Ecological Principles," 624.

[41]Gebara, *Longing for Running Water*, 84.

[42]Ibid., 157.

[43]Constance FitzGerald, "From Impasse to Prophetic Hope: Crisis of Memory," *CTSA Proceedings* 64 (2009): 41-42.

[44]John of the Cross, *The Living Flame of Love*, 2.10, trans. Kieran Kavanugh and Otilio Rodriguez, in *The Collected Works of St. John of the Cross*, rev. ed. (Washington, DC: Institute of Carmelite Studies, 1991).

[45]Willie James Jennings, *The Christian Imagination: Theology and the Origins of Race* (New Haven: Yale University Press, 2010), 9.

[46]Ibid., 6.

[47]Balasuriya, *Planetary Theology*, 164.

[48]McKibben, *The End of Nature*, 182.

A Response to M. Shawn Copeland and an Invitation to Discernment and Open Dialogue

James Logan

My children, love must not be a matter of words or talk; it must be genuine, and show itself in action.
— *1 John 3:18 (NEB)*

Thank you, Dr. Copeland, for offering this meeting of the College Theology Society such an insightful and provocative start to this plenary session. It was insightful and provocative in its proclamation that "what happens to people and what happens to land [and the whole of the natural world] is the same thing." Indeed your understanding of environmental justice rightly includes interlocking human strivings against sexism, racism, classism, and other affronts to human dignity.

My task is offer a response that includes an invitation to group discernment and dialogue, exploring the deeper dynamics of racism and particularly white privilege/supremacy within a framework of conflict transformation.

Dr. Copeland spoke of having experienced a once-bustling cultural and industrial civic body called Detroit be reduced to a city of skeletal ruin. This experience (along with many other life experiences, urban, out in the woods, and otherwise) has helped Dr. Copeland articulate well for us the complexities and subtleties of the ties that bind humans to the environments of places to which we belong—for better or for worse. I would like to suggest that although Dr. Copeland says that she is no environmentalist (at least in the more common delimited understanding of the term) her remarks do, in fact, indicate that black folk have been serious environmentalists throughout our histories in the Atlantic world and beyond. (And, of course, this has been just as true in the life and history of many other exploited and suffering peoples of the world.) Dr. Copeland's word to us suggests just such a truth, as she speaks of respecting and mourning the Atlantic Ocean, where the broken bodies of thousands of Africans were thrown into its waters. Indeed, we have here evidence of a white supremacist misuse of a majestic creation of God, a sacrilege made all the more frightful because it was carried forward in the name of Christ.

The historian Vincent Harding has summarized well the blood-red ironies experienced by Africans who encountered the American Christ on their way to bondage in a so-called "New World." Harding writes,

> We first met the American Christ on slave ships. We heard his name sung in hymns of praise while we died in our thousands, chained in stinking holds beneath the decks, locked in with terror and disease and sad memories of our families and homes. When we leaped from the decks to be seized by sharks we saw his name carved on the ship's solid sides. When our women were raped in the cabins they must have noticed the great and holy books on the shelves. Our introduction to this Christ was not propitious. And the horrors continued on America's soil. So all through the nation's history many black people have rejected this Christ—indeed the miracle is that so many accepted him.[1]

I want to suggest that the black bodies that leapt overboard during the Middle Passage, the ones that struggled to protect themselves from the social death of slavery, the black bodies that endured the sting of Jim and Jane Crow law and custom, and the dark bodies that today wrestle with theologies of consumerism, mass imprisonment, and the numerous intensified degradations of the black female body, both domestically and worldwide, are all participants in history's sacred environmentalist cause. From a Christian perspective, human bodies—like the mountains and valleys, oceans and trees, sunshine and rain, the moonlit skies and stars, and every creature great and small—are sites of God's very good creation. These are all holy sites of beauty forged by the hand of divine love, participants in endless cycles of lament and celebration, death and renewal. So wherever there is a struggle for the dignity of the black body and its holistic presence in opposition to multiple strands of white supremacy, there we have an environmentalist cause.

As Dr. Copeland demonstrates, the black body as a site of environmental concern has always been intimately tied to the wider human corruption of nature in the "New World." Not only has the Atlantic Ocean been employed as a site of black bodily exploitation and death, so too were the trees of the "New World" turned against their God-given purpose to sustain and support life. This violation of both trees and black personhood could be seen vividly in the grotesque practice of American lynching. In 1939, Billie Holiday gave melancholy testimony to the witness of "Strange Fruit," hanging primarily (but not exclusively) from the southern trees of the nation:

> Southern trees bear a strange fruit
> Blood on the leaves, blood at the root
> Black bodies swinging in the Southern breeze
> Strange fruit swinging from poplar trees
> Pastoral scene of the gallant South
> The bulging eyes and the twisted mouth
> Scent of magnolia sweet and fresh
> Then the sudden smell of burning flesh
> Here is a fruit for the crows to pluck
> For the rain to gather, for the wind to suck
> For the sun to rot, for the tree to drop
> Here is a strange and bitter crop.[2]

As white supremacy continues to reign in the church and in the world today, struggles for black inclusion at the political core of social and institutional life remain largely invisible under the banner of environmental justice. We rightly want justice for the world's forests, hills, and mountains, endangered species, bodies of water and air, yet justice for that environmental site called the black body and presence in the United States continues to be widely neglected by even well-meaning environmentalists. We Dark Ones are God's creation, part of the natural order. We are people of both organic and spiritual substance, of flesh and bone, fiber and liquids, minds and souls created by God for co-partnerships of life among all the world's peoples and the rest of the natural world. Side by side with the mountains that groan and weep under the weight of today's corporate appetite for endless profit are the exploited and surplus populations of dark peoples (disproportionately but not exclusively) who continue to face lynching trees, rape camps, human trafficking, torture cells, and torture nations as the powerful fashion diamond-studded lives for themselves formed by the weight of the world. Now we even encounter a world where some advocate for the genetic engineering of designer children, while masses of others spend more time burying their children than they do their elderly loved ones.

Speaking now, more directly, to our beloved white Christian brothers and sisters in this room today, please see it as a high pedagogical calling to remember the unremembered truth that the struggle against white supremacy is an environmental cause. The College Theology Society must, in the service of its own advocacy of world transformation, confess its own sites of white supremacy. If indeed all persons are welcome to fight against the blood-red ironies of environmental racism in the society and world, the ethos of white supremacy within CTS institutions ought to be considered an environmental affront against black bodies and a black presence in the classroom.

Of course confronting white supremacy will mean confronting well-meaning yet hegemonic relationships with other racial, ethnic, gendered, and class-restricted persons whose bodies have been marked by the conscious and unconscious scorn, ridicule, and exploitation of white power and privilege. White supremacy as an unfortunate racial truth operates and is apparent at all levels of academic institutions founded for the comfort and flourishing of white-identified peoples: from boards of trustees, to the overabundance of white males who sit atop the highest administrative structures among faculty and among top staff in many student bodies and in the classroom. And even where the numbers at any one of these levels might suggest good "multicultural integration," the issue becomes the extent to which an institution's overwhelmingly white ethos demands that "others" re/describe themselves (culturally, politically, morally) in its white image.

I do grant without a doubt or reservation the reality that not every problematic fact of our associational lives together can be reduced to race alone; Dr. Copeland has rightly focused on sexism and classism as well. And, of course we should remain vigilant against the scourges of xenophobia, heterosexism, homophobia, ethnocentrism, ageism, imperialism, neo/neo colonialism, and unjust forms of discrimination against persons with physical, intellectual, or behavioral differences. (And some of these too have been touched upon by Dr. Copeland.) Nonetheless, here I focus specifically on white supremacy in the United States, *the racialized orientation of the world according to the dictates of hegemonic Euro-whiteness*. My remarks focus on race not only because the planners invited me to this, but also because the narrative of this nation since before the Middle Passage has known racial strife as its nerve center. Our racial strife has been prominently expressed in the contexts of capitalist exploitation, ideological racial theories, and patriarchal dominance. While racism is not to be viewed as representing the whole body of our difficulties in this society, it is surely fused to the spinal cord of our body politic.

Dr. Copeland has helpfully given us representations of the biblical and Christian historical traditions that have been put to hermeneutical use against matter, against the body, against genitalia, and against human passion, particularly as these stain and mark the female body and the "darker races" of the world. Christian assaults on God's created matter have been a particularly potent sacrilege against the Christ, whose own body was broken for us and whose blood was spilled out onto the pages of history from a tree fashioned into a death-dealing cross. Theological and moral clues concerning conflict transformation related to the subject matter of this plenary can be seen in the Christian knowledge that after Good Friday, Easter came. Jesus' broken body was a site of environmental injustice—as was the hill up which he climbed, the changing weather pattern that accompanied his death alongside two others marked as criminals, the cross-shaped tree on which he (and they) hung, and the stone cave from which he emerges as the Christ.

As today we consider environmental racism (in all its organic and inorganic manifestations, including the darkly human), let us remember God's self-unveiling as the lowly-born, tortured, spat upon, beaten, and crucified Jesus Christ of Nazareth. The way of this humiliated Jesus has been demonstrated for us in a gospel tradition that aims at the restoration of grace-soaked love in the natural world. The grace and love modeled for Christians in the Jesus tradition is a profound love and concern for all creation. Such sublime grace and love speaks of our primal human inter-relatedness with the full measure of God's created world, and our radical mutuality for the cause of liberation from the wages of our broken and battered human associations.

Thankfully, the promise of Jesus Christ's love against environmental racism can be seen in the wider New York/New Jersey area where we sit at this moment. Such love can be seen in the work of Majora Carter and those working alongside her as environmental justice advocates with Sustainable South Bronx, and many other unsung organizations. This love can be seen in the active advocacy of those concerned with confronting the billowing clouds of toxic waste regularly coughed up from the many industries that sit along the I-95 corridor. It can be seen in the victims of crime who call for very difficult restorative justice rather than the violent and vengeful "status humiliation" of offenders. Indeed such love is present with those who remain vigilant at Rikers Island and at Sing Sing against some of the more inhumane, degrading, stressful, and unsanitary conditions of incarcerated life. For Christians, our ties of intimacy to the Earth and to one another are at stake whenever we confront such environmental realities in the name of our creator God and the incarnate co-sufferer with us in the risen Christ, sustaining us through the ruins by the power of the Holy Spirit.

As Dr. Copeland and I now invite you into a time of discernment and discussion around our remarks, please do keep in mind that black people are often asked to speak to our predominantly white colleagues and others interested in confronting white supremacy, privilege, and racism. We do this in the service of our common efforts to eradicate the complex nexus of injustices present in the church, society, and world, which Dr. Copeland has so well documented. It should be noted, and without too much doubt, that the white supremacy of white people in this room may differ from forms of white supremacy expressed in more virulent ideologies and practices of outright racial hate. But even less bitterly hostile forms of white supremacy are nonetheless species of white supremacy, even if cloaked in narratives of relative innocence and religious cultural merit.

White supremacy has never been limited to the racial violence and hatred of the Ku Klux Klan or other groups that unabashedly label themselves "white supremacists." White supremacy is also manifest in other complex and subtle forms. It may even cloak its racial violence in the institutional respectability, piety, and peace witness of Christian churches and institutions. Institutionally, white power and privilege routinely express themselves in the deafening silence of intellectual amnesia, and in the willful ignorance and entitled smugness of alleged openness, toleration, and hospitality. When thinking about the racism that is expressive of white supremacy, the words of Charles Lawrence, writing in 1987 for the *Stanford Law Review*, are important to hear:

> Racism in America is much more complex than either the conscious conspiracy of a power elite or the simple delusion of a few ignorant bigots. It is part of our common historical experience and, therefore, a part of our culture. It arises from the assumptions we have learned to make about the world, ourselves, and others as well as from the patterns of our fundamental social activities.[3]

It is indeed very difficult to talk with white people we scarcely know about white supremacy, privilege, and racism. And, apparently, it is often very difficult for white people to talk in a serious and sustainable way to each other around these issues as well. Nonetheless, one of the most important and difficult Christian foundations of conflict transformation is that we come to speak unflinchingly with the understanding that we will not easily give up on one another—if we can at all help it. None of our narratives of life and struggle is carried on in perfect, unspoiled goodness. Therefore we call upon the grace of God as a most profound and sacred love to guide us all and move us forward. Amen.

Some Questions for Discernment

1. What are the numbers of black students (along with other non-white racial and ethnic groups) you encounter in your class-

rooms? Do you expect black students to be (what bell hooks calls) "cultural informants," who must take primary responsibility for teaching you and their own peers "the black perspective" on subject matter related to the courses you teach? In terms of the teaching/learning expectations in your classrooms, in what ways might the presence, or absence, of black students influence the pedagogy you typically employ in class and in other academic encounters with students?

2. In the development of course syllabi and in your practices of teaching, which racial, ethnic, and gendered voices are heard most often in the materials and resources (books, essays, media, experiential learning, technology, aesthetic forms) you routinely bring to *all* the subject matter you teach? To what extent (or not) does the presence of colleagues from underrepresented groups (including black colleagues) inform (or otherwise influence) your engagements with the multiple voices that have contributed to the praxis of theology and religion?

3. In what complex and subtle ways do you think your responses to the aforementioned questions tend to support white supremacy, privilege, and racism? How might your responses demonstrate promise in the service of dismantling these deleterious human conditions?

Notes

[1] Vincent Harding, "Black Power and the American Christ," in *Black Theology: A Documentary History, 1966–1979*, ed. Gayraud S. Wilmore and James H. Cone (Maryknoll, NY: Orbis Books, 1979), 36.

[2] Billie Holiday, *Strange Fruit*, Commodore 526, 1939, vinyl recording. Reissued on *Strange Fruit*, Atlantic SD1614, 1972, compact disc.

[3] Charles R. Lawrence III, "The Id, the Ego and Equal Protection: Reckoning with Unconscious Racism," *Stanford Law Review* 39, no. 2 (1987): 330.

LGBT Bullying at the Crossroads of Christian Theology

Girard, Surrogate Victimage, and Sexual Scapegoating

Elisabeth T. Vasko

In March 2007, Eric Mohat, a high school student in the suburbs of Cleveland, committed suicide. According to his parents, Eric endured relentless taunting about his sexual identity in the months preceding his death.[1] While he did not publicly identify as gay, Eric was thin in stature and defied traditional gender norms through dress and participation in school activities. Similarly, on September 22, 2010, Tyler Clementi, a college freshman at Rutgers University, took his own life by jumping off the George Washington Bridge. Two nights earlier, his roommate had secretly recorded a sexual encounter Tyler had with another male student and posted a link to the video through Twitter.[2] While the stories of Clementi and Mohat garnered national media attention, they can hardly be considered isolated incidents. Research suggests that approximately one in five students is bullied some time during their school career,[3] and the prevalence rates are significantly higher for members of the LGBT community.[4] Bullying is becoming increasingly sexualized in nature and often involves the denigration of a person's sexual or gender identity. As a form of violence, Christian communities need to recognize the harm incurred by LGBT bullying and seek out pathways that work toward healing.

In this essay, I shall situate LGBT bullying within a theological framework, giving particular attention to its significance for Christian theologies of sin and violence. By and large, Christian theology has focused on individual overt acts of physical harm when making moral injunctions against violence. Yet, comprehensive theological responses to sin and violence must also attend to the coding of violence, emotional and physical, in cultural mores and prejudices. One of the key issues surrounding LGBT bullying is the way in which heterosexism and patriarchy contribute to the normalization of sexual scapegoating within Western culture, thereby veiling collective and individual participation in sexual and gender-based violence.

Adopting a theological framework that unmasks the violence of sexual scapegoating and names such behavior as sinful is a critical step in transforming the violence that encompasses LGBT bullying. I will argue that the work of René Girard, when read with feminist and queer liberation theological commitments, is a helpful resource in this regard. In particular, Girard's notion of surrogate victimage situates bullying at the center of the Christian narrative and names such behavior as contrary to the kin-dom[5] of God. To be clear, Girardian theory is not without its problems and must be supplemented by an analysis of heterosexism and patriarchy so as to explicitly address the ways in which patterns of surrogate victimage and scapegoating have been (and continue to be) inscribed upon sexed bodies in sacred and secular spheres. A theology of bullying violence must take serious account of the social construction of reality. With respect to LGBT bullying, this means countering deeply seeded heterosexism and gender bias.

Bullying as a Form of Violence: Key Definitions

In an era in which reality television dominates the airwaves, we have come to view the humiliation, failures, and degradation of others as a form of entertainment. Can one really say, then, that bullying is a form of violence? Moreover, how does one distinguish bullying from teasing? According to Dan Olweus, one of the leading experts on peer victimization, bullying involves three components: (1) "aggressive behavior that entails unwanted negative actions," (2) a "pattern of behavior that is repeated over time," and is marked by (3) an imbalance of power.[6] In other words, bullying is not a conflict between two individuals or groups for whom the playing field is equal. It is a form of victimization in which the perpetrator has *power over* the victim and uses this power to deliberately and repeatedly inflict emotional or physical harm.

Although bullying is a form of violence, it is not often recognized as such. In part, this is due to the sometimes covert nature of bullying behavior. Nonetheless, it is also tied to the narrow definition of violence that is operative in society at large and in theological circles. As Robert McAfee Brown points out in *Religion and Violence*, the word "violence" often invokes a mental picture of overt physical acts of destruction.[7] While this definition has the advantage of making instances of violence tangible and clear cut, it fails to account for the full spectrum of ways in which we harm one another. As such, McAfee Brown argues that "whatever 'violates' another, in the sense of infringing upon or disregarding or abusing or denying [the personhood of] that other, whether physical harm is involved or not, can be understood as an act of violence."[8] Violence is that which denies the full humanity of another.

Womanist scholar Cheryl Kirk-Duggan concurs with McAfee Brown's definition of violence, but expands it to include a description of unethical passivity. As she explains, "Ignoring the rights of another person, desensitizing oneself by observing more violent acts, and the rationalization and justification of personal or systemic use of damaging thoughts, words, and deeds is violent activity. Some violence manifests itself as one intimidating others for the purpose of domination."[9] What Kirk-Duggan describes is the kind of violence that surrounds bullying. Furthermore, bullying not only violates the personhood of the victim(s), but it also "places everyone and everything in survival mode."[10] Bullying lends toward and flourishes within cultures of relatedness that are shaped by fear and the use of power as domination. While this does not excuse the behavior of those who perpetrate such violence, it does point to the necessity of making a shift in the ways that we view power, privilege, and difference within sacred and secular spheres.

Surrogate Victimage and the Scapegoat Mechanism Unmasking the Dynamics of Power and Privilege

While a number of scholars have rightly called into question Girard's contention that mimetic desire is the root of all violence,[11] his notion of surrogate victimage exposes the harmful ways in which the dynamics of power and privilege are operative in maintaining and defining social identity groups. That is, scapegoating "is often a vehicle for shaping social order and for stabilizing relational [power] differences" along hierarchical lines.[12]

For Girard, violence is a by-product of human relationality. When human beings first attain the ability of speech and of self-reflexive consciousness, they become aware of their desires and how these desires conflict with the desires of others.[13] As S. Mark Heim aptly surmises, "we are face-readers, emotion detectors, who from the beginning of our dependent infancies grow in our desires and patterns of behavior on the basis of models taken from others."[14]

While this understanding of the human person points to the highly relational nature of subjectivity and identity, such relationality is not always positive. For Girard, mimesis leads toward human conflict as the subject imitates the model's desires and seeks to obtain the same object. Over time acquisitive mimesis becomes conflictual mimesis. The object is no longer important as the rival becomes fixated on preventing the model from achieving his or her desire and vice-versa. As the cycle continues in society, it spreads to others by means of mimetic contagion. In an effort to put a stop to violent conflict, the group subconsciously looks for a scapegoat upon whom to project its aggression. As the one whom the community views as the source of evil, sickness, or unrest, the scapegoat detracts from the original conflict and becomes a new rival upon whom to focus. In death or expulsion, the surrogate victim becomes a means of unification, and conflict is temporarily dispersed within the community.[15]

Within a Girardian framework, *pharmakos* are those who are on the fringes of society by virtue of their social identity; they are persons who have been excluded from "establishing or sharing the social bonds of the community."[16] The marginal character of the surrogate victim is important for two reasons. First, the person's "otherness" functions as the rationale for his or her guilt. In the absence of a clearly defined and visible crime, the community seeks justification for expelling the victim by pointing to aspects of his or her personhood that hold the widest variance from the dominant norm. Second, the surrogate victim's marginal location allows the community to make an act of sacrifice without the risk of vengeance.[17] That is, the victim's vulnerability lies in the fact that he or she lacks the social resources to fight back.

In contemporary Western culture, patterns of surrogate victimage often serve as a means for maintaining systems of power and privilege. As Cheryl Kirk-Duggan explains, a person "who looks, acts, or thinks different, and is vulnerable, often ends up being the focus of a group's consolidated effort to define itself and those deemed other, by turning their own pursuit of power against those who cannot react. Thus, a group establishes itself by psychologically or physically eliminating . . . the ones who are different."[18]

At stake is the creation of unity and group identity through the establishment and reinforcement of a social hierarchy whereby the dominant group "[defines] itself and [creates] unity among its members by identifying a susceptible group as 'other' or 'outside.'"[19] In light of the dynamics of power and privilege, this description of surrogate victimage largely mirrors LGBT bullying. By definition, bullying is marked by a power differential between the perpetrator(s) and the victim(s). Therefore, persons most susceptible are those who stand at the community's margins.

Moreover, bullying is not only an expression of the use of *power over*, but it also functions to support social structures of privilege by sending a message about who stands on the inside/outside of the dominant group. Tyler Clementi and Eric Mohat were targeted because their behavior or appearance visibly contested reigning notions of heteronormativity and masculinity. The bullying to which these individuals were subjected crushed their personal sense of dignity; yet, it also sent a message about the appropriate expression of gender identity and sexuality to the larger community. Thus, LGBT bullying is a mechanism for establishing and reinforcing heteronormativity.

The Girardian frame makes explicit the relationship between overt and covert participation in violence. As Girard remarks: "[O]ne of our favorite ways of dealing with scapegoating is to see it as a plot of government leaders, whereas the rest of us have not participated in it."[20] Yet, scapegoating is a collective phenomenon that does not work without the participation of the crowd. While the impetus may be to blame LGBT bullying on the actions of a hateful few, this is an inadequate explanation of what happens to victims and perpetrators because it fails to take serious account of the social construction of reality and the silent complicity of the larger community. Blaming the few bypasses the significance of collective behavior in upholding heterosexism. There were few Twitter posts contesting LGBT bullying at Rutgers prior to Clementi's death, and the school administration did not intervene in the case of Mohat. While there can be legitimate reasons for maintaining silence in violent contexts, the only way to put a stop to bullying is to change the culture in which such behavior flourishes. With respect to LGBT bullying, this means countering deeply seeded heterosexism and gender bias. In addition, given the socio-ethical ramifications of LGBT bullying, it is critical to name participation within these systems as sinful.

Sexual Scapegoating as Contrary to the Kin-dom of God

Within Christian theology sin has been predominantly defined as an individual offense against God in the form of pride or disobedience. As feminist theologians have argued, such constructions obscure the ways in which gender socialization shapes self-understanding and marginalizes the structural aspects of sin.[21] This becomes especially pertinent given the moralization of sexual behavior within the Christian tradition, whereby specific sexual acts are construed as violations of a divinely ordered plan.[22] In view of LGBT bullying, such an interpretive framework risks placing blame on the individual bullied as a kind of divinely ordained condemnation for deviant sexual behavior.

This approach to sin-talk is harmful in that it not only obscures the role of the larger community in resisting violence, but it can also contribute to the internalization of oppression in LGBT persons. As James Alison explains, for those whose sexuality falls outside of what has been deemed a "divinely ordained framework," the implication is that one must deny one's very self in order to be seen as good in God's eyes.[23] When paired with metaphorical constellations of atonement theology that glorify the violent scapegoating of an innocent victim, this interpretation of sin functions to reinforce the notion that Christian virtue is found in a willingness to sacrifice one's personhood and identity.[24]

Given the ways in which Christian traditions have based the alignment of heteronormativity and holiness on a narrow reading of the Christian scriptures,[25] Girard's reading of the gospels offers a critical clue in subverting such meta-narratives, especially when read with feminist and queer commitments.[26] Throughout his *oeuvre*, one of Girard's central contentions is that the Christian religion is subject to participation in violence through the mythologization and ritualization of sacrificial scapegoating.[27] According to Girard, such scapegoating is contrary to the heart of Christian revelation, which belies the notion that surrogate victimage is of God.

Girard argues that the Christian scriptures lay out the truth of scapegoating for all to see, exposing the mimetic nature of rivalry and the mythologization of sacrifice.[28] In presenting Jesus as the innocent victim of a group in crisis, the gospel narratives reveal the violent nature of the scapegoat mechanism. The crucifixion is not a tale of divine love or of the atonement for sin, but a story about surrogate victimage. Christ dies as a result of his efforts to make visible the ways in which religious and social authorities have participated in the sacralization of violent scapegoating. Central here is Girard's assertion that the image of the Divine projected in the Christian scriptures is a "God who is alien to all violence and who wishes in consequence to see humanity abandon violence."[29]

The core of Jesus' preaching of the kin-dom is an invitation to all of humankind to devote itself to the project of "getting rid of violence, a project conceived with reference to the true nature of violence, taking into account the illusions it fosters, the methods by which it gains ground . . . ."[30] The kin-dom is a call to renounce all scapegoating, to "break with the circularity of closed societies, whether they be tribal, national, philosophical or religious."[31] Ultimately, for Girard, the fact that humanity has never really grasped the violent nature of mimetic contagion, much less what is at stake in Jesus' death, is illustrative of our inability to hear the Word of God.

To understand the gospels, one should first realize that violence engenders mythic meanings. As Girard asserts, "instead of reading myths in light of the Gospels, people always have to read the Gospels in light of myths."[32] With this insight as our starting point, any rendering of revelation that holds claim to violent exclusion, including the discrimination of LGBT persons, on the basis of the Christian message must be held suspect. A Girardian framework calls Christian communities to consider the ways in which their participation in violence has been justified in the name of divine revelation. Failure to do so reflects participation in the mythologization of scapegoating violence and an inability to hear God's Word.

Case Study: LGBT Bullying, the "Non-Discrimination of Homosexual Persons," and Roman Catholicism

With the exception of the following statement posted on the webpage for the *National Catholic Education Association* (NCEA), the Roman Catholic Church has remained silent on the subject on LGBT bullying: "When one youth calls another youth a 'queer' deliberately intending it as a painful, prejudice slur, it is critical that school staff and student bystanders respond with more than, 'Boys will be boys.' Schools cannot tolerate such teasing, intimidation, or prejudice."[33] While the NCEA should be applauded for drawing attention to the negative impact of bullying on children and youth, the Roman Catholic Church must directly address the tenuous reception it has offered to homosexuals with respect to LGBT bullying. This is particularly important given the recent efforts members of the Magisterium have directed toward condemning anti-discrimination legislation regarding homosexual persons.[34] Not only do such efforts send mixed messages about the value of LGBT persons, but, for all intents and purposes, it is contradictory to ask young people to refrain from calling LGBT persons "queer" in a derogatory sense while defining homosexual tendencies as "intrinsically disordered."[35]

While the Roman Catholic Church names violence against homosexuals, in speech or action, as deplorable, it also holds that sexual orientation is not a "quality comparable to race, ethnic background, etc. in respect to non-discrimination."[36] Likening homosexuality to a contagious disease or mental illness, the Congregation for the Doctrine of the Faith contends that restricting the rights of LGBT persons may be crucial to "protect[ing] the common good" (*SCC*,12). The implication of this statement is that homogenital activity defiles the God-given moral and social order of society. Moreover, the CDF asserts that discrimination on the basis of sexual orientation is

generally not known to others unless [one] publicly identifies [oneself] as having this orientation or unless some overt
behavior manifests it. As a rule, the majority of homosexu-
ally oriented persons who seek to lead chaste lives do not
publicize their sexual orientation. Hence the problem of
discrimination in terms of employment, housing, etc., does
not usually arise (*SCC*, 14).

The implication here is that LGBT persons must attempt to pass
as heterosexual in order to be considered non-culpable in cases
of discrimination. In view of the stories of Eric Mohat and Tyler
Clementi, this assumption is not only erroneous, but it is harmful.
Mohat did not openly express a homosexual orientation and yet
was subject to anti-gay bullying as his outward appearance defied
traditional notions of masculinity. Even more problematic is the
tacit assumption that someone like Clementi may be responsible
for his own suffering.

Transforming a culture in which LGBT violence is tacitly
and explicitly accepted requires analyzing the ways in which
notions of sexuality and gender sit at the center of the sacrificial
economy. Theories of scapegoating violence must take account
of the gendered ways that bodiliness is inscribed within cultural
and religious systems of meaning. Doing so reveals a long history
of identifying hypersexuality, female bodies, and sin/evil within
the Christian West.[37] Moreover, as Traci West notes, within
such an interpretive framework, the meaning of womanhood
comes to stand for "an invitation to violate" on the grounds
that female sexuality untamed can pollute society.[38] In view of
this particular logic, it is not a far leap to ask whether LGBT
bullying is yet another means of sexual scapegoating, one that
acts to reinforce patriarchy and heterosexism. In other words, the
gendered social hierarchy upon which the symbolic identification
of hypersexuality and sin/evil rests has negative consequences for
nonheterosexual bodies, as systems of inequitable power often
sexualize their victims.[39]

In a framework where homogenital activity is considered to
be "intrinsically disordered" and a source of civic unrest within
the larger community, it is not a stretch to see the condemnation
of homosexual sex as a means of purifying the body of Christ.

For inasmuch as homogenital sex is viewed as a "disease," then so too are the bodies of nonheterosexual people, thereby creating the rationale for practices of surrogate victimage. In the context of LGBT bullying, this rhetorical framework risks sanctifying violence against LGBT persons. In other words, the nursery rhyme "sticks and stones may break my bones, but words will never hurt me" is hardly the case. The words we use to describe others and ourselves play a significant role in shaping the patterns of violent exclusion within sacred and secular spheres.

Concluding Remarks

My goals in this piece have been to situate LGBT bullying, as a form of violence, within the context of Christian theological discourse and to name such behavior as sinful. I have argued that the work of René Girard, when read with feminist and queer liberation theological commitments, is helpful in calling attention to the role of the community in supporting a culture that allows for the acceptance of LGBT violence. Girard's notion of surrogate victimage exposes the harmful ways in which the dynamics of power and privilege function to maintain and define social identity groups. It also calls for a deeper understanding of the ways that human relationality lends toward good *and* evil. For within the Girardian frame there is no such thing as an innocent bystander, nor can the processes that support surrogate victimage be blamed on the powerful few. Rather, all are implicated in the violent expulsion of the scapegoat.

There is, however, more work to be done with respect to the usefulness of Girardian theory in view of theological scholarship on LGBT bullying. First, while Girard's notion of surrogate victimage is helpful in unpacking the relationship of the covert and overt participation in scapegoating, more needs to be said about varying degrees of complicity as well as the ways that one's social location shapes participation within a given culture of violence.

Second, Girard's theory of surrogate victimage runs the risk of veiling gender-based violence, as it essentializes human behavior without giving attention to the particularity of gendered and sexed bodiliness. This is a complex trajectory that needs to be further explored, especially in light of the historical links within

Christendom between masculinity and sanctity. Finally, given the ways in which LGBT bullying aligns with notions of surrogate victimage, it is important to examine further how notions of atonement theology shape the Christian imagination about sacrificial scapegoating. At a minimum, these three trajectories must be explored in order to unpack the relationship between LGBT bullying and Girardian theory.

As psychological literature suggests, expelling the bully from the schoolyard does not put an end to school violence.[40] One must work to transform systems of power and privilege that support such behavior. In view of the problem of LGBT bullying, the way forward involves nothing less than a *kenosis* of heterosexual privilege. Such *kenotic* activity cannot be limited to the actions of a powerful few. Rather, it requires finding new ways to be in relation with one another that refuse to allege obedience to structures that denigrate the livelihoods of many in order to support the dreams of an elite few. Challenging this way of being in the world is no easy task; it requires a revolution in the ways that we educate our children and ourselves.

The recent bullicides call us to ask what our own Christian communities are doing to create a culture that resists violence and welcomes difference. Violence threatens to overwhelm us through conformity to the status quo. With respect to LGBT bullying, for Christian educators and theologians, the difficult work lies ahead. We have to begin to look more closely at where we stand in relation to the crosses of Matthew Shepard, Tyler Clementi, Eric Mohat, and countless others who have died as a result of LGBT violence.

Notes

[1]Susan Donaldson James, "Teen Commits Suicide Due to Bullying," *ABCNews*, April 2, 2009, http://abcnews.go.com/Health/MindMoodNews/story?id=7228335&page=2 (accessed May 12, 2011).

[2]Lisa Foderaro, "Private Moment Made Public, Then a Fatal Jump," *New York Times*, September 29, 2010, http://www.nytimes.com/2010/09/30/nyregion/30suicide.html (accessed May 3, 2011).

[3]"National Youth Risk Behavior Survey 2009 Overview," U. S. Department of Health and Human Services, http://www.cdc.gov/HealthyYouth/yrbs/pdf/us_overview_yrbs.pdf (accessed May 3, 2011).

[4]In a recent national study, 84.6% of LGBT students surveyed reported experiencing harassment at school and 61.1 % reported feeling unsafe because of their sexual orientation. Joseph G. Kosciw et al., *The 2009 National School Climate Survey: The Experiences of Lesbian, Gay, Bisexual, and Transgender Youth in Our Nation's Schools* (New York: Gay, Lesbian and Straight Education Network, 2010), 26 and 22 respectively.

[5]Ada María Isasi-Díaz uses "kin-dom" to avoid the sexist and elitist connotations of "kingdom" and to denote the communal aspects of God's vision for the world. See *Mujerista Theology: A Theology for the Twenty-first Century* (Maryknoll, NY: Orbis, 1996), 65 n.14.

[6]Dan Olweus, "What Is Bullying?" Olweus Bullying Prevention Program, http://www.olweus.org/public/bullying.page (accessed on May 7, 2011).

[7]Robert McAfee Brown, *Religion and Violence*, 2nd ed. (Philadelphia: Westminster Press, 1987), 6.

[8]Ibid., 7.

[9]Cheryl Kirk-Duggan, *Misbegotten Anguish: A Theology and Ethics of Violence* (St. Louis: Chalice Press, 2001), 21.

[10]Ibid., 16.

[11]A number of feminists have critiqued this aspect of Girardian theory. For a review of the literature, see Susan Nowak, "The Girardian Theory and Feminism: Critique and Appropriation," *Contagion: Journal of Violence, Mimesis, and Culture* 1 (1994): 19-29.

[12]Kirk-Duggan, *Misbegotten Anguish*, 38.

[13]See René Girard, "Mimesis and Violence," in *The Girard Reader*, ed. James G. Williams (New York: Crossroad, 1996), 9-19, and *Violence and the Sacred*, trans. Patrick Gregory (Baltimore/London: John Hopkins University Press, 1997), 143-68.

[14]S. Mark Heim, *Saved from Sacrifice: A Theology of the Cross* (Grand Rapids, MI/Cambridge, UK: Eerdmans, 2006), 41.

[15]René Girard, *Things Hidden since the Foundation of the World*, trans. Stephen Bann and Michael Metteer (Stanford: Stanford University Press, 1987), 27.

[16]Girard, *The Girard Reader*, 81.

[17]Ibid., 82.

[18]Kirk-Duggan, *Misbegotten Anguish*, 35.

[19]Ibid., 35.

[20]Girard, *The Girard Reader*, 266.

[21]Marjorie Suchocki outlines this critique in the first chapter of *The Fall to Violence: Original Sin in Relational Theology* (New York: Continuum, 1994).

[22]See Christine Gudorf, *Body, Sex, Pleasure: Reconstructing Christian Sexual Ethics* (Cleveland: Pilgrim Press, 1994), 15-24.

[23]James Alison, *On Being Liked* (New York: Crossroad, 2003), 25-27.

[24]Rita Nakashima Brock and Rebecca Parker make this point in *Proverbs*

of Ashes: Violence, Redemptive Suffering, and the Search for What Saves Us (Boston: Beacon, 2001), 30-6.

[25]In Roman Catholicism, the condemnation of homosexual sex is based upon an interpretation of the letters of Paul (Rom 1: 24-27, 1 Cor 6:10, and 1 Tim 1:10) as well as a reading of the *imago dei* that draws from Genesis 3. See Congregation for the Doctrine of the Faith, "Letter to the Bishops of the Catholic Church on the Pastoral Care of Homosexual Persons," October 1, 1986, par. 6, http://www.vatican.va.

[26]This is not to suggest that Girard's reading of the gospels should be adopted in its entirety. Girard's interpretation of the revelatory power of the cross has been critiqued on the grounds that it leads to a position of religious exclusivism whereby Christianity escapes the mimetic violence of all other world religions. For further discussion, see Leo D. Lefebure, *Revelation, the Religions, and Violence* (Maryknoll, NY: Orbis Books, 2000).

[27]Girard, *Things Hidden since the Foundation of the World*, 225 and 231.

[28]Ibid., 180-220.

[29]Ibid., 183.

[30]Ibid., 197.

[31]Ibid., 198.

[32]Ibid., 179.

[33]National Catholic Education Association, "Students Thrive under No-Tolerance Policy on Bullying," http://www.ncea.org/departments/nabccce/Bully.asp (accessed May 27, 2011).

[34]For example, on May 19, 2010, the USCCB sent a letter to Congress formally denouncing the Employment Nondiscrimination Act (ENDA), H.R. 3017, and Senate (S. 1584), which included provisions that made it illegal to fire someone on the basis of his or her sexual orientation. According to church officials, affirming ENDA could provide grounds for the legalization of gay marriage. A copy of the statement is available at http://www.americamaga-zine.org/blog/entry.cfm?blog_id=2&entry_id=2923 (accessed May 27, 2011).

[35]Sacred Congregation for the Doctrine of the Faith, *Persona Humana* ("Declaration on Certain Questions concerning Sexual Ethics"), December 29, 1975, part 8, par. 4, http://www.vatican.va.

[36]Congregation for the Doctrine of the Faith, "Some Considerations Concerning the Response to Legislative Proposals on the Non-Discrimination of Homosexual Persons," July 24, 1992, (hereafter SCC), par. 7 and 10, respectively, http://www.ewtn.com/library/curia/cdfhomol.htm (accessed September 21, 2011).

[37]See Kelly Brown Douglas, *What's Faith Got to Do with It? Black Bodies/Christian Souls* (Maryknoll, NY: Orbis Books, 2005), chaps. 4 and 5.

[38]Traci West, *Wounds of the Spirit: Black Women, Violence, and Resistance Ethics* (New York: New York University Press, 1999), 111. As noted by West, this has even greater consequences for women of color, as black women have been sexualized according to their race and gender.

[39]Kelly Brown Douglas makes this point in *What's Faith Got to Do with It,* 145-46.

[40]See the study by Juliane E. Fields et al., *Understanding Girl Bullying and What to Do about It: Strategies to Help Heal the Divide* (Thousand Oaks, CA: Corwin, 2009).

Part II

SECULAR AND SACRED:
THEORETICAL CONSIDERATIONS

Violence Religious and Secular

Questioning the Categories

William T. Cavanaugh

When I tell people the title of my book, *The Myth of Religious Violence,* they tend to smile if they are polite and laugh if they are not. I can almost hear them thinking "Is this a sequel to your book *The Myth of a Spherical Earth?*" Everyone seems to know that religion has a dangerous tendency to promote violence. This story is part of the conventional wisdom of Western societies.

I challenge that conventional wisdom, but not in the conventional ways it is sometimes challenged. I do not deny that Christians or Muslims who do violence are really true Christians or Muslims. I do not claim that the wars often cited as evidence against religion are really about economics or politics and not about religion. I think that the idea that there is a rigid line between religion and politics is a questionable assumption. Indeed, many Muslims, for example, make no such distinction. I do not deny that faith systems like Christianity and Islam can and do contribute to violence, given certain conditions.

Implied in the conventional wisdom, however, is that Christianity, Islam, and other faiths are *more* inclined toward violence than ideologies and institutions that are identified as "secular." In order for this indictment of religion to hold, religion must be contrasted with something else that is inherently *less* prone to violence: the secular. It is *this* story that I challenge. In this essay I will argue (1) that there is no good reason for thinking that religious ideologies and institutions are more inherently prone to violence than so-called secular ideologies and institutions, and (2) that this is so because there is no *essential* difference between religious and secular to begin with. These are invented categories, not simply the way things are.

I will look at the political reasons why these categories were invented in the modern West. I will then show that the idea that something called religion is essentially prone to violence is an ideological justification that can be used to justify the violence of so-called secular orders. The myth of religious violence promotes a dichotomy between *us* in the secular West who are supposedly rational and peacemaking, and *them*, the alleged hordes of violent religious fanatics in the Muslim world. *Their* violence is viewed as religious, and therefore irrational and divisive. *Our* violence, on the other hand, is assumed to be secular, rational, and peacemaking. Since we cannot reason with them, our only recourse is violence. So the story goes.

Defining Religious and Secular

Let us start with one of the most famous atheists today, Christopher Hitchens. His bestselling book *God Is Not Great* is subtitled *How Religion Poisons Everything*. There he points to histories of abuses by Christians, Jews, Muslims, Hindus, Buddhists, Confucianists, and so on. But he also acknowledges the fact that atheist regimes, like those of Joseph Stalin and Kim Jong-Il, are responsible for tens of millions of deaths and untold suffering. Hitchens deals with this problem by declaring that such atheist regimes are religious too. Totalitarianism aims at human perfection, which is essentially a religious impulse, according to Hitchens.[1] Religion poisons everything because everything poisonous gets identified as religion. At the same time, everything good ends up on the other side of the religious/secular divide. Hitchens says of Martin Luther King, Jr., "In no real as opposed to nominal sense, then, was he a Christian."[2] He bases this conclusion on the notion that King was nonviolent, while the Bible preaches violence from cover to cover. What is not violent cannot possibly be religious, because religion is *defined* as violent.

Now we could dismiss Hitchens, assume that Stalin is not really religious, and start arguing over who has caused more deaths in the twentieth century, atheists or those who believe in God. But that would be to assume that we really know what religion is and what it isn't. Hitchens is useful because he shows that what counts as religion and what doesn't is very fluid and often depends on the political agenda one is pursuing. Hitchens is by no means alone in this. If we examine arguments that religion causes violence, we find that what counts as religion and what does not is largely incoherent.

Let me give a few examples. In a book on public religion, historian Martin Marty argues that religion has a particular tendency to be divisive and therefore violent.[3] When addressing the question "What is religion?" however, Marty is coy. He begins by listing seventeen different definitions of religion, then begs off giving his own definition, since "[s]cholars will never agree on the definition of religion."[4] Instead Marty gives a list of five "features" that mark a religion. He then proceeds to show how "politics" displays each of these features. Religion focuses our ultimate concern, and so does politics. Religion builds community, and so does politics. Religion appeals to myth and symbol, and politics "mimics" this appeal, and so on down the list.[5] Should we then assume that "politics" is a type of "religion," or vice-versa? If not, what distinguishes the two? Marty nevertheless proceeds in the rest of the book to discuss "religion" as if it were perfectly obvious what he is talking about.

Similarly, sociologist Mark Juergensmeyer, whose book *Terror in the Mind of God*, perhaps the most widely influential academic book on religion and violence, claims that religion exacerbates the tendency to divide people into friends and enemies by ratcheting divisions up to a cosmic level. But he is forced to admit the difficulty of separating religious violence from secular violence. In his 1993 book *The New Cold War?* he writes, "Secular nationalism, like religion, embraces what one scholar calls 'a doctrine of destiny.' One can take this way of looking at secular nationalism a step further and state flatly . . . that secular nationalism *is* 'a religion.' "[6] He repeats this claim in his 2008 book *Global Rebellion*, where he says that "the secular is a sort of advanced form of religion."[7] These are crucial concessions that, taken seriously, would undermine the entire basis for his work on the peculiar relationship between religion and violence. To say that the secular is a form of religion is to demolish the distinction between the two. But without the distinction, there is simply no basis for examining religion and violence as a special category, for religion must be contrasted with something—the secular—in order for religion to stand out as a special subject of interest. Juergensmeyer continues to treat religious and secular as a mutually opposed binary, so that he can continue to make claims about the peculiar relationship of "religion" to violence.

For some religion-and-violence theorists, the confusion around the religious/secular divide is resolved by openly expanding the definition of "religion" to include ideologies and practices that are usually called "secular." In his book *Why People Do Bad Things in the Name of Religion*, Richard Wentz blames violence on absolutism. Religion has a peculiar tendency toward absolutism, says Wentz. But when considering religion, Wentz includes faith in technology, secular humanism, consumerism, football fanaticism, and a host of other worldviews. This type of view is called "functionalist" because it expands the category of religion beyond the usual list of "world religions" (a "substantivist" restricts "religion" to Christianity, Islam, Hinduism, and a handful of others) to include all those ideologies and symbol systems that function in the same way that the "world religions" do in providing meaning and order to a person's life. Wentz thus expands "religion" so widely that he is compelled to conclude, "Perhaps all of us do bad things in the name of (or as a representative of) religion."[8] The problem here is that once the definition of religion has been thus expanded, it becomes necessary to ask "Religion, as opposed to what?" The conclusion to be drawn from the analysis is simply that worldviews and symbol systems of all kinds can promote violence when taken absolutely.

Hitchens, Juergensmeyer, Wentz, and others are not necessarily wrong to include so-called "secular" things in the category "religion." There is, for example, an extensive body of scholarship that explores the prevalence of civil religion in the United States, which, as Robert Bellah says, "has its own seriousness and integrity and requires the same care in understanding that any other religion does."[9] Carolyn Marvin similarly argues that "nationalism is the most powerful religion in the United States, and perhaps in many other countries."[10] A survey of religious studies literature finds the following treated under the rubric "religion": totems, witchcraft, the rights of man, Marxism, liberalism, Freudianism, Japanese tea ceremonies, nationalism, sports, free market ideology, Alcoholics Anonymous, and a host of other institutions and practices.[11]

If one objects that religion is really about belief in God or gods, then we would need to eliminate certain belief systems that are usually called "religions," such as Daoism, Confucianism, and many forms of Buddhism, which don't have a central concept of God or gods. If the definition of religion is expanded to include such belief systems under the rubric of "transcendence" or some such more inclusive term, then all sorts of practices, including many that are usually labeled "secular," fall under the definition of religion. Many institutions and ideologies that do not explicitly refer to God or gods function in the same way as those that do. Expanding the concept of religion to include godless Buddhism makes it difficult to exclude godless Marxism. Likewise, as Juergensmeyer implicitly acknowledges, nationalism is just as "transcendent" as any of the so-called "world religions." The term "transcendence" is a tool of Western scholars of religion, who borrowed the term from the Judeo-Christian tradition, with its distinction between a Creator God and a created order. In order to apply this term to Buddhism, which has no such distinction, one needs to define "transcendence" in an exceedingly vague manner. But the vaguer the term becomes, the less justification one has for excluding other systems of belief and practice, such as nationalism.

This is particularly relevant to the question of violence. Is there any good reason to suppose that people are more likely to kill for a god than for a nation? Suppose we ask two more specific questions: What percentage of Americans who identify themselves as Christians would be willing to kill for their Christian faith? What percentage would be willing to kill for their country? I strongly suspect that the majority of American Christians would consider the idea of killing for God or for Christianity abhorrent, and yet that most would consider killing and dying for the flag and for the nation as sometimes necessary and even laudable. The fact is that people kill for all kinds of things, and there is no coherent way to isolate "religious" ideologies with a peculiar tendency toward violence from their tamer "secular" counterparts. So-called "secular" ideologies and institutions like nationalism and capitalism can inspire just as much violence as so-called "religion."

The problem with Hitchens, then, is not that he thinks Stalinism is a religion. The problem is that, if he is going to use such an expansive definition of religion, he should do so consistently, but he doesn't. For Hitchens, American civil religion is not religion; it is purely secular. The secular/religious distinction is nothing more than the distinction between the things Hitchens likes and the things he doesn't. The problem is not simply that the concept of religion has some fuzzy edges. Rather, it is that the implicit definitions of religion used in religion-and-violence arguments are *unjustifiably clear* about what does and does not qualify as a religion. Certain belief systems, like Islam, are condemned, while certain others, like nationalism, are ignored.

My point here is not to argue either for or against an expansive definition of religion. I have no intention of trying to solve, once and for all, the debate between substantivists and functionalists whether or not Confucianism or Marxism or capitalism is a religion. I don't think there is a once and for all definition of religion. My point is rather that "religion" is a category constructed in different ways in different places and times, and according to the interests of who is doing the construction. To understand why there is so much confusion around the category of religion, we need to examine its history.

History of the Religious/Secular Distinction

The basic problem with the idea that religion causes violence is the category "religion." Those who indict religion assume that religion is a transhistorical and transcultural human activity that is essentially different from secular phenomena. In reality, however, the religious/secular distinction is a relatively recent, Western creation, and what counts as religious or as secular in any given context is determined by certain political configurations of power.

Charles Kimball's book, *When Religion Becomes Evil*, begins with the following claim: "It is somewhat trite, but nevertheless sadly true, to say that more wars have been waged, more people killed, and these days more evil perpetrated in the name of religion than by any other institutional force in human history."[12] Again we must ask, "Religion, as opposed to what?" As opposed to "politics" perhaps? The problem is that there was no "religion" considered as something separable from politics until the modern era, and then primarily in the West. The Romans had the term *religio*, but there was no religion/politics distinction. How could there be, when Caesar was considered a god? For the Romans *religio* covered all kinds of civic duties that we would consider "secular." As St. Augustine says in *The City of God*, "We have no right to affirm with confidence that religion (*religio*) is confined to the worship of God, since it seems that this word has been detached from its normal meaning, in which it refers to an attitude of respect in relations between a man and his neighbor."[13]

In the course of a detailed historical study of the concept "religion," Wilfred Cantwell Smith concluded that in premodern Europe there was no significant concept equivalent to what we think of as "religion."[14] In the medieval era, the religious/secular distinction was instead used almost exclusively to distinguish between clergy who belonged to an order and diocesan clergy. In 1400 the "religions" of England were the various orders. There was no realm of secular pursuits to which God was indifferent, and though there was a distinction between civil and ecclesiastical authorities, there was no distinction between politics and religion as we conceive it.[15]

Today's religious/secular distinction was a creation of the early modern struggles for power between ecclesiastical and civil authorities. In the creation of the modern sovereign state between the fifteenth and seventeenth centuries, "religion" was invented as a universal, essentially interior and private, impulse that is essentially separate from politics and other "secular" concerns. Moreover, the idea that "religion" is a transcultural and transhistorical impulse makes the separation of religion and politics appear natural and inevitable, not a contingent arrangement of power in society.

The religious/secular distinction was subsequently exported to non-Western cultures during the process of colonization. Smith's study concludes that there is no "closely equivalent concept [to religion] in any culture that has not been influenced by the modern West"; there was no such concept in ancient Greece, Egypt, China, India or anywhere else in the ancient world.[16] When we ask a question like "Were the pyramids built for religious or political reasons?" we immediately see how anachronistic it is. This remained the case until the rest of the world was colonized by Europeans. In their initial encounters with the non-Western world, European explorers reported, with remarkable consistency, that the natives had no religion at all. Once colonized, however, the category "religion" became a powerful tool for the classification of native cultures as essentially distinct from the business of government.

"Hinduism," for example, became a "religion" in the course of the nineteenth century, despite the fact that it encompassed the entire Indian way of life, everything we would include under culture, politics, religion, and economy. Frits Staal has concluded, "Hinduism does not merely fail to be a religion; it is not even a meaningful unit of discourse."[17] This is not an insult to Hindus. Staal simply means that talking about "Hinduism" is like talking about "Americanism"; it encompasses too much of disparate meaning to have real accuracy. Nevertheless, the classification of Hinduism as a religion was useful under British rule as a way to take everything Indian and classify it as essentially private. Thus, many contemporary advocates of Hindu nationalism or Hindutva refuse to call Hinduism a religion. As Richard Cohen writes, "The proponents of Hindutva refuse to call Hinduism a religion precisely because they want to emphasize that Hinduism is more than mere internalized beliefs. It is social, political, economic, and familial in nature." [18]

For similar reasons, at the same time that European scholars were discovering Chinese religions in the nineteenth and early twentieth centuries, Chinese scholars like Liang Chichao declared that there is no religion among the indigenous products of China. Such scholars regarded religion as individualistic and nonprogressive. Despite Western categorization of Confucianism as a religion, Chinese scholars regarded it as unitive, progressive, and therefore emphatically not religious.[19] For similar reasons, the Chinese Communist government today excludes Confucianism from its official list of religions in China. It is seen as an expression of the national character, superior to "religions" such as Christianity and Buddhism, which are private and otherworldly.[20]

In her *The Invention of World Religions*, Tomoko Masuzawa concludes, "This concept of religion as a general, transcultural phenomenon, yet also as a distinct sphere in its own right . . . is patently groundless; it came from nowhere, and there is no credible way of demonstrating its factual and empirical substantiality."[21] In other words, the religious/secular distinction is not engraved in the nature of things; it is rather a distinction that is employed in Western or Westernized societies to marginalize certain kinds of beliefs and practices, and to authorize others.

Uses of the Argument

If the idea that religion promotes violence and if the religious/secular distinction upon which it hinges, therefore, are not innocent of political use, then we might ask what purposes these ideas have in current discourse. In domestic life in the United States, the myth of religious violence has played a key role in shifting the dominant mode of jurisprudence. Well into the twentieth century, "religion" was cited in Supreme Court cases as having a unifying social effect. Beginning in the 1940s, however, religion came to be seen as a potentially dangerous and divisive social force. The first U.S. Supreme Court decision to invoke the myth of religious violence was *Minersville School District v. Gobitis* (1940), which upheld compulsory pledging of allegiance to the American flag. Writing for the majority, Justice Felix Frankfurter invoked the specter of religious wars in denying Jehovah's Witnesses the right to abstain from the pledge. "Centuries of strife over the erection of particular dogmas as exclusive or all-comprehending faiths led to the inclusion of a guarantee for religious freedom in the Bill of Rights. The First Amendment . . . sought to guard against repetition of those bitter religious struggles by prohibiting the establishment of a state religion and by securing to every sect the free exercise of its faith."[22] Rather than concluding that Jehovah's Witnesses would be entitled to such free exercise, Justice Frankfurter deemed that their dissent threatened the "promotion of national cohesion. We are dealing with an interest inferior to none in the hierarchy of legal values. National unity is the basis of national security."[23] Furthermore, the government has the right to impose such unity over against dissenters. "What the school authorities are really asserting is the right to awaken in the child's mind considerations as to the significance of the flag contrary to those implanted by the parent."[24]

The Court reversed itself three years later, but Frankfurter had succeeded in introducing the idea that First Amendment decisions could be made against a backdrop of some unspecified history of "bitter religious struggles," the antidote to which is the enforcement of national unity. In subsequent decades, the myth of religious violence would be invoked by the Supreme Court in decisions banning school prayer, forbidding voluntary religious instruction on public school property, forbidding state aid to parochial school teachers, and so on. When the Court banned school prayer in the *Abington* case in 1963, again invoking the specter of religious violence, Justice Potter Stewart dissented, warning of "the establishment of a religion of secularism."[25] His warning went unheeded.

Martin Marty discusses the *Minersville v. Gobitis* case and cites the many instances of Jehovah's Witnesses who were attacked, beaten, tarred, castrated, and imprisoned in the United States in the 1940s because they believed that followers of Jesus Christ should not salute a flag. One would think that he would draw the obvious conclusion that zealous nationalism can cause violence. Instead, Marty concludes "it became obvious that religion, which can pose 'us' versus 'them' . . . carries risks and can be perceived by others as dangerous. Religion can cause all kinds of trouble in the public arena."[26] For Marty, "religion" refers not to the ritual vowing of allegiance to a flag, but only to Jehovah's Witnesses' refusal to do so. In this way the myth of religious violence is used to draw attention away from nationalist violence and toward so-called "religious violence," even though in this case Jehovah's Witnesses suffered rather than perpetrated the violence.

This is possible, of course, only if a strict division is enforced between "religion" on the one hand and the ritual vowing of allegiance to a nation's flag on the other. In an article cited by the Supreme Court in two more landmark religion-clause cases—*Walz v. Tax Commission* (1970) and *Lemon v. Kurtzman* (1971)—Harvard Law professor Paul Freund discusses the unique dangers religious questions pose to public peace. He compares the Jehovah's Witnesses' eventual success in getting themselves excused from having to say the Pledge of Allegiance to the *Abington* case, in which a Unitarian objected to public school prayer and the court banned prayer for everyone. The flag salute continued to be employed in public schools even though the Jehovah's Witnesses found the Pledge of Allegiance "at least as unacceptable and religious in nature"[27] as the Unitarians found the Lord's Prayer.

Freund finds the difference in the rulings perfectly justified. "Why? Because the prevailing, dominant view of religion classifies the flag salute as secular, in contravention of the heterodox definition devoutly held by the Witnesses."[28] Freund continues on to declare, *pace* Stewart, that the idea that secularism is a religion is merely a "play on words."[29]

Neither Freund nor the Supreme Court ever offers a definition of religion or reasons why the implicit "orthodox" definition of religion should hold. It is simply taken for granted that the ritual pledging of allegiance to a piece of cloth is *not religious*. Religion is divisive; nationalism is unifying. And so the idea that religion has a tendency to promote violence becomes one of the principal ways whereby we become convinced that killing and dying for the flag is right and fitting: *dulce et decorum est, pro patria mori*.

This dynamic is most apparent in foreign policy, especially with regard to Muslim countries. Their primary point of difference with the West is said to be their stubborn refusal to tame religious passions in the public sphere. Hitchens, for example, skewers "religion" for its violence, but has been an enthusiastic supporter of the Iraq War and Western military adventures in the Muslim world. Despite his attempt to recruit Martin Luther King to his side, Hitchens has some approving things to say about killing people. "And I say to the Christians while I'm at it, 'Go love your own enemies; by the way, don't be loving mine' . . . I think the enemies of civilization should be beaten and killed and defeated, and I don't make any apology for it."[30] For Hitchens, the Iraq War is part of a broader war for secularism, and compromise is ruled out. "It is not possible for me to say, Well, you pursue your Shiite dream of a hidden imam and I pursue my study of Thomas Paine and George Orwell, and the world is big enough for both of us. The true believer cannot rest until the whole world bows the knee."[31] The true believer Hitchens has in mind is the Islamist. But Hitchens's message is that the true believer in secularism can also not rest until the whole world has been converted to secularism—by force, if necessary.

Hitchens gives us an example from the right, but the myth of religious violence is also employed by those on the left to support America's wars. An example is Paul Berman, contributing editor to *The New Republic*. Describing himself as "pro-war and left-wing" in his bestselling book, *Terror and Liberalism*,[32] he articulates a justification for the U.S. wars in Iraq and Afghanistan based fundamentally on the myth of religious violence, that is, the idea that liberalism has found the solution to the perpetual problem of the inherent violence of religion and we need now to share that solution with the world—by military means if necessary. For Berman, liberalism is founded in the problem of religious violence:

> The whole purpose of liberalism was to put religion in one corner, and the state in a different corner, and to keep those corners apart. The liberal idea arose in the seventeenth century in England and Scotland, and the philosophers who invented it wanted to prevent the English Civil War, which had just taken place, from breaking out again. So they proposed to scoop up the cause of that war, which was religion, and, in the gentlest way, to cart it off to another place, which was the sphere of private life, where every church and sect could freely rail at each of the others.[33]

This problem and solution were not just a matter of local and contingent circumstances. Over the course of the nineteenth century, Western liberalism discovered what Berman calls "the secret of human advancement," which is "the recognition that all of life is not governed by a single, all-knowing and all-powerful authority—by a divine force."[34] Therefore, each sphere or "slice" of life could operate independently of the others, and especially "religion" could operate independently of politics, science, and so on.

The twentieth century saw this secret challenged by the atavistic, irrational impulse to impose totality on the social order. Modern totalitarianism, according to Berman, is just a variation on an age-old religious theme derived from the Bible: the people of God, under attack from evil forces, must be united to achieve victory.[35] Thus Berman, like Hitchens, includes even atheistic regimes like the Soviet Union under the rubric "religion." Since the basic battle is liberalism versus religion, any anti-liberal political system counts as religion too. In this way, the explicitly secular Baathi movement ends up falling under Berman's indictment of religion, as he lumps secular Baathi socialism and Islamic fundamentalism together as species of totalitarianism, thereby justifying Western military intervention in Iraq. "The Baathi and the Islamists were two branches of a single impulse, which was Muslim totalitarianism—the Muslim variation on the European idea."[36]

What seems to be most crucial about the "Islamists and Baathi" totalitarians is their irrationality. "Their ideology was mad. In wars between liberalism and totalitarianism, the totalitarian picture of war is always mad."[37] In a chapter entitled "Wishful Thinking," Berman excoriates liberals whose own rationality leads them to assume that others are rational too. Because of their rationality, liberals assume, for example, that Palestinians must have legitimate reasons for using violence against the Israeli occupation. But Berman assures us that the only explanation is "mass pathology" based on crazy religious ideas. The violence of the Israeli response under Ariel Sharon is regrettable, but rational: "this policy of his conformed to an obvious logic of military reasoning. A conventional logic: to smother violence under a blanket of greater violence."[38] Suicide attacks against Israel, on the other hand, are irrational and futile, and only show the madness of the Palestinian ideology.

What is needed, then, is not sympathy with madness, but "a liberal war of liberation, partly military but ultimately intellectual, a war of ideas, fought around the world."[39] The "Terror War" will be fought with guns, but primarily with philosophy and ideas. If the opposition is mad, however, it is hard to see how rational persuasion is going to work. It would seem, given the inherent irrationality of non-liberals, that they will have to be dealt with by force. Although Berman would prefer employing lectures and books, he deploys his justifications of the Gulf War, the war in Afghanistan, and the Iraq War[40] in the context of a wider argument about the need for liberalism to flex its military might. Berman considers Lincoln's Gettysburg Address in this light. Lincoln spoke about death without glorifying it as a totalitarian would. But nevertheless Lincoln "spoke about death as 'the last full measure of devotion,' which the Union soldiers had given. . . . 'From these honored dead we take increased devotion,' he said. He was explaining that a liberal society must be, when challenged, a warlike society; or it will not endure."[41] Berman then adds that a liberal society differs from other societies because it shuns absolutes; "but liberalism does not shun every absolute."[42] The absolute that it does not shun but requires is the "absolute commitment to solidarity and self-government,"[43] even unto death.

Conclusion

Berman's "liberal war of liberation" is just one expression of a foreign policy that is commonly labeled "Wilsonian" after President Woodrow Wilson made its terms explicit. Wilson was convinced that the future peace and prosperity of the world depended on the extension of liberal principles of government—along with open markets—to the entire globe. This view assumes that liberal democratic governments are inherently more peaceable than other types of government, in part because the former have learned to separate religion from politics. In the American tradition that Wilson articulated, it was assumed that America—and in particular American military might—had a special mission of bringing liberal ideals to the rest of the world.[44] This is a remarkably ambitious project. As John Lukács remarked, "If we judge events by their consequences, the great world revolutionary was Wilson rather than Lenin."[45]

The situation is not different at the beginning of the twenty-first century. As political scientist Colin Dueck says, Americans tend to favor military action "either for liberal reasons, or not at all."[46] This is expressed in the Bush Doctrine that America has access to liberal values that are "right and true for every person, in every society," that we must use our power to promote such values "on every continent," and that America will take preemptive military action if necessary to promote such values.[47]

I do not wish either to deny the virtues of liberalism or to excuse the vices of other kinds of social orders. I wish rather to challenge the religious/secular dichotomy that causes us to turn a blind eye to liberal forms of imperialism and violence. A balanced approach will not ignore violence done in the name of *jihad* and the sacrificial atonement of Christ, but neither will it ignore violence done in the name of the flag or capitalism or freedom. The problem is not "religious violence"; the problem is violence, and we need to see clearly, from both eyes, before we can address it.[48]

Notes

[1]Christopher Hitchens, *God Is Not Great: How Religion Poisons Everything* (New York: Twelve, 2007), 231.

[2]Ibid., 176

[3]Martin E. Marty with Jonathan Moore, *Politics, Religion, and the Common Good* (San Francisco: Jossey-Bass Publishers, 2000), 25-26.

[4]Ibid., 10.

[5]Ibid., 10-14.

[6]Mark Juergensmeyer, *The New Cold War? Religious Nationalism Confronts the Secular State* (Berkeley: University of California Press, 1993), 15.

[7]Mark Juergensmeyer, *Global Rebellion: Religious Challenges to the Secular State, from Christian Militias to Al Qaeda* (Berkeley: University of California Press, 2008), 23.

[8]Richard E. Wentz, *Why People Do Bad Things in the Name of Religion* (Macon, GA: Mercer University Press, 1993), 37.

[9]Robert N. Bellah, "Civil Religion in America," in *American Civil Religion*, ed. Donald E. Jones and Russell E. Richey (San Francisco: Mellen Research University Press, 1990), 21.

[10]Carolyn Marvin and David W. Ingle, "Blood Sacrifice and the Nation: Revisiting Civil Religion," *Journal of the American Academy of Religion* 64, no. 4 (Winter 1996): 767.

[11]Timothy Fitzgerald, *The Ideology of Religious Studies* (New York: Oxford University Press, 2000), 17.

[12]Charles Kimball, *When Religion Becomes Evil* (San Francisco: HarperSanFrancisco, 2002), 1.

[13]Augustine, *City of God*, trans. Henry Bettenson (Harmondsworth, England: Penguin, 1972), X.1, 373.

[14]Wilfred Cantwell Smith, *The Meaning and End of Religion* (New York: Macmillan, 1962), 18-19.

[15]"Religion," *Oxford English Dictionary*, 2nd ed. (Oxford: Clarendon Press, 1989); see also Cantwell Smith, *The Meaning and End of Religion*, 31.

[16]Smith, *The Meaning and End of Religion*, 19.

[17]Frits Staal, *Rules without Meaning: Ritual, Mantras, and the Human Sciences* (New York: Peter Lang Verlag, 1989), 397.

[18]Richard S. Cohen, "Why Study Indian Buddhism?" in *The Invention of Religion: Rethinking Belief in Politics and History*, ed. Derek R. Peterson and Darren R. Walhof (New Brunswick, NJ: Rutgers University Press, 2002), 27.

[19]Peter Beyer, "Defining Religion in Cross-National Perspective: Identity and Difference in Official Conceptions," in *Defining Religion: Investigating the Boundaries between the Sacred and the Secular*, ed. Arthur L. Greil and David G. Bromley (Oxford: JAI, 2003), 174-75.

[20]Ibid., 175-77.

[21]Tomoko Masuzawa, *The Invention of World Religions: Or, How European Universalism Was Preserved in the Language of Pluralism* (Chicago: University of Chicago Press, 2005), 319.

[22]*Minersville School District v. Gobitis,* 310 U.S. 586 (1940), 593.

[23]Ibid., 595.

[24]Ibid., 599. For the court to intervene "would amount to no less than the pronouncement of pedagogical and psychological dogma in a field where courts possess no marked and certainly no controlling competence" (ibid., 598-99).

[25]*Abington Township School District v. Schempp*, 374 U.S. 203 (1963), 313.

[26]Marty, *Politics, Religion, and the Common Good*, 24.

[27]Paul A. Freund, "Public Aid to Parochial Schools," *Harvard Law Review* 82 (1969): 1686.

[28]Ibid.

[29]Ibid., 1690.

[30]Christopher Hitchens, from a public debate in San Francisco, quoted in Chris Hedges, *I Don't Believe in Atheists* (New York: Free Press, 2008), 23.

[31]Hitchens, *God Is Not Great*, 31.

[32]Paul Berman, *Terror and Liberalism* (New York: W. W. Norton & Company, 2003), 7.

[33]Ibid., 79.

[34]Ibid., 37.

[35]Ibid., 46-47.

[36]Ibid., 60.

[37]Ibid., 182-83.

[38]Ibid.

[39]Ibid., 191.

[40]Ibid., 6-7, 198-99.

[41]Ibid., 170.

[42]Ibid.

[43]Ibid., 171.

[44]Colin Dueck, *Reluctant Crusaders: Power, Culture, and Change in American Grand Strategy* (Princeton: Princeton University Press, 2006), 22.

[45]John Lukács, quoted in Andrew J. Bacevich, *American Empire: The Realities & Consequences of U.S. Diplomacy* (Cambridge: Harvard University Press, 2002), 87.

[46]Dueck, *Reluctant Crusaders*, 26.

[47]*The National Security Strategy of the United States of America*, September 2002, prologue and 15.

[48]This essay is a significantly revised version of my plenary address to the College Theology Society Annual Meeting, June 2, 2011, at Iona College. The essay and lecture are a drastically abbreviated version of my book, *The Myth of Religious Violence: Secular Ideology and the Roots of Modern Conflict* (New York: Oxford University Press, 2009).

The Grammar of the Kingdom in a World of Violence

The (Im)possible Poetics of John D. Caputo

Daniel P. Horan

There is a certain logic to violence. Its place, although generally unwelcome in most circumstances, can be understood as a constitutive element of human history. So ubiquitous is violence in contemporary culture—particularly that of mainstream or popular culture in the United States—that the philosopher Jamie Smith identifies violence in the sacrificial iterations in which it is often found as a form of "secular liturgy."[1] An exemplary illustration of this form of secular liturgy is found in what Michael Hanby describes as "the military-entertainment complex," which, as Smith explains, is "a powerful cultural machine that generates stories, images, and paeans of bravery, sacrifice, and devotion to the national cause, choreographed with bodily movements in contexts that are deeply affective."[2] Violence as secular liturgy can be seen as deeply ingrained in the popular expressions of American nationalism. Smith explains:

> Implicit in the liturgies of American nationalism is a particular vision of human flourishing as material prosperity and ownership, as well as a particular take on intersubjectivity, beginning from a negative notion of liberty and thus fostering a generally libertarian view of human relationships that stresses noninterference. Related to this is a sense that competition and even violence is basically inscribed into the nature of the world, which thus valorizes competition and

even violence, seeing war as the most intense opportunity to demonstrate these ideals.[3]

The logic of violence is revealed in the expectations contained within the secular liturgy of American nationalism and the public (and private) performances of it in manifold form. From the ostensibly innocuous manifestations of this logic in motion pictures and television programs like the popular "24" starring Kiefer Sutherland to the more overt and treacherous instances of this logic in the *events* of torture and abuse at Abu Ghraib and Guantánamo Bay, the rituals of this liturgy proclaim a credo that betrays something of an unacknowledged faith of the populous, for the veracity of *lex orandi, lex credendi* is maintained even here.

Of course, the United States is not singular in its cultural advocacy on behalf of such secular liturgies, wherein sacred texts are translated into the logic of violence. However, the particular style of American nationalism is unique in its syncretic appropriation of both violence and Christianity. Of the millions who participate in the rituals of this patriotic faith, the majority are self-described Christians. In a world of unprecedented potential for violence, injustice and division, how can so many not just tolerate but embrace the oppositional paradigms of American nationalism on the one hand and Christianity's good news (literally *Gospel*) on the other? Smith suggests that "many Christians experience no tension between the gospel according to America and the gospel of Jesus Christ because, subtly and unwittingly, the liturgies of American nationalism have so significantly shaped our imagination that they have, in many ways, *trumped* other liturgies."[4] The result is that Christianity is then sifted through the filter of American nationalism and translated into the language that bears the logic of violence.

The Slovenian critical theorist and philosopher Slavoj Žižek offers us yet another take on the ubiquity of violence in society. Žižek suggests that while subjective violence (murder, rape, war, and so on) is the most observed and critiqued form of violence, it is simply the most visible but not the only type. There are also more latent and insidious forms of objective and systemic violence that permeate economic and political structures that never make it to the crime section of the newspaper, but which undergird and perpetuate the condition for the possibility of more visible, if uncorrelated, forms of violence.[5]

An example of this form of objective and systemic violence made manifest in recent times can be seen in the popular, if ostensibly spontaneous, reaction of many to the news of the discovery and state-sponsored assassination of Osama bin Laden by the United States. Additionally, Texas Governor Rick Perry, during a debate in September 2011 prior to the selection of the GOP presidential nominee, was greeted by applause after the moderator introduced a question with statistics highlighting the number of state executions of criminals in Texas. Both of these seemingly popular responses to government-related, nationalistically oriented manifestations of violence serve as heuristic models of what Žižek has posited vis-à-vis our contemporary cultural, political, and religious contexts.

The Christian theological tradition is challenged to respond to this misappropriation of faith that has recast the "good news" into a bronze idol depicting America personified. Theologians must respond in new and creative ways with the transformative message of eschatological hope found in the proclamation of the kingdom of God. Yet, such an effort is not without its own pitfalls, for, as Smith asserts, "the vision of the kingdom implicit in this [secular] liturgy is antithetical to the vision of the kingdom implicit in Christian worship."[6] Disentanglement is necessary; re-articulation is required. Resources must be engaged that help theologians return to the *fides quaerens intellectum* at hand, responding as it were to the questions of theological reflection in a postmodern age.

One resource for such a response is the contemporary theology of John D. Caputo, whose work has produced novel approaches to these issues in recent years. Drawing on the insight of the philosophy of deconstruction, most notably in the work of Jacques Derrida, Caputo offers today's theologians new resources both in terms of method and content. His method, a Christian engagement with deconstruction, serves as a heuristic model for contemporary theological reflection according to the symbolic discourse of poetics in place of the binary grammar of logic. The content of his theology, in part the identification of the kingdom of God as the event of the possibility of the impossible, is both a return to examine the *sensus plenior* of scripture and a (re)presentation of the transformative power of the Christian message.

This essay is a twofold presentation offering a preliminary consideration of Caputo's theological method and content in light of violence. Its thesis, nascent as it is, centers on the claim that postmodern continental philosophy, particularly in the form of deconstruction à la Jacques Derrida, provides contemporary theologians with a means to articulate the content of Christian faith, as capsulized in the *kerygma* of the kingdom, for a world grappling with the reality and effects of subjective, objective, and systemic violence, particularly within the framework of secular liturgies of nationalism and the so-called "American Gospel."

Method: The Faithfulness of Illogical Poetics

In his acclaimed book, *The Weakness of God: A Theology of the Event*, John Caputo is entirely forthcoming about his methodological preference. He writes, "I will make clear that the discourse of the Kingdom rightly understood is governed, not by a 'logic of omnipotence,' which has to do with entities, but by what I will call a *poetics of the impossible*, which has to do with events."[7] Caputo's transparent starting point is the correlation of what the Christian scriptures present as "nothing is impossible for God" (Luke 1:37) with Derrida's concept of "the *impossible*"—in other words, a linkage between the gospel and deconstruction. As Caputo makes clear in his popular book, *What Would Jesus Deconstruct?* the prophetic spirit of Jesus is made intelligible in the proclamation of the kingdom of God. He suggests that we are able to experience that event, to recognize what is already always there through deconstruction, and that "Deconstruction is good news, because it delivers the shock of the other to the form of the same, the shock of the good (the 'ought') to the forces of being ('what is')."[8]

Caputo explains further what he means by deconstruction and its relevance to Christian theology:

> Deconstruction is organized around the idea that things contain a kind of uncontainable truth, that they contain what they cannot contain. Nobody has to come along and "deconstruct" things. Things are auto-deconstructed by the tendencies of their own inner truth. In a deconstruction, the

"other" is the one who tells the truth on the "same"; the other is the truth of the same, the truth that has been repressed and suppressed, omitted and marginalized, or sometimes just plain murdered, like Jesus himself, which is why Johannes Baptist Metz speaks of the "dangerous" memory of the suffering of Jesus and why I describe deconstruction as hermeneutics of the kingdom of God.[9]

Accessing the event of truth, inasmuch as one is able to "access" and not only experience an event, calls for a different hermeneutic, one that is tuned to the key of the kingdom and not of the world—a way of seeing through the eyes of Jesus and not simply repeating the *status quo*. For repetition is a function of the kingdom, a repetition of the impossible made possible in the total gift of forgiveness. As Keith Putt explains, "the kingdom of God is a new creation and, therefore, demands new minds and new hearts; it actually established a new type of economy, a mad economy of excess and extravagance, an economy that does not covet balanced books or safe returns on existential investments."[10]

Deconstruction offers us a method by which to access a new way of seeing that event of truth that is the kingdom. Caputo notes how deconstruction, its recognition of the event of the gift, the truth, the kingdom, stands apart from the previously conceived expressions of Christian faith. He writes:

> Derrida's discourse on the gift delimits and demystifies the economy of sacrifice by showing where the logic of exchange and sacrifice leads, by showing where giving and taking, giving up and getting back, lead, by showing, in short, how such a logic deconstructs or autodeconstructs. Deconstruction shows what happens when the divine madness of the faith of father Abraham becomes an economy pure and simple, when the *credo* of faith deteriorates into a credit system, when the gift turns to poison. The analysis shows the difficulty of keeping the true coin of faith separate from the counterfeit coin of a credit system, that there is nothing to guarantee that the one will not become the other, nothing that says it cannot reverse itself and turn into its opposite, that it does not already contain its opposite, that we must always suspect

it, subjecting it to a "hermeneutics of suspicion," as Paul Ricoeur showed years ago.[11]

This variation on Ricoeur's theme of the hermeneutic of suspicion, namely the hermeneutic of the kingdom, demands a new grammar, a new *logos*, a new way of seeing.

Again, as noted at the outset of this essay, there is a certain logic to violence. This discursive fact invites further consideration, namely that the logical grammar that sustains myriad forms of violence in our world is antithetical to the *kerygma* of the kingdom of God. In keenly observing this oft-overlooked reality, Caputo asserts that the wisdom of deconstruction heuristically identifies the contradiction inherent in so-called worldly wisdom (an *homage* to St. Paul, of course) as it seeks to maintain power amid claims of authentic Christian discipleship. Such a nexus—the "wisdom" of the world and a particular reading of Christian discipleship—enables the context out of which secular liturgies of nationalism and violence (from Constantinian Rome to George W. Bush's America) can be formed, simultaneously (re)scripting the Christian narrative while rendering this novel form of discipleship unrecognizable to the gospel proclamation of the kingdom.

So tainted have certain articulations of the Christian tradition become that the language of its expression no longer offers a resource for accessing the "good news," as it were. One way to describe this phenomenon, this worldly "wisdom" of which St. Paul speaks that is at once and the same time wedded to an obsession with maintaining *arche*, is to talk about the logical grammar of the possible. This worldly discourse is concerned with and bent on the sensible, the logical, the economic exchange of just value and reciprocity. It is a language focused on "fairness" as conceived in finite, human terms, which therefore creates a space where it is not only permissible but logical to seek and endorse systems of retribution and vengeance, economies of debt and control, and liturgies and politics of violence.

To the contrary, Caputo holds that this method of language, this worldly grammar of logic, is not what rightly expresses the kingdom of God proclaimed by Jesus of Nazareth. St. Paul says as much when he confesses the ostensible foolishness and stumbling block the Christian *kerygma* presents to the world. Drawing on his understanding of the "event" of the name of God—inspired as it is from the insight of Derrida—Caputo rejects the logical grammar of the possible as capable of expressing the *kerygmatic* kingdom of the gospel. Jesus does not speak in logical terms, in language of the possible, but instead proclaims a poetic and eschatological theology that denotes the in-breaking of God's reign.

Nevertheless, Jesus is quick to point out that his kingdom is "not of the world" (Jn 18:36), offering Caputo and us yet another deconstructive clue. The kingdom does not conform to the logic of the world, but is structured (or unstructured or *deconstructed*) according to a "divine logic," which is described least badly as a *poetics*.[12] Caputo explains that by "poetics" he means: "a constellation of strategies, arguments, tropes, paradigms, and metaphors, a style and a tone, as well as a grammar and a vocabulary, all of which, collectively . . . is aimed at making a point."[13] This point is, as Caputo creatively describes elsewhere, a "rule of the unruly, the possibility of the impossible."[14]

The kingdom is marked by several things that appear illogical and counterintuitive in a world marred by the logic of violence; because of this, we can understand the kingdom to be an announcement of God's preference for reversals—for preferring sinners over the righteous, for identifying the stranger as the neighbor, for showing that the insiders are actually out and the like. The language of the kingdom must be poetic, cannot be logical, because "the horizon of the world is set by the calculable, the sensible, the *possible*, the reasonable, the sound investment." Caputo goes on, "in the world, we are made to pay for everything. The world is nobody's fool."[15] Yet, it is precisely foolishness that Jesus proclaims and St. Paul confirms. The logical language of the world, the grammar that justifies the perpetuation of violence and vengeance, that inaugurates secular liturgies of nationalism, has no room, no patience, and no time for such poetic discourse and such absurd visions of reality.

In light of this truth, the truth that Jesus proclaimed would set us free, yet set him on a trajectory to be crucified, today's theologians would be wise to consider the illogical and foolish method of deconstruction for its grammar of the impossible. It is not simply the contemporary discourse of politics and secular liturgies that have no time or space for and stand in contrast to the poetics of the kingdom, but the binary and zealously stark grammar of Greek metaphysics also prides itself on its economy (*oikos*), logic (*logos*), and wisdom (*Sophia*). A method of deconstruction recognizes that which is always already unfolding and auto-deconstructing in the *theo-logos* of our day, so significantly shaped as it is by Hellenistic philosophy. How do we square this discourse of God, this God-talk, our *theo-logos* so weighted by binary logic and worldly wisdom with the unsettling, reversing, and an-*arche* proclamation of the kingdom by Jesus? Is it any wonder, then, that from the Council of Nicaea (325) onward the church has had such a difficult time teaching and explaining the *kerygma* in the language of Greek philosophy?

As for supplementary and perhaps a seemingly unlikely source of support for Caputo's method with particular consideration for violence in the world, I again turn to Žižek who, in his book *Violence: Six Sideways Reflections*, recalls Theodor Adorno's remark that "To write poetry after Auschwitz is barbaric."[16] Žižek responds in a way that I believe only bolsters Caputo's claims, writing:

> Adorno's famous saying, it seems, needs correction: it is not poetry that is impossible after Auschwitz, but rather *prose*. Realistic prose fails, where the poetic evocation of the unbearable atmosphere of a camp succeeds. That is to say, when Adorno declares poetry impossible (or, rather, barbaric) after Auschwitz, this impossibility is an enabling possibility: poetry is always, by definition, "about" something that cannot be addressed directly, only alluded to.[17]

What Žižek appears to confirm is Caputo's claim that the ordinary logic of worldly discourse, what he simply calls "prose," is not capable of responding to the horrors of unmitigated evil and violence in the world. In a way, that language of logical prose, because it establishes the condition for the possibility of violence, can only perpetuate that which the poet or prophet seeks to decry in the (event of the) name of God. Prose only speaks in the idiomatic terms of the possible. It is the poetics of the kingdom that breaks open the event of God's non-sovereign reign (to borrow a phrase from Keith Putt)[18] to, literally, ex-press (to push-out, to make real) *the* impossible.

Content: Forgiveness and *Metanoia* as Performance
of the Kingdom

A Christian theological response to the world of violence requires, as we have already seen, a new hermeneutic rooted in the poetic discourse of the kingdom of God as proclaimed by Jesus of Nazareth. If, as Roger Haight and others have so consistently asserted,[19] scripture is the religious and historical medium of God's revelation and the normative source for theology, then theologians are bound to reckon with its *kerygmatic* source and content. Beyond the shift in language necessitated by such exegesis, one uncovers several thematic elements that we might call the theological "content" of the kingdom, features of *theo-logos* (God-Talk) that Caputo maintains form the core focus of what should be our theological enterprise.

Caputo presents the mutually informative Christian/deconstructive themes of "forgiveness" and "*metanoia*" as constitutive elements of the expression of the kingdom poetics of the impossible. I suggest that it is the witness of forgiveness as proclaimed and demonstrated in the deeds of Jesus that most pertinently offers a fecund resource for theological responses to sin, suffering, and violence today. Furthermore, Caputo's notion of *metanoetics*, a reaffirmation of the centrality of *metanoia* in the proclamation of the kingdom, also highlights the (im)possibility of forgiveness of the Christian message. The proximity of forgiveness to the core of the poetic discourse of the kingdom bespeaks something totally new breaking into our quotidian world—the emergence of the event or what Derrida calls "the coming of the Other" (*l'invention de l'autre*). It is this prioritization of the impossible, marked in part by the good news of forgiveness that is reflected in the grammar of the kingdom of God and speaks to a violent world in need of transformation. But what does this forgiveness look like?

Keith Putt, following Caputo, offers a take on what the kingdom means if one understands from the perspective of how Jesus "interprets and embodies that kingdom." He writes:

> Indeed, Jesus's prophetic logic of the kingdom establishes a
> disconnect between it and the world, a critical differentiation

that calls the world into question, that contradicts the world by speaking a word of divine judgment against the world and its adherence to protocols of violence, greed, oppression, and alienation. Jesus claims that the kingdom of God is a reality in which individuals should love their enemies, in which the criterion for giving is the extravagance of "everything," in which the response to evil is not more evil but forgiveness, in which such forgiveness should be granted seventy times seven times, in which the insult of a slap should bring the response of the offer of another cheek, in which the first will be last, the rich cannot buy their redemption, and the innocence and weakness of a child most successfully symbolize the proper model for entry into the kingdom community.[20]

Forgiveness, not vengeance nor violence, is the overarching and distinguishing characteristic of the kingdom of God that all Christians are called to proclaim, following the example of Jesus's preaching and deeds. It demands of us, as Putt says about Caputo's assertion elsewhere, "a disruption of the usual modes of thinking in the world."[21] And a disruption it is.

Caputo claims that forgiveness holds pride of place in the kingdom of God and that this *kergmatic* forgiveness serves as a nexus between Christianity and deconstruction.[22] Forgiveness as exhibited in the preaching and deeds of Jesus anticipates in an eerily accurate way the deconstructive notion of "forgiveness" posited by Derrida two millennia later. For Derrida, "forgiveness" is indeed impossible, for the only thing that can be forgiven is the unforgivable.[23] Derrida goes on to note, that "[forgiveness] *should* remain exceptional and extraordinary, in the face of the impossible: as if it interrupted the ordinary course of historical temporality,"[24] which is precisely what Caputo believes Jesus's proclamation of the kingdom did! This encounter with the impossible is clearly disturbing, unnerving, and outlandish to many—how else would you explain the need to shoot (or *crucify*) the messenger by means of the same system that the *kerygma* seeks to interrupt and undermine?[25]

I experienced this reaction in a personal way when I critiqued on my blog the jingoistic catharsis exhibited by certain Americans joyfully celebrating the assassination of Osama bin Laden.[26] While nearly four thousand people shared that link on Facebook and more shared it elsewhere in other social-media venues, suggesting perhaps that such a critique and call for a more kingdom-based Christian response attracted the compassion (literally: "to suffer with") of some, the backlash was vehement—not just to me, but to anyone who dared to raise the Christian proclamation that we should be responding to violence with forgiveness and not more violence. A friend who wrote an opinion piece for a local newspaper in upstate New York even received attack letters and threats in response to his call for Christians to "forgive" bin Laden.

This sort of reaction—whether in response to theological reflection raised in critique of state-sponsored assassination, increased militarization or wars, responses to domestic crimes, the perpetuation of capital punishment, or the like—seems to reflect what Jamie Smith has described as the effective substitution of "the Gospel of Jesus" with "the Gospel of America," complete with its orchestrated secular liturgies of violence and nationalism expressed in the logical language of the possible. Turning the other cheek, forgiving the unforgivable, protesting the violence of the state—these things remain outside the conceivable limits of the possible, saturated as they are by the strictures of Hellenistic binary systems. Or, as Caputo says so well: "In the kingdom things do not seem to be made of the stiff stuff of Greek *ousia* but to have a wondrous pliability and plasticity that would have left the Greeks themselves wondering, even though the Greeks were supposed to be famous for their wonder."[27]

It is for this reason, this clear shirking of the kingdom of God for the kingdom of the world or of *the possible*, that Caputo believes *metanoia* must be front and center in the minds of those engaged in the Christian theological enterprise today. For Caputo, Christian *metanoia* means to be of "a new mind, a new heart, a new creation, [and] a new order of both spirit and flesh."[28] Demanding more than "personal conversion," whatever that might mean, it includes an entire change of heart and requires the proclamation of the kingdom. There is something illogical, irrational, and mad about the turning-toward the kingdom constitutive of Christian *metanoia*—it demands excess to the point of absurdity. Caputo is quick to point out how moderation, particularly in the thought of Aristotle, is always seen as virtuous according to the grammar of the possible, in the language of Greek philosophy. Yet, the kingdom reveals a God who is excessive in forgiveness, whose reign is not one of *arche*, but humble weakness; whose sense of justice is not violence, but unconditional and non-economic forgiveness.

Metanoia in the grammar of the poetics of the impossible is a turning-away-from the ubiquitous compromises so common in theological reflection and a turning-toward a recentralization of the *kerygma* of the kingdom of God. It is a conversion toward taking Jesus's words seriously in the Gospel of Luke: "But I say to you, Love your enemies, do good to those who hate you, bless those who curse you, pray for those who abuse you" (Lk 6:27-28). It is a realization that the mitigation of excessive forgiveness and uncompromising nonviolence are not exemplary glosses on the *Vita Evangelica*, but exercises of capitulation to a world of violence in the grammatical key of the possible.

Forgiveness is not reserved for ideological admiration, but the product of the kingdom *kerygma*-made-praxis. The invitation of *metanoia* is an invitation to perform the kingdom of God, which is not a place as much as it is a reality made present, a divine time found when the impossible is made possible.

Conclusion: The Theological Import of the Kingdom of God

The question that remains is an ever-popular, relevant, and pragmatic one: so what? What I have sought to do here was, in a very superficial or preliminary manner, highlight the intersection of John Caputo's project of Christian-deconstructive correlation, noting along the way that the method and content of such a project bear relevance for all Christian theologians today. This is particularly true in responding to a world of unprecedented potential for violence, injustice, and division, to which the Christian theological tradition is challenged to respond in a new and creative way with the transformative (the *metanoetic*) message of eschatological hope found in the proclamation of the kingdom of God. While deconstruction might appear to be novel in its recent presentation and popularity, what it reveals for Christian theology is that which is always already under the surface—the madness, the illogic, the impossibility and an-*archic* (literally) content of the Christian proclamation of the kingdom of God. My assertion is that theologians are well advised to follow Caputo's lead, to return to (or begin with) the impossible poetics of the kingdom, responding in prophetic and praxis-oriented discourse. Methodologically this requires a critical examination of the capitulation of our appropriated theological grammar. Concerning the content of that process, we are called to forgive, which is something we often forget, and we are invited to change our hearts (*metanoia*) according to the words and deeds of the one who announces the Good News and whose name we bear.

Notes

[1]See James K. A. Smith, *Desiring the Kingdom: Worship, Worldview and Cultural Formation*, Cultural Liturgies, vol. 1 (Grand Rapids, MI: Baker Academic, 2009), 89-129, esp. 103-11.

[2]Ibid., 104. See also Michael Hanby, "Democracy and Its Demons," in *Augustine and Politics*, ed. John Doody, Kevin Hughes, and Kim Paffenroth (Lanham, MD: Lexington Books, 2005), 117-44.

[3]Smith, *Desiring the Kingdom*, 107.

[4]Ibid.

[5]See Slavoj Žižek, *Violence: Six Sideways Reflections* (New York: Picador Press, 2008).

[6]Smith, *Desiring the Kingdom*, 107.

[7]John D. Caputo, *The Weakness of God: A Theology of the Event* (Bloomington: Indiana University Press, 2006), 102.

[8]John D. Caputo, *What Would Jesus Deconstruct: The Good News of Post-Modernism for the Church* (Grand Rapids, MI: Baker Academic, 2007), 26-27.

[9]Ibid., 29.

[10]B. Keith Putt, "Violent Imitation or Compassionate Repetition? Girard and Caputo on Exemplary Atonement," in *Religion and Violence in a Secular World: Toward a New Political Theology*, ed. Clayton Crockett (Charlottesville: University of Virginia Press, 2006), 32.

[11]John D. Caputo, *The Prayers and Tears of Jacques Derrida: Religion without Religion* (Bloomington: Indiana University Press, 1997), 219-20.

[12]John D. Caputo, "The Poetics of the Impossible and the Kingdom of God," in *The Blackwell Companion to Postmodern Theology*, ed. Graham Ward (London: Blackwell, 2001), 470.

[13]Ibid.

[14]Ibid., 471.

[15]Ibid., 472.

[16]Theodor W. Adorno, "Cultural Criticism and Society," in *The Holocaust:*

Theoretical Readings, ed. Neil Levi and Michael Rothberg (New Brunswick, NJ: Rutgers University Press, 2003), 281.

[17]Žižek, *Violence*, 4-5.

[18]B. Keith Putt, "*Depravatio Crucis*: The Non-Sovereignty of God in John Caputo's Poetics of the Kingdom," in *Peace Be with You: Christ's Benediction amid Violent Empires*, ed. Sharon Baker and Michael Hardin (Telford, PA: Cascadia Publishing House, 2010), 148-82.

[19]See Roger Haight, *Dynamics of Theology* (Maryknoll, NY: Orbis Books, 2001), esp. 68-128.

[20]Putt, "*Depravatio Crucis*," 156-57.

[21]B. Keith Putt, "Reconciling Pure Forgiveness and Reconciliation: Bringing John Caputo into the Kingdom of God," *Crosscurrents* 59 (December 2009): 507.

[22]Caputo, "The Poetics of the Impossible and the Kingdom of God," 476.

[23]See Jacques Derrida, *On Cosmopolitanism and Forgiveness*, trans. Mark Dooley and Michael Hughes (London: Routledge, 2001), 27-60.

[24]Ibid., 32.

[25]See Putt, "Violent Imitation or Compassionate Repetition?"

[26]See http://www.DatingGod.org.

[27]Caputo, "The Poetics of the Impossible and the Kingdom of God," 476-77.

[28]Caputo, *What Would Jesus Deconstruct?* 85.

Scapegoating the Secular

The Irony of Mimetic Violence in the Social Theology of John Milbank

Scott MacDougall

While it is crucial to explore the intersection of theology and violence, an equally pressing topic of concern has to be the extent to which theology can be written *as* violence. Not only must we guard against and critique theologies of violence and the violence legitimated by theology, we must also attend to what happens when we *do* theology violently. This is more than a methodological consideration. It has serious ecclesial and practical import. An examination of John Milbank's theological content and style provides a case study in how this is so.

Milbank's Project and His Understanding of the "Secular"

Milbank is the progenitor of the theological movement known as Radical Orthodoxy. Milbank and Radical Orthodoxy aim to expose, analyze, and critique the processes by which the Christian West moved away from a philosophically realist and transcendent ontology of analogical participation in God and the Good toward a nominalist ontology of immanence. The first, a philosophically realist ontology of analogical participation, relies on the notion of a highly transcendent God and a version of substance metaphysics that views anything with positive existence as sharing ontologically in this transcendent source.[1] Milbank traces this idea along a line running from the neo-Platonic philosophers, patristic theologians, and, supremely, Augustine, to Aquinas, Vico, certain German

Romantic philosophers, such as Hamann and Herder, down to Kierkegaard and theologians such as de Lubac and Blondel, all of whom preserve it to varying degrees.

The other, the nominalist ontology of immanence, is taken to posit a God present in the created order and to emphasize the ontic integrity of individual entities without reliance upon an utterly transcendent divine source, save in the ultimate sense of their existence deriving from the prior act of a creator. Milbank contends this set of views originated with Duns Scotus, was advanced by William of Ockham, apotheosized by the Enlightenment philosophers, Kant above all, and carried forward by Hegel, Nietzsche (held by Milbank to be especially culpable in this), and Heidegger, and by their philosophical and theological progeny, especially the postmodernists. This led directly, Milbank maintains, to the liberalism, positivism, and dialecticism that take their ultimate intellectual and socio-historical form in the atheism and nihilism he thinks characterize "secular" postmodern thought and life.

The only Christian response, Milbank argues, is to reassert the realist ontology of analogical participation. This is the culminating argument of Milbank's highly influential 1990 book, *Theology and Social Theory: Beyond Secular Reason.*[2] His key figure for this is Augustine and his central text is Augustine's *City of God*. Milbank takes up Augustine's distinction between the *civitas terrena* and the *civitas Dei* and he correlates them with ontologies of peace and violence. Augustine's earthly city represents the socio-political order and is juxtaposed against the city of God, which represents the divine order. Milbank's ontology of violence, linked to the earthly city, corresponds to all that we have learned to call the "secular" realm—the area of human life that we have sectioned off from the divine and assign to strictly human agency (the social, the political, the scientific, and so forth). The heavenly ontology of peace associated with the city of God corresponds to the places and times where God's purposes are most fully lived out. Milbank calls this the "Church." The ontology of peace is, so to speak, the "original position" of creation. To return to this divinely intended mode of life is to renounce the violence of the world, to return to peace, to return to God. This is accomplished through the church, where we are able to participate in the Good, in God, and in God's purposes. Outside of the church is violence in the guise of various deployments of power, visible and invisible.[3]

In making this argument, Milbank calls upon the work of anthropologist René Girard, who argues that Jesus' crucifixion is the epitome of a "mimetic violence" that underlies all human social organization. Such violence, Girard contends, occurs as the result of a projection of social conflicts and anxieties onto an innocent victim, a scapegoat, who is brutally slaughtered to cleanse the community of "impurity," but who is then paradoxically sanctified for having been the means by which the community has either established or preserved itself. Violence stands as the unacknowledged heart of our social arrangements. Milbank agrees, and asserts that Girard comes close to revealing the ontology of violence behind the "secular" that he himself describes.[4]

This "secular" realm is a total fiction for Milbank, as there is no component of creation or life within it that can be thought of as separated from divine purposes. Milbank does not deny or downplay the salutary effects of secular*ization*, the retreat of the ecclesial from direct involvement in political and economic life (though he does express a degree of ambivalence about it).[5] His concern is the "secular," a supposed sphere of purely human action. Anything that is separated from divine purpose, whose being is not grounded directly in the divine will, is *de facto* oriented toward evil, toward violence, rather than the Good. It is an illusion with no positive ontological status.

Theological Violence in the Name of Non-Violence

While Milbank's sophisticated attempt to describe and remedy the theological and practical effects of the complex era referred to as (post)modernity is highly laudable and provocative, one can ask whether the style and content of his work regarding his construction of "the secular" are allied with an "ontology of violence." Regarding Milbank's tone, Christopher Insole, for example, contends that even if Radical Orthodoxy is correct in positing that an "ontology of violence" exists at the heart of secular postmodernity, Radical Orthodoxy is itself not able to overcome it in its rhetorical style.[6] Milbank often does use strong language, referring, for example, to the Yale School's "somewhat barbaric deployment of Wittgenstein"[7]; to "that remote and bastard descendant of Luther, Friedrich Nietzsche"[8]; and to "scholars like J. D. G. 'Jimmy' Dunn (who appear to have spent their lifetimes reducing the great apostle [Paul] to banality)."[9]

Not surprisingly, secularity as a phenomenon and as a perspective receives particularly sharp criticism. "Speaking with a microphoned and digitally simulated voice," Milbank writes, the logic of secularism "proclaims—uneasily, or else increasingly unashamedly—its own lack of values and lack of meaning. In its cyberspaces and theme-parks it promotes a materialism which is soulless, aggressive, nonchalant, and nihilistic."[10] The secular is "becoming more hostile," with Christianity being "overthrown by a culture that is sloughing off a respect for Christian values as well as Christian belief."[11] Secularity, or "our current heretical, immoral, and neo-pagan political morass,"[12] is a condition that "destroys life, babies, childhood, adventure, locality, beauty, the exotic, the erotic, people, and the planet itself."[13]

None of this would seem to reflect non-violence or alignment with an ontology of peace. In fact, it appears quite violent. Lucy Gardner notes that she finds in Radical Orthodoxy "a call for non-oppositional opposition, or, more properly speaking, an undoing of opposition in a non-oppositional way. . . . At the same time, however, Radical Orthodoxy exhibits the rhetoric and exercise of a very powerful *oppositional* opposition."[14]

Even if Laurence Paul Hemming is right to say that Milbank's rhetoric simply reflects the no-nonsense intellectual sparring that occurs in the British tutorial system,[15] how does such a practice persuade the unconvinced by the "beauty of truth," which Milbank takes to be essential for any non-foundationalist and non-violent account of truth?[16] Gavin Hyman must surely be correct that Milbank's narration of the ontology of violence in which secular modernity is embedded is itself rife with violence and, accordingly, highly problematic on its own terms.[17] As Hyman puts it, "There seems to be an inconsistency, or at least a tension, between espousing a narrative on the basis of its peaceful content, on the one hand, and expounding it in a way that seems at odds with its content, on the other."[18] But we can go further still and assert that not only does Milbank's language fail to conform to the ontology of peace he extols, but it betrays a deeper violence in his thought, one that springs from a prior violence; in other words, the violence he perpetrates by opposing the earthly city and the city of God, the secular and the sacred, and the world and the church in the first place.

This dualism in Milbank's thinking is highly agonistic. It pits the world against the church,[19] a move that many would consider theologically problematic on its face, and one that appears to do violence to Augustine's thought. As Eric Gregory notes, Augustine's distinction between the two cities is not ethical but temporal. Augustine's distinction is between the secular as *saeculum*, the time between the fall and the *eschaton,* and the eternal, not between the secular as irreligious or anti-religious and the sacred, as Milbank expresses it.[20]

Moreover, Augustine's notion of what constitutes the secular or the earthly city is not reducible to the state or society, nor is the city of God to the church, as in Milbank.[21] There may be in the *City of God* an earthly city defined by violence and a heavenly city defined by peace, but the former is not identified exclusively with the state or the social arena by Augustine any more than the latter is identified exclusively with the church.[22] Augustine did not think that the earthly city with its institutions and its practices should be characterized as "fundamentally sinful," nor that the provisional goods effected by its political order were inauthentic because not referred explicitly to the divine order.[23]

Augustine also understood very well and wrote about the fact that the church itself is full of conflict, not a clear instantiation of an "ontology of peace."[24] Todd Breyfogle notes that the idealized manner in which Milbank construes the city of God thus seems to owe more to Rousseau than to Augustine.[25] Milbank's characterizations of the earthly city and the city of God, therefore, do not seem to be in full accord with Augustine's rendition of them. Milbank has re-worked Augustine's narrative to underwrite his own, and this, as Hyman points out, has led to a distortion of Augustine's views.[26]

Some of his other interlocutors are subject to the same treatment. Milbank's noted dislike of liberation theology, for example, does not stem from his politics—Milbank is a committed Christian socialist. It derives from his disdain for liberation theology's supposed roots in Rahner's overly Kantian transcendental theology, which Milbank claims—based almost solely on his reading of Clodovis Boff—underlies all liberation theology.

Similarly, Milbank routinely reduces the complexity of a person's thought to one unified idea in order to defeat it. Gavin Hyman thinks Milbank perpetrates this intellectual violence against Nietzsche, Heidegger, Deleuze, Lyotard, Foucault, and Derrida, and does so not only to them singly, but as a whole, calling them all "nihilists" and "positivists," lumping this diverse crew into a single category that he proceeds to dismiss, as with the liberation theologians. "In a particularly violent act," Hyman writes, "Milbank obliterates all differences both within as well as among these thinkers."[27]

Paul Hedges understands this to be a conscious strategy of Milbank and Radical Orthodoxy more broadly. Radical Orthodoxy, Hedges says, "is constantly asserting its ability to neatly categorize the Other as whatever best suits its own interpretive agenda, disregarding nuances and subtleties in its interlocutor."[28] Milbank thus sacrifices the full truth about the work of these theologians and philosophers in order to underwrite a new narrative about the development of "nihilistic secularity" of Milbank's own making.

Milbank thus appears to succumb to the very ontology of violence that he claims characterizes modernity and postmodernity. Insole notes that Milbank's use of the two ontologies cannot but re-inscribe the very problematic Milbank thinks he is simply diagnosing and remedying. Instead, as Insole puts it, "the assertion of ontological violence is simply met—violently—by the counter-assertion of ontological peace."[29] Similarly, Hans Boersma is not optimistic about Milbank's contention that violence can be "rooted out" of everyday reality, as seems to be demonstrated by Milbank's use of this idiom—rooting out—a violent image in and of itself, to talk about how we can participate in an ontology of peace.[30]

Milbank calls upon Augustine to help him develop a theological metanarrative that he hopes will "position" and "overcome" the metanarrative of postmodern secularity. Not only is the manner in which Milbank constructs this metanarrative violent in its rhetoric and in how it treats its intellectual allies and adversaries, but these acts of violence stem from a previous violence: the assertion that there are two rival ontologies operating in the world, one of which must be victorious and the other defeated,[31] a claim proffered in the same violent mode for which the so-called "secular" is condemned. In Girardian terms, in both tone and method, Milbank's attempt to demonstrate parallel and conflicting ontologies corresponding to Augustine's *civitas terrena* and *civitas Dei* performs the very brand of mimetic violence that Milbank enlists Girard to illuminate. In Milbank's work, however, the sacrificial victim is not Jesus, but secularity. To make his case, in *Theology and Social Theory* and subsequently, Milbank scapegoats the secular.

Sacrificing the Secular Scapegoat

Miroslav Volf helpfully reminds us that René Girard suggested that the mark of Cain is not placed upon him to brand him a criminal but precisely to protect him from scapegoating, from mimetic violence. It does not negate the fact that Cain has sinned in murdering his brother, but it does protect him from being harmed on account of it.[32] It would seem, then, that even if Milbank's claim that the *civitas terrena* is evil and violent is accepted, this can be acknowledged in a way that does not make it the rhetorical and theological foil of an entirely different ontological order, one that is right and good, and from which the earthly city is utterly separate.

Eric Gregory suggests that if Milbank truly wished to follow Augustine's usage of the two-cities concept, Milbank would be ambivalent about the earthly city, or secularity, making common cause with it wherever possible and critiquing it when necessary, rather than bitterly condemning it.[33] But Milbank maintains that the only way to read the earthly city, the "secular," is through Christian eyes, and that means reading it as heresy, in both ideal and practical terms.[34] There is no authentic secular sphere for Milbank, and claims to the contrary have resulted in nothing but disaster.

Therefore, against the earthly way of doing things, Christian theology must posit three counter-positions: (1) a "counter-history" that reads all of human history through the event of the emergence of the church, (2) a "counter-ethics" that outlines how Christian ethical practice interrupts and corrects the ethical approaches that came before and come after it, and (3) a "counter-ontology" that demonstrates how the Christian understanding of Being differs from and is superior to all others.[35] All of this, of course, is juxtaposed against the "secular," a concept onto which Milbank projects his theological anxieties, so that he can send it out into the wilderness beyond the gates of the city of God, leaving him safe and secure in the ontological peace intended for Christians who participate in the Good. But, as is always the case with scapegoating, somehow the promised peace never seems to arrive. This move does not have the effect he thinks it will, for his theologizing is full of the violence he thinks he has eradicated.

James Alison points out that Girard's theory of mimetic violence also demonstrates that we scapegoat those upon whom we are dependent, those who force us to call into question our own uniqueness.[36] This can also be found in Milbank's writings. Milbank regularly excoriates postmodern philosophers, whom he takes to be the supreme exponents of the ontology of violence, even while making recourse to their core philosophical views and methods. For example, Christopher Insole notes that it is somewhat problematic that Milbank uses Foucauldian genealogical analysis to uncover the nihilism of modernity, following Foucault just far enough to turn Foucault's thinking back on itself in order to pronounce that Foucault was wrong. Insole wonders, if Foucault was wrong, how can Milbank use Foucauldian methods to prove Foucault's error?[37]

Similarly, Gavin Hyman thinks that both Hegel and Milbank labor diligently to construct metanarratives designed "to 'explain' and 'master' reality." Hyman takes this likeness in their approaches to be precisely "why Milbank is so eager to distance his own project from that of Hegel."[38] Wayne Hankey understands Milbank to be very exercised about the eradication of ontotheology, an endeavor Milbank pursues throughout his work, but doing so deeply in debt to Heidegger and in a sort of Heideggerian manner, despite his utter rejection of Heidegger's philosophy.[39] In order to make his case against secularity, therefore, Milbank relies on some of the very figures he condemns, while continuing to condemn them. This is a mechanism Girard associated with the brand of mimetic violence that Milbank asserts characterizes the ontology of violence he is attempting to overcome.

Milbank's social theology, in which there is no secular and therefore the only legitimate sociology is theology, and more specifically, ecclesiology, provide the grounds for Milbank to assert a "new version of 'no salvation outside of the Church'" basedon what Mary Doak calls Milbank's "pragmatic linguistic idealism."[40] Milbank, Doak contends, verbally constructs a reality that he then advances as utterly and exclusively true in adversarial terms that brook no conversation or dialogue and in which the "secular" is construed in a manner that seems contrary to what we think we know about it. According to Alison, this is precisely what Girardian theory warns against: The scapegoat mechanism relies upon a "*linguistic construction of human reality* over against the expelled one, and it is a self-deceived linguistic construction, which is the same as saying that it is a reality based on a lie, and a violent lie."[41] Milbank linguistically constructs the scapegoat he seeks to sacrifice: the "secular," the "modern."

As James K. A. Smith, an author associated with Radical Orthodoxy, puts it, for Milbank and his fellow travelers, "modernity is the heuristic label used to name what's wrong."[42] But how can this be for Milbank, who is so clear that the "ontology of violence" or the "earthly city" is the name for what is wrong, since there was a fall away from the ontology of peace that predates the rise of anything like "modernity" by many millennia? If "modernity" names the error, would this not mean there was a time, up to the advent of "modernity," when things were "right"? Milbank and his exponents claim—despite a constant refrain that marks 1300 as the year that theology went astray and that the socio-political realm quickly followed—that they do not think this is the case.[43] Yet, they write as if they do, and Smith's comment therefore says more than he intends: Milbank *does* think modernity, the secular, names what is wrong. The secular is Milbank's scapegoat, the sacrifice that makes his theological system run.

Some Effects of Violence in Milbank's Social Theology

Milbank claims that what might appear at first to be violent may not be. Coercion of the linguistic or the ontological variety is not actually violence when it is carried out in the name of truth. Such coercion always contains within itself the possibility that the person it is aimed at will turn toward the Good, making it clear in retrospect that such coercion was not violence at all but persuasion. This, Milbank says, is always a risk, and a tragic one. But it does mean that recourse to what may seem like the rhetoric of violence may not actually be so.[44] However, this attempt to exonerate his views from the charge of violence fails to be convincing. Milbank's language leans toward the violent, his method of argumentation is intellectually violent, and the content of his theology, particularly his oppositional juxtaposition of competing ontologies, is violent. As a result, his theology displays some troubling features.

Milbank's theological perspective exhibits an overly realized eschatology (the suggestion that the eschatological reign of God is available presently), understood as the restoration of a prior state.[45] We may enter into this now by returning to the ontology of peace that characterized this previous (Edenic?) condition. No room remains for the ongoing work of God in bringing about the truly new as the eschatological promises in scripture are fulfilled. For Milbank Christian practice concerns aligning oneself with the ontological truth that all created things have essences, "that there is a true way for things to be and a way things eternally are."[46] Under such a scenario, the eschatological consummation of God's purposes for creation can mean only a return of all that exists to a proper purpose from which it has been diverted. The future can only be the past—something Milbank wants to deny. But his position logically forces him to construe eschatological ultimacy as a repristinization rather than as a perfection or completion of creation and of God's divine purpose for it. If change occurs, it is not because new emergences have drawn the world closer to God's intention, but because a static, stable, known quantity called "the eternal" has broken into the flux of time.[47] Eschatology is stripped of its dynamism.

In terms of what constitutes Christian practice, virtually the only act that defines a Christian mode of life is participation in the Eucharist, as this is what brings a person into unity with the ontology of peace made available through Jesus Christ and with the ongoing work of atonement being carried out under the power of the Holy Spirit in the life of the church. The Eucharist is the model for all Christian practice and for the mode of life that represents the ontology of peace.

Milbank does not consider that baptism, for example, might also be a pattern for Christian life, nor the notion that actions and practices carried out in the earthly city consonant with divine purposes might also count as authentic Christian practices. By positing that the church and its practices are normative for humanity and constitute the only true social theory, rather than grounding such a theory in the actual behavior of real human beings across space and time, he downgrades the status of creation. Instead of finding it revelatory of divine purpose and intent, he sees creation as (mostly) negative, fallen, and in need of divine supplementation through the church to attain to some level of dignity.[48]

For Milbank, the church is the only authentic model for human sociality, and only the church is indicative of the presence of the ontology of peace, which represents a deeply problematic ecclesiology. Milbank contends that the church, at its best, is what the social aspires to become and replace.[49] In construing the relationship between two functionally sealed and identifiable realms called "church" and "world" as essentially conflictual, Milbank calls into question the tenets of democratic pluralism and all knowledge gained on the basis of science and historical criticism instead of theological reflection.[50] Outside the church, everything tends to be construed as nihilism and violence, phenomena with no positive ontological or ethical value. Even other religions cannot foment the true sociality achieved by the Christian church.[51]

Milbank's ecclesiocentric social theology must result in either the church's withdrawal from the world into the peaceful city of God (though Milbank himself finds this is unacceptable[52]) or the colonization of the "secular" by the ecclesial, a kind of re-instantiating of Christendom that would make all human endeavor over in the image of church practice, especially Eucharistic worship. Politically, there is thus in Milbank's work an intermingling of church and state and an ecclesially imperialistic stance that many, particularly political and theological progressives, would find profoundly disquieting.[53]

Milbank's argument is only one example of the effects of theologizing violently. In his case, it occurs through scapegoating. But it can happen in many ways. In each case, however, the resulting theology will be deeply deficient because violence, as Milbank quite rightly points out, contravenes Christian revelation and leads to error.

Notes

[1]Milbank himself denies the presence of substance metaphysics in his work. See his "The Linguistic Turn as a Theological Turn," in *The Word Made Strange: Theology, Language, Culture* (Malden, MA: Blackwell, 1997), 85.

[2](New York: Wiley/Blackwell, 2002).

[3]John Milbank, *Theology and Social Theory: Beyond Secular Reason*, 2nd ed. (Malden MA: Blackwell, 2006), 392.

[4]Ibid., 395–402.

[5]Nathan Schneider, "Orthodox Paradox: An Interview with John Milbank," The Imminent Frame: Secularism, Religion, and the Public Sphere, March 17, 2010, http://blogs.ssrc.org/tif/2010/03/17/orthodox-paradox-an-interview-with-john-milbank/ (accessed March 20, 2010).

[6]Christopher J. Insole, "Against Radical Orthodoxy: The Dangers of Over-coming Political Liberalism," *Modern Theology* 20, no. 2 (2004): 220–21, 223.

[7]John Milbank, Foreword to James K. A. Smith, *Introducing Radical Orthodoxy: Mapping a Post-secular Theology* (Grand Rapids, MI: Baker Academic, 2004), 14.

[8]John Milbank, "Can Morality Be Christian?" in *The Word Made Strange*, 225.

[9]John Milbank, "Paul against Biopolitics," in *Paul's New Moment: Continental Philosophy and the Future of Christian Theology*, ed. John Milbank, Slavoj Žižek, and Creston Davis (Grand Rapids, MI: Brazos, 2010), 57–58, n72.

[10]John Milbank, Catherine Pickstock, and Graham Ward, introduction to *Radical Orthodoxy: A New Theology* (London: Routledge, 1999), 1.

[11]John Milbank, "The New Divide: Romantic versus Catholic Orthodoxy," *Modern Theology* 26, no. 1 (2010): 27.

[12]John Milbank, preface to *The Future of Love: Essays in Political Theology* (Eugene, OR: Cascade Books, 2009), xix.

[13]John Milbank, "Liberality versus Liberalism," in *The Future of Love*, 263.

[14]Lucy Gardner, "Listening at the Threshold: Christology and the 'Suspension of the Material,'" in *Radical Orthodoxy?: A Catholic Enquiry*, ed. Laurence Paul Hemming (Aldershot, UK: Ashgate, 2000), 127.

[15]John Milbank, *Being Reconciled: Ontology and Pardon* (New York: Routledge, 2003), 4.

[16]See, for example, John Milbank, "Enclaves, or Where Is the Church?" in *The Future of Love*, 140.

[17]Gavin Hyman, *The Predicament of Postmodern Theology: Radical Orthodoxy or Nihilist Textualism?* (Louisville, KY: Westminster John Knox Press, 2001), 73–74, 88.

[18]Ibid., 77.

[19]Christopher McMahon, "Theology and the Redemptive Mission of the Church: A Catholic Response to Milbank's Challenge," *Heythrop Journal* 51, no. 5 (2010): 786.

[20]Eric Gregory, *Politics and the Order of Love: An Augustinian Ethic of Democratic Citizenship* (Chicago: University of Chicago Press, 2008), 10–11.

[21]Insole, "Against Radical Orthodoxy," 223.

[22]Daniel Franklin Pilario, *Back to the Rough Grounds of Praxis: Exploring Theological Method with Pierre Bourdieu* (Louvain: Peeters Publishers, 2005), 487.

[23]Gregory, *Politics and the Order of Love*, 52–53, 134.

[24]Pilario, *Back to the Rough Grounds of Praxis*, 484.

[25]Todd Breyfogle, "Is There Room for Political Philosophy in Postmodern Critical Augustinianism?" in *Deconstructing Radical Orthodoxy: Postmodern Theology, Rhetoric and Truth*, ed. Wayne J. Hankey and Douglas Hedley (Aldershot, UK: Ashgate, 2005), 42.

[26]Hyman, *The Predicament of Postmodern Theology*, 74.

[27]Ibid., 108.

[28]Paul Hedges, "Is John Milbank's Radical Orthodoxy a Form of Liberal Theology? A Rhetorical Counter," *Heythrop Journal* 51, no. 5 (2010): 806.

[29]Insole, "Against Radical Orthodoxy," 219–21.

[30]Hans Boersma, "Being Reconciled: Atonement as the Ecclesio-Christological Practice of Forgiveness in John Milbank," in *Radical Orthodoxy and the Reformed Tradition: Creation, Covenant, and Participation*, ed. James K. A. Smith and James H. Olthuis (Grand Rapids, MI: Baker Academic, 2005), 197.

[31]Hyman, *The Predicament of Postmodern Theology*, 66.

[32]Miroslav Volf, *Exclusion and Embrace: A Theological Exploration of Identity, Otherness, and Reconciliation* (Nashville, TN: Abingdon Press, 1996), 98.

[33]Gregory, *Politics and the Order of Love*, 138.

[34]Milbank, *Theology and Social Theory*, 3.

[35]Ibid., 383.

[36]James Alison, *Raising Abel: The Recovery of the Eschatological Imagination* (New York: Crossroad, 1996), 18–25.

[37]Insole, "Against Radical Orthodoxy," 224.

[38]Hyman, *The Predicament of Postmodern Theology*, 78.

[39]Wayne J. Hankey, "Theoria versus Poesis: Neoplatonism and Trinitarian Difference in Aquinas, John Milbank, Jean-Luc Marion and John Zizioulas," *Modern Theology* 15, no. 4 (1999): 388.

[40]Mary Doak, "A Pragmatism without Plurality? John Milbank's 'Pragmatic' New Christendom," *Contemporary Pragmatism* 1, no. 2 (2004): 123.

[41]Alison, *Raising Abel*, 103; emphasis in original.

[42]Smith, *Introducing Radical Orthodoxy*, 95.

[43] John Milbank, "Ecclesiology: The Last of the Last," in *Being Reconciled*, 119.

[44] Milbank, *Theology and Social Theory*, 424.

[45] See, for example, Milbank, "Can Morality Be Christian?" 229; and John Milbank, "On Theological Transgression," in *The Future of Love*, 170.

[46] Milbank, "Ecclesiology," 106.

[47] John Milbank, "Politics: Socialism by Grace," in *Being Reconciled*, 180.

[48] Jonathan Chaplin, "Suspended Communities or Covenanted Communities? Reformed Reflections on the Social Thought of Radical Orthodoxy," in *Radical Orthodoxy and the Reformed Tradition: Creation, Covenant, and Participation*, ed. James K. A. Smith and James H. Olthuis (Grand Rapids, MI: Baker Academic, 2005), 171–72.

[49] Milbank, "On Theological Transgression," 169.

[50] McMahon, "Theology and the Redemptive Mission of the Church," 786.

[51] John Milbank, "Stale Expressions: The Management-Shaped Church," in *The Future of Love*, 272–73; emphasis in original.

[52] Gregory, *Politics and the Order of Love*, 135.

[53] Graeme Smith, "Mission and Radical Orthodoxy," *Modern Believing* 44, no. 1 (2003): 51–53.

Georges Rouault

Encountering God's Beauty
through the Face of the Other[1]

Gael Mooney

Georges Rouault's art is characterized by a "powerful spiritual cohesion" such that the diversity of themes in his work acquires an ever widening significance as they are seen in relation to each other and to his oeuvre as a whole.[2] His work possesses a symphonic quality in that each image contributes to the harmony of the whole. The result is that the ultimate vision that his work expresses, exceeds, and transcends the individual parts. Perhaps this explains Rouault's affinity for the Gothic cathedral, which embodies these same characteristics and whose aim is likewise to compel our participation in a divine and eternal reality. This essay reflects upon one of the most surprising and important aspects of Rouault's spiritual vision; namely, the way he unveils the meaning of divine beauty through the face of the other.

Otherness is present in the repetitiveness and diversity of themes of Rouault's oeuvre in which he relates the sufferings of Christ to "every aspect of the human condition"—the plight of the poor, the disenfranchised, and other oppressed members of society, the despair of the condemned, the anguish of soldiers and victims of war, violence, and neglect, and "the solitude of the individual."[3] The dispossessed and marginalized are depicted alongside more esteemed members of society—such as judges, academics, and high society women. The themes of the sacred and the profane are interwoven in his paintings, as well as in the series of prints made in connection with his several books, in which clowns and other profane subjects are often depicted in a manner that recalls his portrayals of Christ. In Rouault, no one is left out of the equation—and as we will see through our consideration of Rouault's late period, this includes you and me. What was Rouault seeking to express through these images that merge boundaries between social classes and between the sacred and profane?

Rouault provides us with some compelling insights to this question when he says through "this human tide" he was seeking to show "a mysterious interlinking of the blessed and the damned, of crime, of innocence, of sublime devotion, both apparent and hidden." He then added, "There, for me, lies a horizon of some grandeur."[4]

In this essay I wish to suggest that Rouault's art, as well as his definition of grandeur, contains an important theological insight: namely, that divine illumination unfolds not individually but collectively, not in isolation but in community. That is, we encounter truth and beauty through the face of the other –which is to say, through both God and neighbor. My argument is twofold: first, that otherness is expressed through the *subject matter*, *form*, and *evolution* of Rouault's work. Second, that by making this *horizon of grandeur* his aim, through the evolution of his oeuvre Rouault unveils the meaning of divine beauty. More specifically, I will suggest that the evolution of Rouault's oeuvre conforms to three distinct stages—*recognition, embrace, and becoming*—each of which highlights a different aspect of the meaning of otherness as part of a spiritual uplifting that leads us toward the horizon of grandeur. In so doing, through the evolution of his oeuvre Rouault reveals the centrality of otherness—"this human tide"—to the *via pulchritudinis*—way of beauty and path of spiritual illumination.

Recognition

I begin this reflection with a consideration of Rouault's clowns, a prevalent theme of his oeuvre from the beginning through his late period. By virtue of their itinerant lifestyle, the wandering circus performers, to use a phrase from Hebrews 13:11, represent the viewpoint "outside the camp," of the dispossessed and marginalized who are not considered to be part of the status quo. They therefore hold a privileged place with respect to the theme of otherness, as Rouault makes clear through his depictions of them.

Unlike Rouault's predecessors (Watteau and Daumier) and

his contemporaries (Degas, Picasso, and Toulouse Lautrec) who regarded the clown or *pierrot* as a vehicle for social satire or as the embodiment of a Romantic ideal, Rouault was seeking to portray clowns *objectively* from the standpoint of the clowns themselves so as to compel our self-identification with them.

Key to the pictorial conception of Rouault's early clowns was an experience the artist had one day when, while strolling through the streets of Paris, he came upon a gypsy caravan of circus performers. Rouault was particularly moved by the sight of an old clown seated by the side of the road mending his motley costume. In a 1905 letter to Edouard Schuré, Rouault described the impact of this incident, which made him suddenly aware of "this *contrast* between bright shiny things, made to entertain, and this life of *infinite sadness*, if seen from a distance."[5] The sight of the old clown evoked feelings of empathy, making him see clearly that "the 'clown' was me, was us . . . all of us almost . . . we are all *clowns more or less*, each of us wears a 'spangled costume'. . . ."[6] The contrast between surface and appearance is expressed in Rouault's *Head of Clown*[7] in which the artist unmasks the clown to betray his inner anguish and sorrow. By portraying the clown close-up and devoid of props, Rouault compels our self-identification with him, prompting us to reflect upon the sad circumstances of his life.

This encounter reveals that *recognition* is not merely a matter of physical sight but instead involves openness and receptivity to the other. Such receptivity displaces the center from the self to a more objective viewpoint from which we are able to approach others from a standpoint of disinterested love and empathy. Baudelaire referred to this type of objective seeing as *dédoublement*, "a self-identification in another provoking self-awareness and self-knowledge."[8]

Recognition is the first step of a spiritual conversion through which we turn away from self-centered love (*cupiditas*) to love of God and neighbor (*caritas*). Drawing on the work of Augustine and St. Bernard of Clairvaux, Ann Astell characterizes this process in terms of a "projection" or "expansion" through which one "puts oneself physically and emotionally at the Other's place."[9] Such self-identification with the other alters our sight such that "When one returns, altered, to oneself, the Other appears differently to one's eyes—that mystical Otherness being at the root of all properly allegorical interpretation. What was hidden before is suddenly revealed. What was ugly before now appears beautiful and love worthy."[10] Such was apparently true in the case of Rouault, who was so profoundly altered by this encounter that it prompted him to evolve a whole new aesthetic aimed at revealing the truth of his revelation that "the 'clown' was me, was us . . . all of us almost. . . . Life gives us that *rich spangled* costume, we are all *clowns more or less*, each of us wears a 'spangled costume'. . . ."[11]

Rouault wanted his art to "lead to the awakening of meaning" such that "this head of a buffoon or of a clown would, if it were to take on a serious character . . . become something exceptional (the *Christ à la Passion*, for example, that was what my material was made for)."[12] From the very beginning, Rouault did in fact paint clowns in a manner that recalls his portrayals of Christ. Rouault's *Head of Clown* (1907-08)[13] resembles in both composition and facial expression his *Head of Christ* (1905)[14] from around the same period. As Leo J. O'Donovan has observed, by depicting clowns and other disenfranchised members of society in a manner that recall his portraits of Christ, Rouault is saying that they "are all much more than they initially appear to be—all belong together, and depict the drama of life in its deeper, mystical dimension."[15]

Through this association of the clowns with Christ (which is made more explicit in the mature work), despite their sad demeanor, Rouault's clowns evoke not our pity but our admiration. Rouault makes us see that their act of putting on a mask and costume is an act of selfless love through which they suppress their identities in order to bring joy into the lives of others. They therefore illuminate the virtues of humility and selfless love, qualities that will be further highlighted in the next section that focuses on the meaning of "embrace."

Embrace

David Schindler has defined beauty as the patient sense "of the other—of the world—as gift," that is to say, as "as inherently meaningful and lovable . . . in its very otherness."[16] Giftedness is key to the experience of genuine transcendence that draws us out of ourselves to experience an "'ecstatic' relation to the Infinite (Other) *in* the finite (other)."[17] According to Schindler, giftedness then is not the achievement of the autonomous ego but instead is the product of our conformity to the twin commandments of love of God and love of neighbor. Through the evolution of his work of the 1930s and 1940s, Rouault brings this dimension of the embrace of the other to light as he leads us in the second stage of unveiling the meaning of truth, beauty, and grandeur.

Such qualities are evident in the series of prints Rouault made in connection with two books on the theme of the circus, *Circus* (1930) and *The Shooting Star Circus* (1938). As Stephen Schloesser and I have previously suggested with regard to the clowns of this period,[18] these prints highlight the bonds of patience, kindness, and friendship that order their modest lives lived out in close-knit community on the road and under the circus tent. The two clowns on the title plate for Rouault's book, *The Shooting Star Circus*, entitled *Frontispiece-Parade* (1935),[19] who greet each other with bowed heads and outstretched arms set the stage for the clowns' role as archetypes of selfless love.[20] In *Parade/Green Background* (1934),[21] a painted study based on this print, the figures are cropped, so as to magnify the way their gestures mirror each other.[22] Through their welcoming gestures of mutual respect, the clowns exemplify the "patient sense of the other as other," as *gift*.[23]

Parade(Green background), 1934. Ink and gouache on engraved paper, 17.7 x 18.7 cm., Musée National d'Art Moderne, Centre Georges Pompidou. © 2011 Artists Rights Society (ARS), New York/ADAGP, Paris. Photograph: CNAC/MNAM/Dist. Réunion des Musées Nationaux/Art Resource, NY.

The impression of a mirror image is made even more explicit in Rouault's series of double portraits or diptychs. One such pairing entitled *Two Elders* (1943), from Rouault's book *Divertissements/distractions*, features two face-to-face clowns whose heads are depicted in profile. This image conforms to the convention of the diptych, which consists of two adjacent figures who face each other like pages of a book, thus establishing a relationship between the two.[24] A common feature of Roman art that was later adopted by Christianity, the diptych is a hieratic and symmetrical composition that denotes the figures' submission to a higher, spiritual order.[25]

As a sign of openness and receptivity to the other, the mirror image both here and throughout Rouault would appear to be the visual equivalent of "I am you." That is, as the work's title would seem to suggest, the *Two Elders* represent the wisdom of the ages, prevalent in Western religion, literature, and art, suggesting that each person discovers him or her self in relation to others. The foregoing premise and the subject of a book by Karl F. Morrison investigating the hermeneutics of empathy in Western culture, "I am you" would appear to be the logical extension of the Baudelairean notion of *dédoublement*, which suggests that we see ourselves more objectively and transparently through the eyes of the other.[26]

From a Christian perspective, *I am you* is not a dyadic relationship but a triadic relationship that reflects not merely the finite "other" but the infinite "Creator-Other."[27] As the mystic Meister Eckhart (ca.1260-1327) has written, mimesis is sign of sacramental unity stemming from our common source and union with each other through Christ's body.[28] Awareness of the "Creator-Other" is represented both here and throughout Rouault through the harmony of the whole, as sign of a hidden and spiritual order. As Ann W. Astell, drawing on the work of Karl F. Morrison, has observed, this type of "sacramental assimilation," which is present in a special way in the sacrament of the Eucharist, fosters a "mutual in-one-anotherness, which is the pre-condition for empathetic understanding."[29] Through their submissive poses and mirroring gestures, the *Two Elders* create a neutral space in which to embrace each other from a standpoint of disinterested love and empathy.

In contrast to the *Two Elders*, the *Two Stubborn Men* (1943, *Divertissements*) jostle for dominance as their forms, pushing and overlapping, disrupt the harmony of whole. Caught up with "so many precarious interests" and "stuck on a name," Rouault writes, neither will "cease or step back an inch in the face of his adversary."[30] Rather than reconciling themselves to each other and their respective halves of the picture, it seems they have succumbed to chaos. The *Two Stubborn Men* illustrate how pride and the ego can prevent us from acquiring the "patient sense of the other" as "gift."[31]

In the series of prints made in connection with Rouault's two books on the circus, *Circus* (1930) and *Shooting Star Circus* (1938), the analogy between the clowns and Christ that we saw earlier is made even more explicit. *Bitter Lemon* (1935, *Shooting Star Circus*) assumes the attitude and posture of submission of the *Christ in Profile* (1936, *The Passion*). *Bitter Lemon*'s head appears to be literally fastened to the horizontal red bar/cross that is likewise featured behind the head of the *Christ in Profile*.[32] The clown's submissive pose, together with the red bar/cross, suggests his symbolic role as an *alter Christus* who models the self-emptying of Christ the Suffering Servant, the archetype for divine love and the radical embrace of the other.[33] In an ironic twist, Rouault adopted the same compositional format for his *Lady with a Crest* (1936) from his book of illustrations of Charles Baudelaire's poem *The Flowers of Evil*; given both the context and her richly dressed attire, she would appear to be the antithesis of disinterested love.

As Roberto S. Goizueta has argued, suffering and woundedness in Rouault represent a call to conversion.[34] Through his example of selfless love, mercy, and compassion, Christ becomes one with the crucified people so as to show us the meaning of the embrace of the other.[35] *The Wounded Clown* (1932)[36] depicts three clowns walking arm-in-arm. The two adjacent clowns literally bear the suffering of the wounded clown located in the center through their compassionate embrace of him. The title would appear to be a specific reference to Christ. Plate 58 of Rouault's masterful series of prints, the *Miserere*, which depicts the Holy Countenance on Veronica's veil, is entitled, *It is by his wounds that we are healed*.[37] Both the image and title suggest that through woundedness and self-emptying we increase our capacity for compassion and mercy, strengthening the bonds of community. Uniting the themes of human suffering with those of Christ the Suffering Servant suggests that the *via dolorosa* and *via pulchritudinis* are one and the same, for each point to Christ as the archetype of love and divine beauty.[38]

In his 1936 essay, "To Exist with the People," Jacques Maritain distinguishes between "acting for" and "existing with":

> To act belongs to the realm of mere benevolence. To exist with and to suffer with, to the realm of love and unity. . . . To exist with is an ethical category . . . it means to love someone in the sense of becoming one with him, of bearing his burdens, of living a common moral life with him, of feeling with him and suffering with him.
>
> If we love that living human thing which we call the people . . . we will want first and foremost to exist with them, to suffer with them, and to remain in communion with them.[39]

This brings us to the final stage of our journey that reveals the communal aspect of the rise to human grandeur as part of a process of becoming the other.

Becoming

Rouault's late work expresses a striving for homogeneity and assimilation aimed at reconciling differences of class, gender, social status, and other barriers that divide us as a society. The sacred and profane are often depicted in an analogous manner, and at times within a given work, prompting a reflection between the two. Through his interweaving of the sacred and the profane, Rouault emphasizes the communal aspect of the horizon of grandeur that is our mutual source and destiny.

Triptychs

One particularly striking example of this can be seen in the evolution of Rouault's triptychs. The triptych consists of a central figure flanked by two adjacent figures. The triptych first appeared in Rouault's judges from the 1910s and 1920s. In his early triptych entitled *Three Judges* (1913),[40] the judge in the center stares blankly into space while the other two look off to the side, seemingly disconnected from each other and their surroundings.

In contrast to the *Three Judges,* Rouault's *Three Clowns* (1933, *The Shooting Star Circus*), executed two decades later, are not so much disconnected as disinterested. This work is more hieratic. That is, the central clown faces the viewer in the full frontal style characteristic of a Byzantine icon while the two adjacent clowns conform to the profile pose of an Egyptian priestess. The attitudes and demeanor of all three suggest their submission to a higher spiritual order.[41]

Five years later, Rouault adopted a similar composition for his *Christ and the Pharisees* (1938).[42] The figures are set in an architectural framework that recalls a medieval altarpiece. Adjacent to Christ, where one would expect a saint or disciple, are two Pharisees who, as doctors of the law, were opposed to everything Christ stood for.[43] This dynamic equilibrium of things in opposition to each other reflects the new form of justice that Christ came into the world to establish, one based upon peace and reconciliation, stemming from Christ's example of selfless love, mercy, and forgiveness.[44]

Rouault adopted a similar composition for another triptych from approximately the same time period entitled *Trio* (1935-40).[45] Judging from their attire, both the central figure and the one on the right conform to the bourgeois type in Rouault's oeuvre known as *Madame X*, while the one on the left would appear to be a circus girl.[46] The painting expresses "a clear consciousness of class or of social status and a structure of opposition" that is nonetheless resolved and transcended through the harmony and symmetry of the whole.[47] Madame X adopts the same pose of submission as Christ in the preceding painting. Unlike the high society woman from the series of etchings made in connection with Rouault's book *Miserere, who believes that she has a reserved seat in heaven,* here Madame X is an archetype of divine love who demonstrates the role of self-emptying in the search for human grandeur.

These two triptychs, both in the Idemitsu Collection in Tokyo, express a feeling of the "structured interdependence" that Thomas Berry has written about in reference to Gothic architecture and polyphonic music of "part upon part, each opposed, yet each sustaining the other in a vital flowing rhythmic whole."[48] As Berry has observed, this juxtaposition of opposites embodies social, ethical, and spiritual significance as a sign of "an organic structuring in which every idea, every principal, every mental process found its proper place" as part of an integral whole.[49] This wholeness would appear to be the outward manifestation of the "mysterious interlinking of the blessed and the damned" that Rouault, by his own acknowledgment, was striving to express through all of his work and that he equated with "a horizon of some grandeur."[50]

Rouault's striving for unity culminates in the triptychs of his mature period, beginning with a work such as *Trio* (1935-1940).[51] Here, not only is everyone being "brought into the tent," but the three judges are so similar as to be one and the same. Their individual identities are suppressed.[52] What emerges instead is the mysterious unity stemming from humanity's mutual source, which is our collective calling and destiny.

Rouault adopted the same composition associated with the previous images for a late triptych entitled *Trio* (1949-1956).[53] Judging from their attire, the central figure and the one on the left appear to be women, whereas the one on the right would appear to be a male clown. This work is more spatially compressed and luminous with its rich palette, comprised of vivid reds and yellows with touches of cerulean blue. The form, space, and light of this work reflect the medieval concept of *ordo*. As Hans Urs von Balthasar has written, *ordo* expresses the mutuality and interconnectedness of human existence stemming from the transcendentals of goodness, beauty, and truth that "are not delimited from each other but penetrate each other."[54]

Both the foregoing images and the evolution of his oeuvre as a whole suggest that Rouault's "blessed trinity" of "form, color, harmony," a phrase that he frequently invoked in speaking about his work, is but a reflection of the Trinitarian doctrine that expresses "the essential truth that God who saves through Christ by the power of the Spirit lives eternally in the communion of persons in love."[55]

Mirror Reflection

The foregoing features are magnified by the practice characteristic of many of the artist's late works in which he painted a decorated frame around the border. One striking example is *Pierrot Mélancholique* (1949-56)[56] who, with his head depicted in the full frontal disposition of a Byzantine icon and eyes lowered, is a model of contemplation. The painted border recalls medieval tapestries and stained glass windows.[57] Further, the shallow space (that brings the figure up to the surface) combined with the shimmering translucent light and decorated border reinforces the impression that we are looking into a mirror that merges the pictorial space with the actual space of the viewer.

Melancholy Pierrot, 1949-1956. Ink on canvas, 56 x 47 cm., Musée National d'Art Moderne, Centre Georges Pompidou. © 2011 Artists Rights Society (ARS), New York/ ADAGP, Paris. Photograph: CNAC/MNAM/Dist. Réunion des Musées Nationaux/Art Resource, NY.

This merging of actual and pictorial space embodies spiritual significance as sign of mutuality stemming from our common and divine source. Yet, in this instance, it is not the reflection of another figure in the painting that we are seeing, but our own reflection. The painting thus represents a reflection in both the literal and metaphoric senses of the word, for in seeing the *Pierrot Mélancholique*, we are seeing our inner truth and light reflected through the light, form, and contemplative gaze of this *pierrot*, who serves as an archetype of divine love. By displacing the center from the subjective and limited self to the objective standpoint of the *pierrot*, Rouault helps us to see ourselves and our neighbors more objectively and transparently, as if through God's eyes. In so doing, he engages us in a process of becoming beauty.

Conclusion

Born in a cellar during the Franco-Prussian war, raised in the poor suburb of Belleville, and having lived through two world wars, the Spanish Civil War and the Great Depression, Rouault was no stranger to violence and human suffering occasioned by war, poverty, and injustice. Rouault was seeking to make art that would redeem a broken world in order to restore it to its original beauty. The diversity of the themes of his work—*this human tide* and *mysterious interlinking of the blessed and the damned*—as well as his incessant gaze on the poor and other disenfranchised members of society as recurrent motifs of his oeuvre, reveal the centrality of the embrace of the other to this aim.

Through his embrace of the other Rouault highlights social justice as not merely an ethical category, but as an aesthetic and theological one that is central to the meaning of divine beauty. Through the evolution of his oeuvre, Rouault raises our awareness of the meaning of true beauty and true grandeur as part of a spiritual conversion by which we conform our lives to the twin commandments of love of God and of neighbor that are the basis of a loving community. In so doing, Rouault demonstrates art's power not only as source of visual delight but as a call to a radical transformation in truth and love. Through his embrace of the other, Rouault reveals the contours of the horizon of grandeur that as children of God is our collective calling and true inheritance.

Notes

[1]Where possible I have provided a web link for the images referred to in this article. For those works for which no web link was available, the reader should consult the books referenced in the endnotes pertaining to the section in which the work appears. I would like to thank Giles and Jean-Yves Rouault and the Rouault Foundation for their assistance with referencing and reproducing the images for this article. Parts of this essay appear in a different form in Gael Mooney and Stephen Schloesser "Hieratic Grandeur: Weightless World, Hidden Order, Magnifying the Modest. 1930-1943," *Mystic Masque: Semblance and Reality in Georges Rouault, 1871-1958*, ed. Stephen Schloesser (Boston: McMullen Museum of Art, 2008). I am grateful to Professor Schloesser for the opportunity to have participated in this publication. It was a pleasure and an honor to work with him and this article represents an effort to continue the conversation begun with him and the other contributors to the exhibition catalogue.

[2]François Chapon and Isabelle Rouault, *Rouault: Oeuvre gravée*, 2 vols. (Monte Carlo: Éditions André Sauret, 1978), 1:53.

[3]Ibid., 1:68, n. 124.

[4]Ibid., 1:72, n. 187.

[5]Ibid., 2:49, n. 283.

[6]Ibid.

[7]*Head of Clown*, 1907-08, Dumbarton Oaks House Collection. http://museum.doaks.org/Obj199?sid=454&x=90309.

[8]Gael Mooney and Stephen Schloesser, "Hieratic Grandeur," 312-13.

[9]Ann Astell, *Eating Beauty: The Eucharist and the Spiritual Arts of the Middle Ages* (Ithaca, NY: Cornell University Press, 2006), 83.

[10]Ibid.

[11]Chapon and Rouault, *Rouault*, 2:49, n.283.

[12]Ibid., I:55, n. 25.

[13]*Head of Clown*, 1907-08, Dumbarton Oaks Museum of Art. http://museum.doaks.org/Obj199?sid=3032&x=315221.

[14]*Head of Christ*, 1905, Chrysler Museum of Art, http://www.bc.edu/bc_org/rvp/pubaf/08/Commonweal-Rouault.pdf.

[15]Leo J. O'Donovan, SJ, "Unmasked: Georges Rouault at Boston College," *Commonweal*, October 10, 2008, 19.

[16]David L. Schindler, "Beauty, Transcendence, and the Face of the Other: Religion and Culture in America," *Communio* 26, no. 4 (Winter 1999): 916-17.

[17]Ibid., 917.

[18]See Mooney and Schloesser, "Hieratic Grandeur," 309-19.

[19]http://travex.syr.edu/exhibitions/slides/rouault/Pages/1.html.

[20]For a discussion of the symbolism of this as well as the version of this print made in connection with Rouault's earlier book on the theme of the circus, *Circus* (1930), see Mooney and Schloesser, "Hieratic Grandeur," 312-13.

[21]*Parade/Green background*, 1934, Musée National d'Art Moderne, Centre Georges Pompidou. http://www.photo.rmn.fr/cf/htm/CSearchZ.aspx?o=&To tal=619&FP=20417993&E=2K1KTSULUN1M9&SID=2K1KTSULUN1M9 &New=T&Pic=513&SubE=2C6NU0KJRS1J.

[22]Mooney and Schloesser, "Hieratic Grandeur," 313.

[23]Schindler, "Beauty, Transcendence, and the Face of the Other," 917.

[24]Ian Chilvers and Harold Osborne, eds., *The Oxford Dictionary of Art*, new ed. (New York: Oxford University Press, 1997), 163.

[25]For a discussion of the symbolism of Rouault's adoption of the hieratic style for his clowns of the 1930s, see Mooney and Schloesser, "Hieratic Grandeur," 309-19.

[26]See generally Karl F. Morrison, *I Am You: The Hermeneutics of Empathy in Western Literature and Art* (Princeton: Princeton University Press, 1988).

[27]Schindler, "Beauty, Transcendence, and the Face of the Other," 917.

[28]Morrison, *I Am You*, xx, 17.

[29]Astell, *Eating Beauty*, 11, n. 50 (referring to Morrison, *I Am You*, 9-10).

[30]Mooney and Schloesser, "Hieratic Grandeur," 315.

[31]Schindler, "Beauty, Transcendence, and the Face of the Other," 917.

[32]For a discussion of the red bar/cross, see Angela Lampe, "Work in progress. Les Oeuvres inachevées," *Georges Rouault: Forme, couleur, harmonie*, commissariat Fabrice Hergott (Strasbourg: Musées de Strasbourg, 2006), 219-21 and Mooney and Schloesser, "Hieratic Grandeur," 314.

[33]Rouault reinforces the impression of his clowns as an *alter christus* in the poem written for his book, *The Shooting Star Circus*, when in addressing his leading protagonist, he says, "Weary bones, my friend, we are beaten dogs, loyal dogs who walk in the shadow of Jesus" (Mooney and Schloesser, "Hieratic Grandeur," 314). On the role of Christ as archetype of divine beauty and the radical embrace of the other, see Hans Urs von Balthasar, *The Glory of the Lord: A Theological Aesthetics, Vol. 1: Seeing the Form* (San Francisco: Ignatius Press, 1998).

[34]For a discussion of Rouault's incarnational and sacramental aesthetics, see Roberto Goizueta, "Rouault's Christ: A Call to Aesthetic Conversion," *Mystic Masque*, 449-57.

[35]Ibid.

[36]*The Wounded Clown* (1932, Musée National d'Art Moderne, Centre Georges Pompidou) http://www.photo.rmn.fr/cf/htm/CSearchZ.aspx?o=&T otal=618&FP=2797987&E=2K1KTSU9XBSE5&SID=2K1KTSU9XBSE5& New=T&Pic=540&SubE=2C6NU0KIT2YU.

[37]This impression is further reinforced by the print originally intended for *The Miserere* but not included in the final book entitled *Le Blessé/The Wounded*, which depicts a wounded soldier seated on the ground with head bowed. Suspended above him is the Holy Face of Christ imprinted on Veronica's veil. For a discussion of this image and the theme of the "wounded"

in Rouault, see Stephen Schloesser, "1929-1939: Mystic Masque, Hieratic Harmony," *Mystic Masque*, 301-02.

[38]For a discussion of the *Via Dolorosa* as the nexus of a spiritual transformation, see Goizueta, "Rouault's Christ," 454.

[39]Bernard Doering, "*Lacrymae rerum*: Creative Intuition of the Transapparent Reality," *Mystic Masque*, 393, n. 20. See Jacques Maritain, *The Range of Reason* (New York: Charles Scribner's Sons, 1942), 121.

[40]*Three Judges* (1913, Museum of Modern Art) http://www.moma.org/collection/provenance/provenance_object.php?object_id=33, 219.

[41]Mooney and Schloesser, "Hieratic Grandeur," 311. On Rouault's use of photographs of paintings and sculptures of Egyptian priestesses from the Louvre as models for his work, see also Lampe, "Work in progress. Les Oeuvres inachevées," 215-16.

[42]*Christ and the Pharisees or High Priests*, 1938, Idemitsu Collection, Tokyo.

[43]*Georges Rouault: Les Chefs-d'oeuvre de la Collection Idemitsu*, exposition, Pinacothèque de Paris, 17 September, 2008-18 January, 2009, commissariat Marc Restellini, 167.

[44]In another example of merging the sacred and the profane, *Jesus on the Cross until the End of Time* (1952-56, Pompidou) depicts two judges (or perhaps a judge and the condemned) at the foot of the cross where one would expect to find John and Mary.

[45]*Trio*, 1935-40, Idemitsu Collection, Tokyo.

[46]*Georges Rouault: Les Chefs-d'oeuvre de la Collection Idemitsu*, 124.

[47]Ibid. (translated from the French).

[48]Thomas Berry, "Dante: The Age in Which He Lived" (unpublished and undated manuscript), 4. I wish to thank Judith Emery for providing me with a copy of this unpublished manuscript given to her by Thomas Berry.

[49]Ibid., 5.

[50]Chapon and Rouault, *Rouault*, 1:72, n. 187.

[51]*Trio*, 1935-1940, Metropolitan Museum, http://www.metmuseum.org/Collections/search-the-collections/210005650.

[52]Camille Giertler has observed a similar phenomenon with respect to the compositions of *Sarah* (1956, Rouault Foundation), wife of Abraham, and *Theodora* (1946, Private Collection), undoubtedly the Byzantine empress, who are depicted in a similar fashion so that there is no discernable distinction between the two ("Les dernières oeuvres," *Georges Rouault, Forme, Couleur, Harmonie*, 192).

[53]*Trio*, 1949-56, Musée National d'Art Moderne, Centre Georges Pompidou. http://www.photo.rmn.fr/cf/htm/CSearchZ.aspx?o=&Total=500&FP=2785344&E=2K1KTSU9XT6D2&SID=2K1KTSU9XT6D2&New=T&Pic=454&SubE=2C6NU00DO6NB.

[54]Hans Urs von Balthasar, "Earthly Beauty and Divine Glory," *Communio* 10, no. 3 (Fall 1983): 203.

[55]Catherine Mowry LaCugna and Michael Downey, "Trinitarian Spirituality," *The New Dictionary of Catholic Spirituality*, ed. Michael Downey (Collegeville: The Liturgical Press, 1993), 968.

[56]*Melancholy Pierrot*, 1949-56, Musée National d'Art Moderne, Centre

Georges Pompidou. http://www.photo.rmn.fr/cf/htm/CSearchZ.aspx?o=&Total=500&FP=19824685&E=2K1KTSULSPTOZ&SID=2K1KTSULSPTOZ&New=T&Pic=433&SubE=2C6NU00DOO55.

[57]Lampe, "Work in progress. Les Oeuvres inachevées," 215; on the mirror motif, see also Fabrice Hergott, "Das Licht des Abends: Die letzten Werke," in Rudy Chiappini, ed., *Georges Rouault*, catalogue exp. Museo d'Arte Moderna, Lugano, 1997, 124-25.

PART III

TRANSFORMATION OF VIOLENCE

Virtue, Vulnerability, and Social Transformation

Kevin J. Ahern

The violent and tragic events of September 11, 2001 have had a profound impact on the collective psyche of the people of the United States. The graphic images of destruction brought to us on our television screens, computer monitors, and newspaper pages opened the eyes of many Americans to the reality of what one September 12 *New York Times* headline called "America the Vulnerable."[1]

In the decade since the terrorist attacks, Americans have struggled to find the most appropriate response to this reality. Strongly portrayed by our media and political figures as a negative reality to be overcome, this vulnerability has been used to justify questionable practices from unilateral military intervention and the use of torture to more restrictive immigration policies. In the end, however, many of these efforts have seemingly done more to create a culture of fear than to offer genuine security.

In light of these experiences of vulnerability and fear, what resources might the Catholic social tradition offer our present society? One possible resource can be found in the virtue tradition of St. Thomas Aquinas, especially in his consideration of the virtues of magnanimity and humility. As a personal virtue, the acquired virtue of magnanimity, in a Thomistic sense, serves as a middle way between the sins of prideful self-interest and destructive self-emptying. Applied socially and politically, magnanimity, aided by its parent virtue of fortitude and the virtue of humility, has the potential to enable national and global communities to constructively embrace the reality of vulnerability and to identify shared goals that we can collectively work toward. In contrast to the dominant realist frameworks that perceive vulnerability negatively, a socially magnanimous approach has the potential to liberate us from irrational fears and move us toward a new empowering sense of positive freedom. Certainly, seeking to apply Thomas's personal virtue framework socially in a very different historical context is not without risk. Nevertheless, I believe the virtue of magnanimity has the potential to offer a hopeful and transformative response in our divided and anxious context.

Destructive Responses to the Reality of Vulnerability

Unlike any other event in recent history, the attacks of 9/11 publically revealed a reality that many of us in the United States still find difficult to accept. Over the course of few hours as we watched the dramatic and terrifying footage of the World Trade Center's destruction, Americans came face to face with the fact that we, as a nation, are vulnerable; a reality that has been concealed for much of our history by the geographic protection of two vast oceans, relatively peaceful neighbors, and the myth of manifest destiny. The publically orchestrated destruction of important cultural icons on September 11 continues to have a profound impact on our way of life as illustrated by the recent outbursts of emotions following the news of Osama bin Laden's death in May 2011 and the immediate reaction to unsubstantiated threats around the tenth anniversary.

Over the past decade since 9/11, other high profile events have further illustrated our vulnerability, including: the worldwide economic downturn, the anthrax scare, the dangers presented by the global spread of diseases such as the Influenza A (H1N1) virus, and the ever-present risks to our security from natural disasters such as Hurricane Katrina. In light of these and other recent events sensationalized by the twenty-four-hour news cycle, how have Americans responded to this reality?

The most simplistic response to this vulnerability and insecurity is that of denial. Prior to 2001, in the decade following the end of the Cold War, there was a sense that Americans could do anything. The denial of death that Ernest Becker highlighted in the 1970s manifested itself collectively and nationally in the 1990s.[2] With the collapse of the Soviet Union, the United States was unrivaled militarily, politically, and economically. Combined with the mythic beliefs of American power and predestination, it was easy to reject any notion of collective vulnerability.

Although the narratives of American triumphalism remain operative and this prideful denial continues to shape some people's response to global problems (such as climate change), the public and dramatic nature of 9/11 has made it nearly impossible to deny our collective vulnerability in the face of terrorism. Unaccustomed to not being in control of the situation, both ordinary citizens and members of the political elite have responded in the other extreme by being consumed by fear.[3] Allowing our vulnerability to consume our lives has manifested itself in several destructive ways, from being paralyzed by despair to becoming obsessed with an almost Machiavellian desire for security through power. In the end, the result of this dangerous mix is what Dominique Moïsi has called the "culture of fear."[4]

In a 2007 article in *Foreign Affairs*, Moïsi makes the argument that the United States and Europe, while facing different realities, can be distinguished from the rest of the world by a "common culture of fear." This outlook emerges largely from the threats posed by Islamic extremism, new immigration patterns, rapid cultural changes, and the diminishment of Euro-American hegemony. For him, these fears and the different ways in which they manifest themselves are emblematic of "a sense of loss of control over one's territory, security, and identity—in short, one's destiny."

Over the past decade, this culture of fear has been used to justify a number of ethically questionable foreign and domestic policy actions. On the domestic front, one of the most striking examples has been the USA Patriot Act. The controversial bill made a number of legal changes impacting civil liberties, intelligence collection, border policies, and even library records. Using the threats to our security posed by terrorism, and with almost no debate, the Act was overwhelmingly passed by Congress shortly after 9/11.

More significantly perhaps, this culture of fear and control has been used to justify unjust foreign policy decisions. In 2003, the Bush administration pointed to supposed threats to our security by weapons of mass destruction and terrorism to make the case for preemptive war in Iraq. Despite resistance from most of the international community and prominent religious leaders, many in the United States supported the invasion on the pretense that it would make us more secure and prevent an attack with Iraqi weapons of mass destruction. Over seven years and one hundred and fifty thousand violent deaths later, we still have yet to find serious evidence of such weapons and do not seem to be any safer from terrorist threats as a result of our actions in Iraq.[5] Since 2001, arguments in favor of security have also been used to justify the use of torture. While most people will admit that torture is wrong, many appear to accept and even support the practice, if it is seen to make us less vulnerable to a threat.

From an extreme realist perspective, the reduction of civil liberties, the use of torture, and preemptive war seem justifiable in light of potential threats to our security, power, and hegemony. Such an inordinate desire for security is extremely dangerous as it easily leads to seeing nature, other nations, and even individual human beings as either threats to our power or commodities to be controlled. In *Being Consumed*, William T. Cavanaugh laments the consumer culture, which falsely assumes that "we live in a world of scarce resources" and limitless desire.[6] Such an ultra-consumerist culture, as he points out, lacks any shared *telos* or goal to unite people. In the end, this outlook can only lead to conflict and "sheer arbitrary power, one will against another."[7]

In a worldview of consumerism and control, the "other" is obviously threatening. Other people and other nations need to be depersonalized "so that they may be consumed" and controlled.[8] Ultimately, however, as Edna McDonagh warns, this obsessive desire to control the real and supposedly real threats to our security is paradoxical and tragic in that a person's desire to control or to possess will often translate into that person or community becoming possessed and enslaved.[9] Ten years after launching the so-called "War on Terror," American policies and attitudes remain captive of this culture of fear. As we move into the second decade of this long war, Americans must seriously consider if it is all worth it.

Magnanimity: A Transformative Response to Vulnerability

Given the complex problems facing our country and planet today, are there alternative paths to security and flourishing other than through denial, fear, and the obsessive desire for control? For certain realists and neoconservatives who see freedom as being free from the interference from anyone or anything, the answer is clearly no. For them, vulnerability and dependency must be rejected or overcome.

The Thomistic virtue tradition, however, offers an alternative response to the reality of vulnerability. With the virtues of magnanimity and humility, Aquinas lays out an approach that has the potential to liberate us from both inordinate fear and the destructive desire to be in complete control of others and ourselves.

Thomas embraces vulnerability as a core dimension of our created nature and as a condition for genuine flourishing and security both in this life and in the next. True and lasting happiness can be found only if we are open to receiving the gifts of grace and charity that unite us with God since, in the words of Thomas, "neither man, nor any creature, can attain final Happiness by his natural powers."[10] A certain amount of vulnerability and dependency are also needed in this life, where, according to Thomas, openness to virtue and "the fellowship of friends" are necessary conditions for imperfect happiness and security.[11]

From this more positive outlook on vulnerability, Thomas develops a framework in which genuine security is found not in power or control but in the elimination of inordinate fear. Security, for Thomas, even the imperfect security that is found in this life, is a good object that is "attractive to the appetite" and worthy of hope.[12] The appetitive impulse toward security and other similar good objects requires a "twofold virtue" to help moderate our appetites and to avoid the vices of despair, presumption, and pride. On the one hand, he argues that we need the virtue of humility to restrain "the appetite from aiming at great things against right reason."[13] On the other, we need the virtue of magnanimity to "to strengthen the mind against despair, and urge it on to the pursuit of great things according to right reason."[14] While they appear to tend to go in "contrary directions," Thomas explicitly points out that magnanimity and humility are not opposed to one another but are complementary.[15] For him, both are necessary in achieving those difficult goods that are in accordance with right reason, including security and justice.

Although he builds off of Aristotle's understanding of the virtue in Book IV of the *Nicomachean Ethics*, he departs from "the Philosopher" on a number of important points. For Aristotle, it is only the rare wealthy and self-sufficient man who is magnanimous. Thomas, by contrast, perceives magnanimity as a more accessible virtue that is compatible with humility and vulnerability. In treating the virtue through the lens of faith in a God who "humbled himself" (Phil 2:8), he departs sharply from Aristotle, who saw humility as a vice. For Aristotle, to "be humble was to be low, despicable, beneath respect. Christianity turned this way of looking at the world upside down by proclaiming that humility is the typical Christian virtue and pride the greatest vice."[16]

Thomas defines magnanimity or high mindedness as the "stretching forth of the mind to great things" amid difficulty.[17] In this outward movement, the acquired virtue of magnanimity resembles aspects of the passion and theological virtue of hope. In contrast to a realist approach, the goals of magnanimity do not include power, honor, or the goods of fortune in and of themselves, but with an eye to the final *telos*, magnanimity enables us to be oriented toward true security and the common good.

For Thomas, it is magnanimity together with its parent virtue of fortitude that can best help us to get past our inordinate fears to achieve security, without falling into the trap of pride or presumption. In question 129 of the *Secunda Secundæ*, Thomas defines security as denoting "perfect freedom of the mind from fear."[18] Importantly, however, he qualifies this with two points. First, as he points out in question 126, not all fear is inherently bad. It is the role of magnanimity and fortitude to moderate this "fear according to reason" so that one fears only what it is reasonable to fear.[19] Second, while security is a good goal, he stresses that "Not all security is worthy of praise." Some security, he recognizes, can inordinately come about through denial or trust in objects that are not worthy of trust. Accordingly, true security, "a condition of fortitude and magnanimity" occurs "only when one puts care aside, as one ought."[20]

At first glance, it may seem as if magnanimity and its parent virtue of fortitude stand in opposition to vulnerability and dependence. However, as Josef Pieper points out, the two virtues "presuppose vulnerability; without vulnerability there is no possibility of fortitude. An angel cannot be brave, because he is not vulnerable."[21] If one denies this vulnerability, one is not magnanimous, but prideful, a vice that Thomas articulates as being opposed by excess to both magnanimity and humility.[22]

While magnanimity looks outward, humility looks inward and is concerned with authentic self-knowledge and the moderation of our deepest desires of self-preservation. Humility helps moderate our movement towards security by offering a true self-estimation as a vulnerable and dependent creature. It is this virtue that gives us a realistic understanding of who we are and what we should magnanimously aim to be. Such a realistic and humble self-knowledge is important, for Thomas, in that it helps us to overcome the sin that is rooted in an inordinate, all too often prideful vision of the self.

In our present context, where humility is again seen as a vice, it is helpful to remember, as Pieper clarifies, that humility for Thomas in no way suggests "an attitude, or principle, of constant self-accusation, of disparagement of one's being and doing, of cringing inferiority feelings."[23] On the contrary, humility as proper self-understanding linked with magnanimity should liberate us from our shallow and destructive fears and desires to be in control, all the while empowering us to work toward appropriate goals.

Humility and magnanimity, therefore, are not mutually exclusive, but actually are, as Pieper points out, "neighbors and akin."[24] Seen together, they offer a different response to vulnerability and dependence than those destructive responses of denial and control. While he does not refer to her in relation to this virtue, it seems that Mary with her prophetic Magnificat (Lk 1:46-55) aptly embodies Thomas's understanding of magnanimity and its proximity to humility. While Mary's role as a "humble servant" has often been stressed in the tradition, feminist theologians such as Elizabeth Johnson have more recently pointed to her role as an empowered agent in the pursuit of God's reign.[25]

Even if these virtues cannot be applied directly to our contemporary social structures, which are often divided over notions of the good, this virtue tradition has the potential to inform our efforts at developing domestic and international policies that can lead us to genuine security. When applied socially, even if only analogously, a number of broad principles and implications arise from Thomas's vision of magnanimity that have the potential to help transform our culture of fear into a culture of hope.

The first and perhaps most characteristic feature of magnanimity is that of empowered agency. This emphasis of magnanimity offers a corrective to some of the destructive interpretations of humility that have been justifiably critiqued by feminist scholars.[26] In his ethical vision, Thomas offers a middle way between the sins of extreme self-interest (or pride) and those of destructive self-emptying. In his approach to magnanimity and humility, he outlines a way to empower agency while maintaining a humble perspective. Applied socially, this principle challenges us to find ways to put aside those inordinate fears that can lead to despair and to model a humble agency in the world. As the magnanimous agent is concerned for the well being of the neighbor, this principle also calls us to empower other nations in becoming magnanimous agents themselves.

A second principle that arises from social magnanimity is that of interdependence or solidarity. Here, Thomas stands in contrast to both Machiavelli and Aristotle who valorize total self-sufficiency.[27] Thomas seeks to correct this by affirming that everyone needs help from both God and the neighbor: "For it surpasses man to need nothing at all. For every man needs, first, the Divine assistance, secondly, even human assistance, since man is naturally a social animal."[28] A lack of recognition of this interdependence and the social nature of humanity leads to vice. One is guilty of pride, for example, when one is only concerned about honor for the self or when one sets oneself "inordinately above his neighbor."[29] Similarly, one is guilty of the vice of ambition, when one seeks good things without reference to God or "without referring it to the profit of others."[30]

In light of the strongly individualistic American culture, theologians, social scientists, and philosophers have affirmed the need to recognize our social nature and dependency on others at the personal level. Looking more globally, this principle of interdependence, as Pope John Paul II often recognized, demands a rethinking of our relationships with other nations in terms of solidarity. To be socially magnanimous, therefore, entails a recommitment to our intergovernmental institutions and international legal obligations, a strengthening and reform of the United Nations, an end to unilateral military actions, a reform of immigration policies in light of solidarity, and a rethinking of those myths that perceive us as superior and detached from the rest of the world.

A third dimension that emerges from social magnanimity is that of positive freedom. As a virtue that entails the stretching forth of the mind to great things, magnanimity invites and empowers us to a distinctive form of freedom that stands in contrast to the dominant notions of negative freedom. Genuine freedom in this sense is a positive and transformative force that, in the words of Cavanaugh, is "not simply a negative freedom *from*, but a freedom *for*, a capacity to achieve certain worthwhile goals."[31] By its very nature, magnanimity aspires to good goals that cannot be limited only to the self. In order to avoid falling into the vice of ambition, the magnanimous agent must desire to profit others with her actions.[32] In other words, to be magnanimous, an agent must be oriented to a good goal, such as the promotion of the common good.[33]

In *We Hold These Truths*, John Courtney Murray argues in favor of adopting such a socially magnanimous orientation to a good goal. Writing in the midst of the cold war, Murray points to the need to develop a common consensus to ethically guide the American society. He laments the fact that the public consensus of the 1950s seemed to be guided primarily by a negative reaction against communism. "We have achieved a consensus that communism is an evil thing," he writes, "but where does that leave us? We cannot establish a philosophy based only on a negative consensus of this kind."[34] A consensus needs to be able to be a proposal to the world in favor of the common good. In the eyes of Murray, a policy guided primarily by anti-terrorism, anti-government, anti-Democrat, or anti-Republican cannot be a genuine public philosophy.[35]

A fourth and important principle that Thomas relates to the virtue of magnanimity is that of justice. In his question on magnanimity, Thomas writes that it is unbecoming of the magnanimous person to abandon justice or to conceal truth. Here, he makes an interesting observation that injustice and the concealment of truth are often an "outcome of fear."[36] Since the events of 9/11, it is clear that fear for our security and power has led to a number of instances of injustice and a lack of transparency. An example of this can be seen in the treatment and detention of those suspected of terrorism, where the norms of due process and transparency have, in many cases, been suspended. Social magnanimity, therefore, can help to reaffirm justice and the need for transparency and accountability in our domestic and international affairs. Taken together, these four principles of magnanimity, I believe, can help us to find creative and durable solutions to the real threats to our security in liberating us from inordinate fear and desires for power.

Toward a Social Transformation: Some Practical Recommendations

The tenth anniversary of the September 11 attacks present us with an opportunity for a realistic and honest assessment of the position of the United States in the world and our collective hopes for the future. In the language of virtue ethics, the anniversary offers us an opportunity to respond collectively as Americans and as members of a global human community to three key questions: Who are we? Who ought we to become? How do we get there?

In responding to these questions, the Thomistic virtue of magnanimity has the potential to develop socially transformative approaches to the reality of vulnerability and the real threats to our security. While the principles of empowered agency, interdependence, positive freedom, and justice offer guiding values to help us to answer these questions, what concretely might we do to engender social magnanimity?

A simple way to bring about the virtue of social magnanimity is to support those structures of magnanimity that are already operative in our society today. Historically, as Robert Bellah and others have noted, civil society and nongovernmental organizations (NGOs) have played an important role in creating community and combating the destructive forces of individualism in various ways. In today's globalized world, a diversity of international NGOs, from Catholic religious congregations to the Lions Clubs, are playing a particularly important role in facilitating an awareness of global solidarity.

A second and more formidable task in engendering magnanimity is a reform in the way our local and national media support the culture of fear. Sadly, most local news outlets in the United States pay very little attention to positive global news stories. Instead, much of the media coverage in our culture of consumerism is based on the manipulation of desire. Furthermore, the advent of adversarial and polarized cable news has encouraged an approach that sensationalizes suffering, desire, and fear. We must find new ways to present complex events and opinions in more hopeful ways.

A third task relates to the selection of political leaders. If we want to be magnanimous as a nation and as a global community, it is not enough to support magnanimous NGOs and hopeful news outlets; we also need to select magnanimous and hopeful leaders. Virtuous leaders are essential to help us develop the common consensus that Murray spoke of fifty years ago. An unfortunate reality of our politics today, however, is the dominant role played by fear and pride, which easily reduce our political discourse into "thirty-second commercials composed of vivid images stimulating fear or desire but inhibiting thought."[37] Political figures and parties, it seems, are more and more defined by what they are against and less about what they are for. A concrete way to address this is to enact reforms, similar to those in some European countries, that ban campaign advertizing on television and the radio.

Fourth, again echoing Robert Bellah's proposals in the *Good Society*, universities need to become magnanimous communities of learning and formation.[38] Colleges and universities around the country might try to take advantage of the 9/11 anniversary to have interdisciplinary reflections on the reality of the country and our possible goals heading into the future. In these reflections, intellectuals have a specific responsibility to initiate and facilitate dialogues across disciplines, universities, and national borders. Such spaces can go a long way in helping the wider community discern between what fears are reasonable and what fears or threats are irrational and should be put aside.

Finally, we can promote social magnanimity if we as church model this virtue in our own communities. As Christians, we are called to reflect the theological virtue of hope in our personal lives and in our communities. Unfortunately, especially after the clergy sexual abuse crisis, there has been a serious lack of hope and magnanimity within the American Catholic Church. Sadly, it seems that the present Catholic Church communicates more about what it is against than what it offers to the world. This, especially around social issues, often gives the impression that the Catholic community lacks a positive consensus, has nothing to offer, and is simply against everything.

As we move ahead into the second decade of the twenty-first century, no nation will be able to live in isolation. Our deeply interconnected global reality will continue to bring cross-border challenges and threats to our security and well-being. But this reality will also bring many new opportunities for us to do great things as members of one human family. Applying magnanimity socially in this context can help guide us as we seek to meet these challenges and work to promote the global common good.

Notes

[1]John F. Burns, "America the Vulnerable Meets a Ruthless Enemy," *New York Times*, September 12, 2001, http://www.nytimes.com/2001/09/12/international/12OSAM.html.

[2]Ernest Becker, *The Denial of Death* (New York: Free Press, 1975).

[3]Dominique Moïsi, "The Clash of Emotions: Fear, Humiliation, Hope, and the New World Order," *Foreign Affairs* 86, no. 1 (February 2007): 8.

[4]Ibid., 9.

[5]World Health Organization, "New Study Estimates 151,000 Violent Iraqi Deaths Since 2003 Invasion," January 9, 2008, http://www.who.int/mediacentre/news/releases/2008/pr02/en/index.html.

[6]William T. Cavanaugh, *Being Consumed: Economics and Christian Desire* (Grand Rapids, MI: William B. Eerdmans, 2008), xii.

[7]Ibid., 16.

[8]Timothy Radcliffe, *What Is the Point of Being a Christian?* (London; New York: Burns & Oates, 2005), 101.

[9]Enda McDonagh, *Vulnerable to the Holy: In Faith, Morality and Art* (Blackrock, Co. Dublin: Columba Press, 2004), 16.

[10]Thomas Aquinas, *Summa Theologica*, trans. Fathers of the English Dominican Province (Westminster, MD: Christian Classics, 1981), Ia IIae, q.5, a.5.

[11]Ibid., Ia IIae, q.4 a.8.

[12]Ibid., IIa IIae, q.161, a.1.

[13]Ibid., IIa IIae, q.161, a.1, ad.3.

[14]Ibid., IIa IIae, q.161, a.1.

[15]Ibid. IIa IIae, q.129.3, ad.4.

[16]Ibid., IIa IIae, q.129, a.3, ad.4. See IIa IIae, q.129, a.8, ad.1.

[17]Ibid., IIa IIae, q.129, a.1.

[18]Ibid., IIa IIae, q.129, a.7. See also Ia IIae, q.45, a.2.

[19]Ibid., IIa IIae, q.126, a.1.

[20]Ibid., IIa IIae, q.129, a.7, ad.2.

[21]Josef Pieper, *The Four Cardinal Virtues: Prudence, Justice, Fortitude, Temperance* (Notre Dame, IN: University of Notre Dame Press, 1966), 117.

[22]See Aquinas, *Summa Theologica*, IIa IIae, q.162, a.1, ad.3.

[23]Pieper, *The Four Cardinal Virtues*, 189.

[24]Ibid., 189.

[25]See Elizabeth A. Johnson, *Truly Our Sister: A Theology of Mary in the Communion of Saints* (New York: Continuum, 2003).

[26]Valerie Saiving, "The Human Situation: A Feminine View," in *Womanspirit Rising: A Feminist Reader in Religion*, ed. Carol P. Christ and Judith Plaskow (San Francisco: HarperSanFrancisco, 1992).

[27]Aquinas, *Summa Theologica*, IIa IIae, q.129, a.6, ad.1.

[28]Ibid., IIa IIae, q.129, a.6, ad.1.

[29]Ibid., IIa IIae, q.162, a.5, ad.2.

[30]Ibid., IIa IIae, q.131, a.1.

[31]Cavanaugh, *Being Consumed*, 29.

[32]Aquinas, *Summa Theologica*, IIa IIae, q.131, a.1.

[33]See IIa-IIae q.123, a.5.

[34]John Courtney Murray, *We Hold These Truths: Catholic Reflections on the American Proposition* (Lanham, MD: Rowman & Littlefield Publishers, 2005), 94.

[35]Ibid., 95.

[36]Aquinas, *Summa Theologica*, IIa IIae, q.129, a.4, ad.2.

[37]Robert N. Bellah, Richard Madsen, Steven M. Tipton, and William M. Sullivan, *The Good Society* (New York: Vintage, 1992), 143.

[38]See ibid., chap. 5.

Deceit, Desire, and the Desert

René Girard's Mimetic Theory in Conversation with Early Christian Monastic Practice

Brian D. Robinette

In his recent book, *The Genesis of Desire*, psychologist Jean-Michel Oughourlian speaks of the need for "day-to-day asceticism," a "constant watchfulness" for the mechanisms of desire that lead us into conflict with others.[1] A long-time collaborator with René Girard,[2] whose theories on mimetic desire and scapegoat violence have provided penetrating insights into the dynamics of human culture, Oughourlian maintains that if free and loving relationships are to become a sustained possibility, a process of conversion must be undertaken in which the *askesis*, or spiritual discipline, of interior vigilance becomes habitual. It "requires self-control and a careful, ubiquitous, never ending asceticism," he writes. "And it is often difficult in daily life to maintain this sort of constantly watchful attentiveness."[3] One might assume by the vocabulary that the author is addressing novices in a monastery. He is not. It is counsel given to persons in committed loving relationships. Yet its truth extends to all human relationships. Love and jealousy, friendship and rivalry, erotic attraction and vehement repulsion: these are the poles between which relationships swing, and whose inner workings can be illuminated by mimetic theory.

But what is mimetic theory, and how is it illuminating? And what are we to make of Oughourlian's reference to "day-to-day asceticism"? This latter question is especially pertinent for my present purposes; for while I am convinced that mimetic theory helps us better understand many dynamics governing human life, particularly the mechanisms generating exclusion and violence, it is not clear in my reading of Girard (and his many interpreters) what kinds of everyday practices—or *askeses*—are critical for bringing about conversion. How might perception, affectivity, and cognition be restructured so as to establish a new "way of life" for releasing deep-seated antagonisms in human life?[4]

In light of this question, I will pursue a two-fold inquiry by staging a conversation between mimetic theory and aspects of early Christian desert monasticism, particularly as exemplified in the writings of Evagrius Ponticus and John Cassian. I shall argue that several insights and practices enshrined in these fourth- and fifth-century texts reveal a profound intuitive grasp of mimetic desire that can be clarified when examined in light of mimetic theory. At the same time, such examination provides an opportunity to deepen mimetic theory by rooting it more explicitly in ascetical-contemplative practice. Although the latter inquiry will focus on practices historically associated with fourth- and fifth-century desert spirituality, the effort presumes that their creative adaptation by men and women today is not only possible but in many ways crucial for the sort of human flourishing that is the fruit of reconciled relationship with neighbor and God.

Mimetic Theory in Outline

In his first major work, *Deceit, Desire & the Novel: Self and Other in Literary Structure* (1961), Girard provides an account of what he calls the "triangularity of desire."[5] According to this view, human desire is inherently mimetic, or "imitative," insofar as what it desires—its "object"—is mediated by the desires of others. In contrast to a "romantic" understanding of the self, which views desire as spontaneously and privately generated within the self, a mimetic approach views all human desire, even that which seems most original to us, as *suggested* by others who are our models, and therefore our potential rivals. Whereas we typically imagine desire arising from a simple subject-object relation (for example, I desire this toy, this occupation, this style of dress, and so on), in fact the object is mediated and transfigured by the light of another's attention. Desirability lies not in the object, per se, but in the value others confer upon it. The relationship is triangular, not binary: I desire "according to the desire of the other," as Girard frequently puts it; and it is this mimetic attraction that lies at the heart of both human belonging and conflict. Mimetic desire is therefore ambiguous: it can tend either toward creative mutuality or violent rivalry, and with many different shades in between.

Regarding creative mutuality, mimetic theory underscores the fundamental goodness of imitation in human relationships. Indeed, it is necessary for human development. We have all observed, for instance, how infants naturally imitate facial expressions, or how toddlers' motor skills are learned by mirroring and interiorizing the bodily gestures of others. Long before the acquisition of language, which itself is learned through imitation, mimetic responsiveness to gesture, touch, and articulated sound draws the infant into an intersubjective world that makes its nascent individuation possible.

What we call the "self" is hardly an atomized ego but is rather a dynamic reality arising "between" others who remain mutually implicated and constantly "exchanged" through perception, language, and culture.[6] Such "universal mimesis," which Oughourlian likens to a force of gravity in human relationships, does not diminish as persons pass from childhood to adulthood; rather, it becomes more complex and nuanced, even to the point where we can learn to hide or obscure the borrowed character of our desires. Neither should we imagine that mimetic theory denies personal uniqueness or freedom; instead, mimesis "both individualizes us and universalizes us, binds us and at the same gives us liberty."[7]

Iain McGilchrest makes just this point after summarizing much of the recent neuroscientific research on "mirror neurons" in the human brain. "Imitation gives rise, paradoxically as it may seem, to individuality. That is precisely because the process is not mechanical reproduction, but an imaginative inhabiting of the other, which is always different because of its intersubjective betweenness."[8] Such "imaginative inhabiting" is made possible, in part, by a special class of neurons distributed throughout the brain that internally "mirror" the intentions, feelings, and behaviors of others. Crucial for language acquisition and sociality—and thus for freeing humans from genetic determinism for the myriad creations of culture—mirror neurons are vitally important for human empathy.[9]

Empathy is not arrived at through a process of inference but is an immediate, viscerally felt, and pre-reflective response to the perceived actions and expressions of others. The consequences of such capacities are far-reaching: "The enormous strength of the human capacity for mimesis is that our brains let us escape from the confines of our own experience and enter directly into the experience of another being: this is the way in which, through human consciousness, we bridge the gap, share in what another feels and does, in what it is like to be that person."[10] This is why McGilchrest, like Girard and Oughourlian, argues that imitation makes freedom and individuality possible. Mimesis is not necessarily mechanical or slavish, but a creative process that introduces novelty and uniqueness along the way. "We are imitators," he emphasizes, "not copying machines."[11]

Scapegoat Violence and Otherness

Nevertheless, our capacity for imitation can indeed become mechanical and destructive. If the other models my desire, he or she may become my rival in its fulfillment. Because desire is triangular—the "impulse toward the object is ultimately an impulse toward the mediator"—it harbors here potential for all manner of conflict, including such "passions" as envy, fear, anger, loathing, hatred, and *ressentiment*.[12] Consider how children can suddenly converge upon the same toy but with great potential for conflict in its sole possession. Or consider how gadgets, styles of dress, or property can transfigure arbitrary items into absorbing necessities. Such "objects" are never mere "things": they are "metaphysical," by which Girard means symbolic realities laying claim on one's sense of *being*, such as recognition, identity, status, or power.[13]

A major feature of Girard's work is its insight into the contagion of violence that emerges when persons or groups in rivalry find resolution by projecting the source of their rivalry onto an outside party; this may be objectified through exclusion, subordination, or expulsion. The "scapegoat mechanism" is the dynamic that appears when some "other" is perceived as an ambiguous, polluting element that requires purging for the maintenance of self or group identity.

If, for instance, you and I find ourselves rivals, we may "reconcile" the tension by finding a common enemy against which our relationship may be redefined. Consider how frequently we fashion our identities and allegiances by polarizing ourselves against some "other" who thereby serves, as the result of nationality, culture, religion, race, gender, sexual orientation, or any other marker of difference, as an oppositional index.

The ambiguity and volatility of mimetic desire, which so easily shifts from pacific to conflictual patterns, can achieve a deceptive sense of clarity to the extent that its stability is established over and against an "outsider." I say "deceptive" because my sense of ownership and identity, when secured against an Other, is bought at the price of misunderstanding, even willfully denying the origins of my desires. "Hatred is individualistic," writes Girard. "It nourishes fiercely the illusion of an absolute difference between the Self and that Other from which nothing separates it. Indignant comprehension is therefore an imperfect comprehension . . . for the subject does not recognize in the other the void gnawing at himself."[14] The upshot here is that only when I accept the other as *constitutive* of my identity, and so recognize that the origins of my desires are anterior to me, flowing through me in ways I may discern, negotiate, resist, or cooperate with graciously, rather than acquisitively, that I may be released from the antagonisms that lock me into distorted, possibly violent relationships.

According to mimetic theory, personal authenticity is not premised upon freedom *from* others in self-determination. Instead, "the most 'authentic' self would be one that recognizes the mimetic nature of its desire and thereby frees itself from the deceptive individualism that impedes understanding of oneself, of others, and of their relations."[15] This is not to collapse self and other: the remedy for a hypertrophied individualism is not a pseudo-mystical collectivism in which the self is regarded a mere epiphenomenon, blissfully unaccountable for its burden of desire. Rather, authentic selfhood is premised upon an attitudinal and behavioral hospitality to the otherness that founds it. The self is born of otherness, and so is other to itself. Growth in such hospitality requires a proficiency in discerning those relational patterns that lead either to creative reciprocity or strained polarization. Here is the starting point for that "day-to-day asceticism," which, according to Oughourlian, "requires a clear understanding of the mimetic mechanisms that are always working to undermine love and pervert it."[16]

Deceit, Desire, and the Desert

In light of this brief account of mimetic theory we turn now to the wisdom of the desert, particularly as exhibited by Evagrius Ponticus and John Cassian who together helped craft the first major theological syntheses of early Christian desert monasticism. A number of reasons might be offered to justify initiating this conversation, but let me address a potential objection by way of preface. If mimetic theory denies that genuine freedom can be realized through self-determination *from* others, as though one's "true" desires might be wrested from the intersubjective field in which they arise, is this not the very ambition of those who renounced the social entanglements of the city for desert solitude? Does such "flight from the world" presuppose a facile dualism between city and desert in a way quite at odds with the central insight of mimetic anthropology?

Certainly there were those who approached the monastic experiment with something of this attitude. But we will thoroughly misread the deepest impulse of desert monasticism, in the terms articulated by Evagrius and Cassian, if we fail to appreciate the centrality of the neighbor in its exercise. "The goal of the ascetic life is charity," writes Evagrius in his *Praktikos*.[17] Cassian echoes the point when he declares that all of the activities of monastic life are "subordinate to our main objective, purity of heart, that is to say, love. . . ."[18] Later, in his *Conferences*, Cassian writes movingly of the purgative process that allows love of God and neighbor to become unmotivated by fear or reward, a love that delights in the good for its own sake. Such "disinterested" (or *agapeic*) love, which Evagrius claims is the "progeny of *apatheia*," allows God and neighbor to be truly *other*, for it manifests a creative liberty from the countless resentments and comparative (mimetic) judgments that so frequently charge relationships with rivalry and conflict.[19]

Because the monk discovers creaturely poverty in a radical way—this is the best way to understand the cultivation of *apatheia*, as we shall see—he can more clearly perceive and resist the temptations to project his own illusions and frailties onto others. The desert is thus a school for desire, a *topos* for conversion in which the practice of interior vigilance, discernment, and dispossession allow God and neighbor "to be." "You 'flee' to the desert," writes Rowan Williams, "not to escape neighbors but to grasp more fully what the neighbor is. . . ."[20] As Thomas Merton put it, the Desert Fathers give witness to an "interior and spiritual identification with one's brother, so that he is not regarded as an 'object' to 'which' one 'does good.' . . . Love takes one's neighbor as one's other self, and loves him with all the immense humility and discretion and reserve and reverence without which no one can presume to enter into the sanctuary of another's subjectivity."[21]

Skillful Imitation and Eschatology

Sharing in the sanctuary of another's subjectivity is one way to appreciate the emphasis Cassian places on the skillful imitation of elders in the monastic life. Cassian makes clear from the outset of his *Conferences* that the monastic life, so far from enacting heroic escape from mimetic desire, demands its thoroughgoing reformation, first through the imitation of those who are proficient in the ascetical life, and second through deepening contemplative awareness of God who alone is the source and of all pacific desire. Likening monastic life to various practical arts, including archery, farming, and seafaring, Cassian explains that if purity of heart is the ultimate aim of the monk, he should point his spirit in its direction and, with unwavering purpose, "travel the road laid down for us by the tradition of our elders and by the goodness of their lives" (*Conf.* II.11).

The metaphor of following a path cleared by others appears frequently in the *Conferences* and in fact permeates the sayings tradition as a whole. "It is a very necessary thing," insists Evagrius, "to examine carefully the ways of the monks who have traveled, in an earlier age, strait along the road and to direct oneself along the same paths. Many excellent sayings and deeds are found that have been left behind by them" (*Prak.* 91).

The transmission of the elders' sayings and deeds, along with their "performance" in community, can be thought of as establishing a *habitus* of imitation extending from the disciples of Jesus, who themselves were summoned to "follow me." One also thinks of Saint Paul's frequent appeal that others imitate him just as he imitates Christ. This is non-rivalrous imitation, or "positive mimesis," by which Girard means a creative form of imitation that progressively releases persons from conflictual patterns of relationship.

Because of his self-emptying in imitation of the Father, even unto death on a cross, Jesus Christ is the model whose imitation establishes a "living chain" of mutual self-emptying rather than mutual projection and expulsion.[22] His is a human life unmoved by compulsion or fear of others, empty of any acquisitiveness that would lay claim to divinity (Phil 2), a self free to share itself with others in love because it is utterly available to the Father's inexhaustible gratuity (Jn 6-8).

Cassian speaks of Christ as the "fullness of purity," and thus the absolute exemplar in the monk's path toward purity of heart. Imitation of Christ allows the monk to "reproduce some image of that blessedly eternal life promised for the future to the saints so that among us it may be a case of 'God—all in all' (1 Cor 15:28)" (*Conf.* X.6). The goal of monastic mimesis is communion with others in God, the formation of a reconciled community in which God will be "all our living" and "our very breath." The aim of the monk is eschatological, for "all his striving" is in hope of realizing "in this life an image of future happiness" and "the beginnings of a foretaste in this body of that life and glory of heaven" (*Conf.* X.7). Skillful imitation of Christ in community both anticipates and realizes the future of God's kingdom.

Attention and the Mill of the Mind

For Cassian, the most important practice in the monastic life is discernment. Its attainment comes through "avoiding extremes" in the spiritual life, a prospect greatly assisted by following the "royal road" charted by those who have gone before (*Conf.* II.2). This means far more than mimicking what one observes from afar. It involves humbly entrusting one's practice and inner discourse to the scrutiny of others (*Conf.* II.10). The presumption of "private judgment" is disastrous for the monk; for harboring "passionate thoughts" like envy, anger, or lust, rather than exposing them through confession to one's neighbor allows them to fester into compulsions and delusions. The *Conferences* is laced with colorful, sometimes disturbing examples of those who, presuming

themselves free from the dialogical process of discernment, strike
out on their own only to suffer illusions of grandeur, depression,
and in some cases suicide.

A common theme in early Christian monasticism is the recognition that our desires—or what the desert monks generally
called "thoughts"—are largely involuntary. We naively ascribe
self-authorship to our desires when in fact they are mostly adven-
titious. They phenomenalize themselves unbidden, even as they
absorb our attention. The constant flow of perceptions, memories,
inclinations, and half-formed thoughts—or what today we might
call the "stream of consciousness"—follows a course largely its
own, drawing attention hither, thither, and yon in a cascade of
currents not easily traced and treating their so-called "author" to
what Martin Laird describes as the "cocktail party" of the unquiet
mind.[23] Should anyone doubt this, sitting quietly in contemplative
repose for just the duration of five minutes would reveal it. Indeed,
it is difficult to appreciate just how cacophonous our minds can
be until we cultivate some climate of interior silence; for silence,
when so nurtured, enables us to become witness to the desires that
course through us. Little wonder why so much desert literature is
dedicated to anatomizing the passionate thoughts—how to quiet
them, trace their origins, mark their effects, and transform them
through *askeses* of heart and mind.

Cassian compares this flow of desire to a grain mill "activated
by the circular motion of water" (*Conf.* I.18). Though the mind
cannot prevent its flow, like a miller who grinds wheat, now barley,
and now darnel on the rotating wheel, the monk may, through
interior vigilance, memorization of scripture, and non-discursive
prayer, become witness to the process, grow progressively free
from its gripping immediacy, and learn to choose which thoughts
to tend. Evagrius likewise maintains that while it is "not in our
power to determine whether we are disturbed by these thoughts,"
we may "decide if they are to linger within us or not and whether
or not they are to stir up our passions" (*Prak.* 6).

Laird helpfully points out that this does not imply whipping
up commentary over the content of thoughts. Instead, the monk
learns, especially in times of prayer, but also habitually in day-
to-day activity, how to meet the endless stream of thoughts with
interior silence, with a contemplative awareness that allows them

"to be." Such "letting be" is at the heart of Evagrius's understanding of *apatheia*, which we shall discuss later. But it is worth emphasizing here that its cultivation says much about the quality of attention underwriting it. Attention, or *prosoche*, is a foundational practice for the monk, for by it he may become a dispassionate and discerning witness to the operations of his heart and mind. Attentiveness allows the monk to observe and anticipate those movements that undermine loving relationship with others, to borrow Oughourlian's language above.

It is illuminating to compare this "detached" attentiveness with Oughourlian's assessment: "But I can also choose to resist being swept along by my desire, to let it flow through me without my submitting myself to its motion. If one of my desires begins to conflict with my convictions, I always retain the ability to reject it—not simply to follow it, but to choose another model. That often requires a clear understanding of the mechanisms that move us."[24] To see how desert spirituality typically understands such mechanisms, we turn now to Evagrius's taxonomy of the "passionate thoughts."

The Passionate Thoughts

As St. Athanasius puts it in his classic hagiography, St. Antony lived in the desert "giving heed to himself and patiently training himself."[25] The desert landscape plays a crucial role in this work of attention and training. Like an anechoic chamber that allows blood flow in the ear to be heard, the silence of the desert allows the passionate thoughts to appear in sharp relief. Modern readers may wince at the language associated with the passionate thoughts, as for instance when Evagrius speaks of the "demons" of anger, envy, and pride, or when Antony is described thrown about in his cell by temptations; but we might appreciate that such quasi-objectivity bears an important phenomenological insight into the way our desires are *suggested* rather than solely originated by us: neither exterior nor interior, but stretching across spaces "between" self and other.

Consider that most of the "eight passionate thoughts" detailed by Evagrius in his *Praktikos* are mimetic in origin, each exhibiting some form of conflictual energy that distorts human relationships and frustrates contemplative awareness. *Avarice* "suggests to the mind" that hoarding can fend off the "great shame that comes from accepting the necessities of life from others" (*Prak.* 9). Avarice thus denies our creaturely frailty and dependence while charging desire with acquisitiveness, distrust, and anxiety. *Anger*, the "most fierce passion," is moved by real or imagined injury and easily metastasizes into indignation and revenge. Especially at times of prayer anger "seizes the mind and flashes the picture of the offensive person before one's eyes" (*Prak.* 11). *Vainglory* is the subtlest of them all, for it grows readily among those who ardently practice virtue. It leads us "to hunt after the praise of men," including esteem for our great humility. *Pride*, the most damaging of the passions, leads the monk to consider himself the cause of virtue rather than its recipient and quickly arouses anger or sadness when he learns that his brethren do not share the same opinion of himself as he does (*Prak.* 13).

A key Evagrian strategy for dealing with such passionate thoughts is to resist spurious modes of solitude or society in the effort to escape them. Instead we should "follow the opposite course" of their momentum and attack them at their roots (*Prak.* 22). Avarice should be met with a simplification of appetitive desire and a reduction of accumulated preferences. Such non-possessiveness allows us to accept our ontological poverty and learn gratitude for the simplest of life's provisions, even a morsel of bread (*Prak.* 16).

Anger, resentment, and sadness might suggest flight in order to escape the offending neighbor, but such flight cannot afford genuine solitude (*Prak.* 22). "Hatred is individualistic," to recall Girard's statement, and thus a deception. Only by attending to the neighbor who offends me can conflictual desire enter into the light of truth, and only a spirit of almsgiving and meekness toward that neighbor establishes the conditions for reconciliation (*Prak.* 21). "A gift snuffs out the fire of resentment, as Jacob well knew" (*Prak.* 26).

As for the enticements of vainglory that draw us into company with others in order to ferret out their praise, Evagrius advocates deepening contemplative awareness of God in solitude. Not only is such awareness humbling, as it entails a long letting go of our illusory self-separateness, but the delight that derives from spiritual contemplation infinitely surpasses all lesser delights (*Prak.* 32). The antidote to pride is found in recalling our weaknesses and the mercy of Christ who alone is the full measure of *apatheia* (*Prak.* 33). Since pride leads us to judge our neighbor in a spirit of rivalry, its remediation through humility undermines the potential for anger and sadness since these passions are aroused when we do not attain the admiration we seek.

Conclusion: *Apatheia* and the Neighbor

In his conference on perfection, Cassian makes clear that only by renouncing our tendencies to judge our neighbor may we grow free from the mechanisms binding us in rivalry. Herein lies the relationship between *apatheia* and *agape*—as a "cutting loose" from the sin of "censoriousness" that blocks our capacity for feeling "sympathizing pity" for others, including our enemies (*Conf.* XI.9). Such detachment in no way entails a numbing of feeling. Both Cassian and Evagrius stand squarely in a tradition that regards tears of compunction and contemplative joy as important markers of conversion.[26] Rather, the practice of detachment enables us to grow increasingly unmoved or "empty" of those conflict-laden passions that prevent us from "carrying one another's burden" (Gal 6:2).

From the point of view of mimetic theory, the problem with judging my neighbor is that it allows me to "project" upon others what in fact I lack and most need; it displaces truthful attention to myself, including my weaknesses and failings, while reinforcing the self-deceptive security of knowing I am *not* my neighbor. Such false distance between self and neighbor only exacerbates unhealthy proximity, for my endlessly inventive comparisons serve to turn my neighbor into a prop for maintaining the illusion of a freestanding, unambiguous self. "I put the neighbor in touch with God by a particular kind of detachment from him or her," declares Rowan Williams.[27]

Through the practice of *apatheia* the monk learns how to resist simply reacting to impulses and instead discover a pacific distance from them so that they may be witnessed, discerned, or simply "let go" in non-judgment and non-actuation. This puts the neighbor in touch with God because now I may enter into gratuitous and loving relationship with him or her. I allow the other "to be," and thus model pacific desire in a way that frees my neighbor for the same in creative mimesis. No longer must I cling to identity over *alterity*, and no longer need I project my frailties onto others. I learn to accept them in myself and in others in recognition of our shared poverty. Only when we "convert one another by our truthful awareness of frailty," writes Williams, will we be able to discern and disable "the scapegoat mechanisms that the cross of Christ" has "exploded once and for all."[28]

By way of conclusion, Williams's reference to Girard allows us to underscore the gospel-centered character of desert monastic practice. Though obviously the language and practice of attention (*prosoche*) and detachment (*apatheia*) in Evagrius and Cassian have much in common with the "spiritual exercises" found in several Hellenistic schools of philosophy, the centrality of the neighbor, along with the intense emphasis on a cross-shaped love and humility, show that "all these virtues were transfigured by the transcendent dimension of the love of God and of Christ." The desert monks were not, first and foremost, "cultivated men," writes Pierre Hadot, "but Christians who wanted to attain to Christian perfection by the heroic practice of the evangelical prescriptions, and the imitation of the Life of Christ."[29] By situating such imitation at the heart of the ascetical-contemplative path, early Christian monasticism premised the discovery of God in the discovery of the neighbor, and vice versa, for both are one in Christ.

Notes

[1]Jean-Michel Oughourlian, *The Genesis of Desire*, trans. Eugene Webb (East Lansing: Michigan State University Press, 2010), 15.

[2]See their co-authored volume, along with Guy Lefort, *Things Hidden since the Foundation of the World*, trans. Stephen Bann & Michael Metteer (Stanford: Stanford University Press, 1987).

[3]Ibid., 21. See also 27, 34, and 146 for references to asceticism.

[4]The allusion is to Pierre Hadot's study of ancient philosophy as a "way of life" (*Philosophy as a Way of Life: Spiritual Exercises from Socrates to Foucault*, ed. Arnold I. Davidson, trans. Michael Chase [Oxford: Blackwell Publishers, 1995]).

[5]René Girard, *Deceit, Desire and the Novel: Self and Other in Literary Structure*, trans. Yvonne Freccero (Baltimore: The Johns Hopkins University Press, 1966), esp. 1-52.

[6]Oughourlian, *The Genesis of Desire*, 34.

[7]Ibid., 14.

[8]Iain McGilchrist, *The Master and His Emissary: The Divided Brain and the Making of the Modern World* (New Haven: Yale University Press, 2009), 249.

[9]Girard engages the science of mirror neurons (and neuroscience more generally) in his recent *Evolution and Conversion: Dialogues on the Origins of Culture* (New York: T&T Clark, 2007). See also Oughourlian's treatment (*Genesis of Desire*, 92-95, 101-6).

[10]McGilchrist, *The Master and His Emissary*, 248.

[11]Ibid., 247.

[12]Girard, *Deceit, Desire, and the Novel*, 10.

[13]Ibid., esp. 85ff. See also Girard, *Things Hidden since the Foundation of the World*, 294-98.

[14]Girard, *Deceit, Desire, and the Novel*, 73.

[15]Oughourlian, *The Genesis of Desire*, 34.

[16]Ibid., 15.

[17]Evagrius Ponticus, "The Praktikos," in *The Praktikos & Chapters on Prayer*, trans. John Eudes Bamberger (Collegeville, MN: Cistercian Publications, 1972), 84, 37.

[18]John Cassian, *Conferences*, trans. Colm Luibheid (New York: Paulist Press, 1985), I.7, 42. Though Cassian never mentions Evagrius by name, the Egyptian monk was "the single most important influence on Cassian's monastic theology." See Columba Stewart, *Cassian the Monk* (New York: Oxford University Press, 1998), 11.

[19]"*Agape* is the progeny of *apatheia. Apatheia* is the very flower of *ascesis*" (Evagrius, "The Praktikos," 81, 36).

[20]Rowan Williams, *Where God Happens: Discovering Christ in One Another* (Boston: New Seeds, 2005), 33.

[21]Thomas Merton, Introduction to *The Wisdom of the Desert: Sayings from the Desert Fathers of the Fourth Century*, trans. Thomas Merton (New York: A New Directions Book, 1960), 18.

[22]Girard, *Conversion and Evolution*, 222-23.

[23]Martin Laird, "The 'Open Country Whose Name Is Prayer': Apophasis, Deconstruction, and Contemplative Practice," *Modern Theology* 21, 1 (2005): 144.

[24]Oughourlian, *The Genesis of Desire*, 27.

[25]Athanasius, *The Life of Antony and the Letter to Marcellinus*, trans. Robert C. Gregg (Manwah, NJ: Paulist Press, 1980), III, 32.

[26]See esp. Evargius, "Chapters on Prayer," 5-9, 56-57; Cassian, *Conferences*, IX:29-30, 118-19. For helpful background, see Stewart, *Cassian the Monk*, 122-29.

[27]Williams, *Where God Happens*, 14.

[28]Ibid., 27.

[29]Hadot, *Philosophy as a Way of Life*, 140.

The Embrace of Radical Poverty

Clare of Assisi's Unconventional Response to a World of Violence

John V. Kruse

A world of violence. Families are ripped apart by domestic violence. Society is plagued by tension between classes. Regionally, violence erupts between competing interests. There are outbreaks of violence as secular and religious forces clash, and there are even wars spurred by religion itself. This description could be applied to the modern world, but it could equally apply to the late twelfth- and thirteenth-century world of Clare of Assisi (d. 1253). Clare lived in a world torn asunder by violence.

In this essay, I will first explore Clare's violent context by examining four specific episodes in her life: (1) Clare's encounter with violence within her own family as she sought to embrace a Franciscan lifestyle of absolute poverty; (2) a not dissimilar experience of domestic violence as Clare's blood-sister Catherine sought to follow Clare in living a life of radical poverty; (3) the siege of Clare's monastery of San Damiano by Saracen forces loyal to the Emperor Frederick II; and (4) the attack of Vitalis de Aversa, the commander of Frederick's army, on the city of Assisi. I will then examine the conflict Clare had with the papacy as she sought to live a Franciscan lifestyle committed to absolute poverty. It is this very struggle with the papacy that points to Clare's most fundamental response to a world of violence.

Although Marco Bartoli has asserted in his recent biography, *Clare of Assisi: Beyond the Legend*, that the "weapon with which Clare responded to violence was that of prayer,"[1] deeper examination of Clare's life and writings reveals that her more fundamental response to a world of violence was an embrace of radical poverty. By her response to her own world of violence, Clare provides us with valuable insights into how to respond to the violence we encounter in our own lives.

Childhood Environment and Domestic Violence

As Bartoli notes in his above-mentioned biography, Clare grew up in a world of four concentric circles of violence. First, there were emerging class conflicts. In Assisi, this involved conflicts between the *minores*, which included a growing merchant class with an increasing desire for more power and autonomy, and the *majores*, of which Clare's noble family was a part. In fact, conflicts between the *minores* and the *majores* became so intense during Clare's childhood that Clare's family was forced to flee to the neighboring city of Perugia. Second, there were also conflicts between neighboring towns that sometimes had competing interests. Third, there was the conflict between the papacy and the Holy Roman Emperor, with cities taking sides between these dueling powers. Finally, there was the clash between Christendom and Islam in the crusades. As Bartoli points out, these levels of violence were often interrelated.[2] Within this context, however, Clare faced her own unique experiences of violence.

The first instance to be explored occurred after Clare surreptitiously fled her noble family on Palm Sunday, 1212, in order to join Francis in living a life of absolute poverty.[3] After Clare had been tonsured by Francis at the Church of Santa Maria degli Angeli (or the Porziuncola) in the valley below Assisi, Francis, fully aware that Clare could not take up residence with the friars, took her to the Benedictine monastery of San Paolo delle Abbadesse. As a member of a noble family, Clare was expected to marry and establish connections of power for her family; instead, Clare had given her dowry to the poor, committed herself to living a life of absolute poverty, and been tonsured, an act that rendered her unmarriageable.[4] Her family, understandably, was not pleased. Given the monastery's legal recognition as a place of sanctuary, Clare was to have enjoyed some protection from her family there.[5] Her family, however, was undeterred and sought to physically remove Clare and to "help" her to come to her senses. The pontifically commissioned *Legend of Saint Clare* provides a somewhat dramatic account of events based on witnesses at her process of canonization:

> But after the news reached her relatives, they condemned with a broken heart the deed and proposal of the virgin and, banding together as one, they ran to the place, attempting to obtain what they could not. They employed violent force, poisonous advice, and flattering promises, persuading her to give up such a worthless deed that was unbecoming to her class and without precedent in her family. But, taking hold of the altar cloths, she bared her tonsured head, maintaining that she would in no way be torn away from the service of Christ. With the increasing violence of her relatives, her spirit grew and her love—provoked by injuries—provided strength. So for many days, even though she endured an obstacle in the way of the Lord and her own [relatives] opposed her proposal of holiness, her spirit did not crumble and her fervor did not diminish. Instead, amid words and deeds of hatred, she molded her spirit anew in hope until her relatives, turning back, were quiet.[6]

In the face of the violent opposition of her family, Clare refused to abandon her commitment to absolute poverty, as emphasized by her exposure of her tonsured head. Instead of submitting to her family, Clare clung to an altar, with all its connections to self-emptying sacrifice. Ultimately, Clare discovered that the force of the love with which she responded gave her added strength as she resisted the intensifying hatred and violence of her relatives.

Clare's family had not suffered the last of its humiliation or finished resorting to violence in its efforts to restore some semblance of family honor. After Clare had been at the Benedictine monastery of San Paolo for a relatively short period of time, a time during which she assumed the role of a servant sister, one who had entered the monastery without the privilege of wealth,[7] Clare resettled with a community of penitential women at San Angelo in Pranzo.[8] Sixteen days after Clare's own embrace of the Franciscan lifestyle of absolute poverty, her sister Catherine, who was to be given the name Agnes by Francis, joined Clare in the same embrace of poverty.[9] For Clare's family, insult had been added to injury. Knights of the family came after Agnes. In this instance we do not find a detailed account of events from the witnesses in *The Process of Canonization of Clare of Assisi* or the later *Versified Legend*.

One of the few accounts we find in the early sources is in *The Legend of Saint Clare*,[10] which describes a scene of violence even more intense than that when Clare herself had first embraced a life of radical poverty. As twelve men of the family beat and attempted to drag Agnes away by her hair,[11] "Clare prostrated herself in prayer with tears, begged that her sister would be given constancy of mind and that the strength of humans would be overcome by divine power."[12] At this, Agnes became too heavy to lift.[13] When a man attempted to kill Agnes with a blow, his hand was stricken with intense pain.[14] Clare entreated the men to stop their attack on her "half-dead" sister and to surrender Agnes to Clare.[15] After the men left, Agnes was tonsured by Francis, who "directed her together with her sister in the way of the Lord."[16]

While it is true that Clare did meet violence in this case with prayer, one may question if the emphasis on her prayerful response may be a result of later papal promotion of Clare as a model of strict enclosure. At any rate, it is interesting to note that part of this prayer was a plea that her sister "would be given constancy of mind." Clare remained faithful to her commitment to absolute poverty and prayed that Agnes would be strong enough to be faithful to this same life-giving and peace-filled commitment to "the way of the Lord" as taught by Francis.

Military Violence in the Life of Clare

After a brief period as a member of the community at San Angelo in Pranzo, Francis relocated Clare to the rebuilt church of San Damiano just outside of Assisi. Here Clare was to live a life of enclosure for the remainder of her life, but it did not insulate her from the forces of violence. Emperor Frederick II, who had been excommunicated twice by the pope, desired to gain more power over the Italian peninsula and to capture the key city of Assisi.[17] In 1240, Saracen troops fighting for the emperor stormed the walls of the San Damiano monastery. One of the more detailed accounts of this event comes from Sister Francesca, a nun at San Damiano and one of the witnesses at Clare's process of canonization:

> Asked what she [Sister Francesca] saw in her [Clare], she replied, one time, when the Saracens entered the cloister of the said monastery, the Lady made them bring her to the entrance of the refectory and bring a small box where there was the Blessed Sacrament of the Body of our Lord Jesus Christ. Throwing herself prostrate on the ground in prayer, she begged with tears, saying among other things: "Lord look upon these servants of yours, because I cannot protect them."[18]

After this, Sister Francesca heard the voice of the Lord tell Clare that he would protect the sisters and the city of Assisi, for which Clare had also sought protection.[19] "Then the Lady turned to the sisters and told them: 'Do not be afraid, because I am a hostage for you so that you will not suffer any harm now nor any other time as long as you wish to obey God's commandments.'"[20] At this, the Saracens turned away.[21]

It is interesting to note that according to this account Clare turned to the Eucharist for protection,[22] as she had clung to the altar when her family had sought to remove her forcibly from the monastery of San Paolo delle Abbadesse earlier in her life. In short, in the face of violence she turned to the protection of the one she embraced as the poor, humble Christ to defend her convent.[23] Referring to her sisters and herself as "servants," the humble Clare acknowledged her vulnerability and total dependence upon God's power and protection. Such a sense of humility and dependence stemmed from Clare's experience of poverty.

It is also true that, as in the case when Clare's family came to remove her sister from San Angelo in Pranzo, Clare turned to prayer in the face of violence. In fact, in *Clare of Assisi: Beyond the Legend*, Bartoli portrays Clare, weakened by illness, as using prayer to overcome yet one more hardship encountered in her life of poverty.[24] As I will discuss below, however, for Clare poverty was not some obstacle that one had to overcome through prayer but instead was the prerequisite that opened one to prayer and disposed one to peace. In short, poverty was not secondary to prayer in one's quest for peace but was essential for the kind of life and prayer that led to genuine peace.

The attack of the Saracens on the San Damiano monastery was not to be the last time Clare was to be called upon to defend those she loved from military attack. In 1241, Vitalis de Aversa, commander of Frederick's army, again attempted to take Assisi for the emperor. While the monastery of San Damiano was not specifically threatened this time, Clare did seek to defend the city of Assisi from the violent attack. The testimony of the above-mentioned Sister Francesca describes Clare's response to the attack in this way:

> The sisters came, as directed, in the morning for some time with her. When they had come, the Lady made them bring her some ashes. She took all the coverings from her head and made all the sisters do the same. Then, taking the ashes, she placed a large amount on her head, as if she had been newly tonsured; after this she placed them on the heads of the sisters. Next, she directed them to go pray in the chapel. So it happened; being broken and defeated, the army left the following morning.[25]

Bartoli emphasizes that once again Clare turned to prayer, this time to a specifically liturgical variety, in the face of violence.[26] However, as part of this prayer she also performed a penitential ritual in which she and her sisters became Job-like figures.[27] The ritual calls to mind Clare's original commitment to absolute poverty (as indicated by her tonsure of ashes) and points to the "nothingness" and humility of herself and her sisters, a humility fostered by the sisters' poverty and that recognized their absolute dependence on God in this dire situation.

Clare's Struggle to Live a Life of Poverty: A Key to Understanding Her Response to Violence

As indicated above, Clare's embrace of radical poverty was key to her response to a world of violence. Clare clung uncompromisingly to this ideal even in the face of strong papal opposition. Both Gregory IX and Innocent IV used their hierarchical authority to try to coerce Clare to abandon her sense of her own vocation. While this clearly did not constitute an instance of physical violence, it might be construed as a form of spiritual violence. Absolute poverty lay at the core of Clare's vocation and was essential to her vision of how a Christian was called to live in a world of violence. Her struggle to live a life of poverty in the face of papal opposition and the centrality of poverty in her eventual *Form of Life* (or Rule) point to this fact.

One may question why there was a conflict between the papacy's agenda and Clare's desire to live a life of absolute poverty. As noted above, for Clare, poverty was the key to living an authentically Franciscan vocation. Her insistence on this aspect of her calling, however, was not compatible with the model of women's religious life envisioned by the papacy, which wished to standardize women's religious movements based on the Benedictine Rule, enclosure, and a system of endowments.[28] This model was unacceptable to Clare, who tenaciously held onto her ideal of absolute poverty, though she received a number of visits from popes who tried to convince her to accept their model of religious life.[29] For example, Pope Gregory IX visited Clare at the Monastery of San Damiano in 1228 during Francis's canonization. *The Legend of St. Clare* includes a description of this encounter and is supported by a number of witnesses in *The Process of Canonization of Clare of Assisi*:

> When he was [attempting to] persuade her that, because of the events of the times and the dangers of the world, she should consent to have some possessions which he himself willingly offered, she resisted with a very strong spirit and would in no way acquiesce. To this the Pope replied: "If you fear for your vow, We absolve you from it." "Holy Father," she said, "I will never in any way wish to be absolved from the following of Christ."[30]

From her response to Pope Gregory's urging that she accept some property, it is clear that Clare saw the vow of absolute poverty as central to her vocation and to a genuine Franciscan identity. This was a non-negotiable absolute for Clare, so much so that she was willing to resist papal attempts to coerce her to accept the possession of property.[31] Because poverty was so foundational to Clare's vocation and identity, it also played a crucial role in her response to a world of violence.

Clare had an ally in her battle to defend the ideal of absolute poverty in the person of Agnes of Prague, a daughter of the king of Bohemia who had refused marriage to Emperor Frederick II. Agnes and Clare wished to transform the monastery of St. Francis of Prague from the form of life established by Gregory IX to the model of San Damiano (meaning the form of life of Francis), a transformation that Gregory at first prohibited.[32] In the four letters that we have that Clare sent to Agnes, the central topic is poverty.

In her first letter (1234), Clare praises Agnes for having taken Christ as a spouse, for it was in the person of Christ that God had embraced poverty. Clare assures Agnes that those who have followed this model of poverty will inherit God's riches.[33] Significantly, Clare states in the same letter that attachment to earthly things can only get in the way of "the fruit of love."[34] Of particular importance here is Clare's use of the metaphorical language of fighting. She acknowledges Agnes's awareness "that one clothed cannot fight another naked, because she who has something to be caught hold of is more quickly thrown to the ground." Clare continues, "Therefore, You have cast aside Your garments, that is, earthly riches, so that instead of being overcome by the one fighting You, You will be able to enter the kingdom of heaven through *the straight and narrow gate*."[35] According to Clare, attachment to material possessions is a hindrance and burden to anyone who is faced with "the fight," or battle, for salvation. One might extrapolate that attachment to material possessions is a hindrance and burden to anyone who is faced with violence in general. One cannot be overcome by violence when the other who is threatening violence has nothing to claim.

In her second letter to Agnes (1235), Clare continues to exhort her friend to hold firm to her commitment to absolute poverty. By this point, Gregory IX, in order to bring Agnes's convent into line with his own vision of women's religious life, had given the Hospital of St. Francis, which the royalty of Bohemia and Agnes had endowed, to Agnes's convent. Thus, Agnes's monastery "became a [de facto] heavily endowed papal institution."[36] In this second letter, Clare instructs Agnes never to abandon the vocation of absolute poverty. Clare advises her to remain faithful to her commitment to poverty in a manner "so that even . . . [her] steps stir up no dust"[37] and to persevere regardless of obstacles placed in her way.[38] She goes as far as to state, "If anyone has said anything else to you or suggested any other thing to you that might hinder your perfection or that would seem contrary to your divine vocation, even though you must respect him, do not follow his counsel."[39] Agnes must remain faithful to absolute poverty even if it means disobeying a pope. Clare notes that, like the poor Christ, Agnes too might suffer for her commitment, but Clare assures Agnes that her name will be inscribed in the book of life if she remains firm.[40] Poverty, for Clare, is of the essence of what it means to be, not only Franciscan, but also Christian.

In her third letter to Agnes (1238), Clare encourages Agnes to be satisfied with the level of poverty she had been permitted to live by Pope Gregory IX and not to be consumed by further interactions with the pontiff, who continued to pressure Agnes's community at Prague to accept possessions.[41] Clare instructs Agnes to transcend the situation by contemplating Christ.[42] Clare goes on to tell Agnes that she is to empty herself of possessions so that she might make room to become a vessel for Christ:

> As the glorious virgin of virgins carried [Him] materially, so you, too, *by following in* her *footprints*, especially [those] of humility and poverty, can, without any doubt, always carry Him spiritually in your chaste and virginal body, holding Him by Whom you and *all things are held together* possessing that which, in comparison with the other transitory possessions of this world you will possess more securely. In this, certain worldly kings and queens are deceived, for even thought their *pride may reach the skies and their heads touch the clouds, in the end they are as forgotten as a dung-heap!*[43]

Poverty was the prerequisite for Agnes to become a Christ-bearer as she transcended the conflict with Pope Gregory.[44] Poverty would make room for Christ in a world where there was conflict and strife.

The theme of transcendence through contemplation of the poor Christ that is found in the third letter is further developed in Clare's fourth letter to Agnes (1253). After describing Agnes as "half of her soul" and her "favorite daughter,"[45] Clare encourages Agnes to experience transcendence and transformation through contemplation of the "mirror" of the crucifix. In her method of contemplation, Clare places special emphasis on the humility and poverty of Christ:

> Indeed,
>   in that mirror,
>   blessed poverty,
>   holy humility,
>   and inexpressible charity shine forth
>   as, with the grace of God,
>   you will be able to contemplate them throughout
>   the entire mirror.
> Look, I say, at the border of this mirror, that is, the poverty
>   of Him
>   Who was placed in a manger and wrapped in
>   swaddling clothes.
>   O marvelous humility!
>   O astonishing poverty!
>   The King of angels,
>   The Lord of heaven and earth,
>   *is laid in a manger!*
> Then reflect upon, at the surface of the mirror,
>   the holy humility, at least the blessed poverty,
>   the untold labors and punishments
>   that he endured for the redemption of the whole
>   human race.
> Finally contemplate, in the depth of this same mirror,
>   the ineffable charity that He chose
>   to suffer on the tree of the Cross
>   and to die the most shameful kind of death.[46]

In short, Agnes is to become like Christ through the embrace of poverty and humility. In doing so, Agnes will grow in self-giving love, which was Christ's own response to violence and hatred.

As she encouraged Agnes in living a life of poverty, Clare believed that she would have to have her own rule of life, not one imposed on her by the papacy, in order to preserve her own commitment to absolute poverty. Desiring to use Clare as a figure around which to centralize diverse movements of women religious, and reluctant to give a stamp of approval to Clare's insistence on the right to live a life of absolute poverty, Popes Gregory IX and Innocent IV did not wish to grant this privilege of following her own rule to Clare. It was only on her deathbed that Innocent IV in his bull, *Solet annuere*, approved Clare's Rule, the first to be written by a woman.

The observance of a life of absolute poverty is at the center of her Rule—literally. Of the Rule's twelve chapters, the chapter on poverty is number six, and it is the only one to adopt an auto-biographical tone. Here, Clare recalls her original commitment to follow Francis and his example of absolute poverty as well as the simple form of life he had given her.[47] She quotes Francis as stating near his death, "I little brother Francis, wish to follow the life and poverty of our most high Lord Jesus Christ and of His Holy Mother and *to persevere* in this *until the end*; and I ask you, my ladies, and I give you my advice that you live always in this most holy life and poverty. And keep careful watch that you never depart from this by reason of the teaching or advice of anyone."[48] Clare then goes on to state that her sisters are to observe the Franciscan ideal of absolute poverty "to the end"[49] and clarifies explicitly the meaning of that poverty: "that is, by not receiving or having possession or ownership either of themselves or through an intermediary, or anything that might reasonably be called ownership."[50] Poverty was the heart of what it meant to be a follower of Christ and a follower of Francis. Poverty was what had set Francis apart and continued to set Clare and her sisters apart from the world and much of Christendom.

One may question the reasoning for Clare's emphasis on absolute poverty as a response to a world of violence.[51] Clearly, she wanted to follow the model of Francis. In doing so, she was following the model of Christ and, consequently, she saw the embrace of poverty as an investment that would lead to a shar-ing in Christ's glory. But Clare rejected ownership of things for reasons beyond that of a heavenly reward. As noted in her first letter to Agnes of Prague, clinging to possessions prevented "the fruit of love."[52] Furthermore, as noted in Clare's third letter to

Agnes, it was poverty that opened one to be a vessel of Christ[33] in a violent world.

In addition, as Joan Mueller notes in *The Privilege of Poverty*, poverty was a choice for solidarity with the poor in a world torn by systematic oppression. In this world, not to own property meant "not to oppress, tax, or levy control over the lives of the poor."[54] Mueller argues that Clare and Agnes of Prague embraced poverty in order to directly benefit the poor and oppressed.

> They envisioned the property and wealth of women being transformed into resources for the poor. In a church that was gaining control over the lives of more and more people, Clare and Agnes's way of life was an act of faith that was seeking dignity for the poor, the sick, and the downtrodden. More than that, it was revolutionary—the wealthy accepted poverty so that the poor could survive.[55]

In other words, Clare embraced poverty so as not to participate in a system of alienation from and oppression of the poor. For Clare, it was a clinging to things that led to alienation and ultimately to violence in the world. Clare refused to be a part of the economic and ecclesiastical systems that alienated groups of people from each other and that, consequently, fueled cycles of oppression and of violence. In this sense, Clare modeled Christ's response to a world of violence. Like Christ, she identified with and did not put herself above the poor, the oppressed, and the outcast. Ultimately, like Christ, she emptied herself in order to give violence, oppression, and hatred a place to die and to allow for an influx of life and love.

Conclusion

While violence seems to be growing exponentially in the modern world, Clare of Assisi, living in the late twelfth and thirteenth centuries, was no stranger to violence herself. She grew up in a world brimming with class conflict, experienced violence within her own family, found herself caught in the crossfire between emperor and pope, and was even pressured by popes to abandon what she considered her vocation. Although Marco Bartoli has argued that prayer was Clare's ultimate response to violence, a deeper study of her life and works demonstrates that her most fundamental and unique response to a world of violence was not prayer but the embrace of absolute poverty. Poverty was Clare's way of rejecting economic and ecclesiastical systems that led to alienation and oppression that, in turn, manifested violence. Through poverty, Clare identified with the poor Christ. Poverty represented a reflection of Clare's ultimate dependence on God, "emptying" her and making her a vessel receptive to an inflow of God's love. All of these factors point to poverty as the basis for Clare's relationship with God, for prayer, and for her response to a world of violence.

Clare offers much by way of example regarding contemporary responses to a world of violence. She demonstrates that detachment from obsessive ownership leads to a reduction in tension over possession claims between individuals and factions. Detachment from things facilitates identification with the world's poor and oppressed and reduces participation in unjust systems of power that foment violence and wars.

Though modern media voices constantly urge the possession of more material goods, Clare of Assisi shows that the way to genuine peace, which of course is more than the absence of conflict, unfolds through detachment from things in identification with the poor Christ. Like Christ, one thus freed may meet a world of violence through surrender to God and loving, non-violent resistance that interrupts the self-perpetuating cycle of violence. Like Christ, Clare responded to violence with the power of absolute dependence on God that had been strengthened by her own embrace of poverty.

Notes

[1]Marco Bartoli, *Saint Clare: Beyond the Legend*, trans. Sr. Frances Teresa Downing (Cincinnati: Saint Anthony Messenger Press, 2010), 137.

[2]Ibid., 126, 128–29.

[3]For a description of the event, see *Legend of Saint Clare* 4.7.1–12(in *The Lady: Clare of Assisi: Early Documents* [CA:ED], rev. ed., ed. and trans. Regis J. Armstrong [New York: New City Press, 2006], 285–86). See also *The Acts of the Process of Canonization of Clare of Assisi* 8.2–3 (CA:ED, 185).

[4]See Joan Mueller, *The Privilege of Poverty: Clare of Assisi, Agnes of Prague, and the Struggle for a Franciscan Rule for Women* (University Park: Pennsylvania State University Press, 2006), 9, and Marco Bartoli, *Clare of*

Assisi, trans. Sr. Frances Teresa, OSC (Quincy, IL: Franciscan Press, 1993), 48.

[5]Mueller, *The Privilege of Poverty*, 9.

[6]*The Legend of Saint Clare* 5.9.1–6 (CA:ED, 287). See also the corresponding accounts of witnesses in *The Acts of the Process of Canonization of Clare of Assisi* 12.4.9–10 (CA:ED, 183) and 20.6.13 (CA:ED, 196).

[7]Bartoli, *Clare of Assisi*, 54.

[8]Mueller, *The Privilege of Poverty*, 9.

[9]*The Legend of Saint Clare* 16.24.10 (CA:ED, 303).

[10]There is also an account in *The Life of Sister Agnes*. See Mueller, *The Privilege of Poverty*, 10-12, and accompanying endnotes.

[11]*The Legend of Saint Clare* 16.25.14–21 (CA:ED, 303).

[12]Ibid., 16.25.22 (CA:ED, 303).

[13]Ibid., 16.26.23–26 (CA:ED, 303–4).

[14]Ibid., 16.26.27 (CA:ED, 304).

[15]Ibid., 16.26.28 (CA:ED, 304).

[16]Ibid., 16.26.30 (CA:ED, 304).

[17]Bartoli, *Clare of Assisi*, 170.

[18]*The Acts of the Process of Canonization of Clare of Assisi* 9.2.4–7 (CA:ED, 174). There are similar accounts in the testimony of numerous other witnesses (for example, I, II, III, IV, VI, VII, X).

[19]Ibid., 9.2.8–12 (CA:ED, 174–75).

[20]Ibid., 9.2.13–14 (CA:ED, 175).

[21]Ibid., 9.2.15 (CA:ED, 175).

[22]Bartoli notes that medieval spirituality shifted from an emphasis on crusades and Holy Land pilgrimages to Eucharistic devotions (Bartoli, *Clare of Assisi*, 169-70).

[23]See, for example, Clare's *First Letter to Agnes of Prague* 13 (CA:ED, 45) and *Second Letter to Agnes of Prague* 18 (CA:ED, 49).

[24]Bartoli does acknowledge Clare's sense of utter dependence on God. He describes her cry for help as "the cry of one who no longer has any power and therefore trusts in God" (Bartoli, *Saint Clare*, 143). He goes on to describe the incident "as an example of the power of Clare's prayers at this moment of her greatest weakness" (Bartoli, *Saint Clare*, 143-44).

[25]*The Acts of the Process of Canonization of Clare of Assisi* 9.3.25–30 (CA:ED, 175–76). Supporting accounts are found in the testimony of numerous other witnesses (for example, I, II, III, IV VI, VII, X).

[26]Bartoli, *Saint Clare*, 141. Bartoli compares Clare to Francis, who also devised a liturgy (an additional stanza in the *Canticle of Creatures*) during the conflict between the bishop and podestà of Assisi (see Bartoli, *Saint Clare*, 138–40).

[27]Job 2:8; 42:6. For references to Clare assuming the role of servant to her sisters, see *The Legend of Saint Clare* 25 (CA:ED, 312), and *The Fourth Letter to Agnes of Prague* 2 (CA:ED, 54).

[28]Pope Gregory IX believed that financial stability was an absolute necessity for enclosure. By endowing religious communities himself, he could exercise a degree of control over their enclosure (Mueller, *The Privilege of Poverty*, 66).

[29]Gregory IX also visited Clare in 1220 before he became pope and while

he was a papal legate and the cardinal protector of the Franciscan Order. See John Kruse, "Apostolic Visitations: Clare of Assisi's Insights from the Thirteenth Century," *Review for Religious* 70, no. 2 (2011): 179–93.

[30]*The Legend of Saint Clare* 9.14.13–14 (CA:ED, 294).

[31]Clare was eventually granted the *privilegium paupertatis* by Gregory IX in *Sicut manifestum est* (1228/9; CA:ED, 348–50). See also Bartoli, *Clare of Assisi*, 134, and Maria Pia Alberzoni, *Clare of Assisi and the Poor Sisters in the Thirteenth Century*, ed. Jean François Godet-Calogeras, trans. William Short and Nancy Celaschi (Saint Bonaventure, NY: Franciscan Institute Publications, 2004), 45.

[32]In a letter to Agnes of Prague, *Angelis gaudium* (May 1238), Gregory IX describes the *forma vitae* given to Clare and her sisters by Francis as baby food: "Blessed Francis gave them, as new-born children, not solid food but rather a milk drink, a formula of life, which seemed to be suited for them" (CA:ED, 361). Clearly, what Agnes needed was the solid food of his own Rule, which Gregory points out was being observed by Clare's own community at San Damiano (CA:ED, 361). Later, after Clare's death, Innocent IV and Alexander IV did grant Agnes permission to observe Francis's *forma vitae* (Alberzoni, *Clare of Assisi and the Poor Sisters*, 55).

[33]Clare of Assisi, *The First Letter to Agnes of Prague* 19–22 (CA:ED, 45–46). Mueller refers to this investment in God's riches as Clare's concept of the *sacrum commercium* (Mueller, *The Privilege of Poverty*, 61).

[34]Clare of Assisi, *The First Letter to Agnes of Prague* 25 (CA:ED, 46). One could argue that clinging to possessions would have obstructed the emboldening love Clare experienced when her family tried to violently remove her from San Paolo delle Abbadesse.

[35]Ibid., 27, 29 (CA:ED, 46).

[36]Mueller, *The Privilege of Poverty*, 67.

[37]Clare of Assisi, *The Second Letter to Agnes of Prague* 12 (CA:ED, 48).

[38]Ibid., 14 (CA:ED, 48).

[39]Ibid., 17 (CA:ED, 48–49).

[40]See Clare of Assisi, *The Second Letter to Agnes of Prague* 20–22 (CA:ED, 49).

[41]See Mueller, *The Privilege of Poverty*, 78–83.

[42]Clare of Assisi, *The Third Letter to Agnes of Prague* 12–17 (CA:ED, 51).

[43]Ibid., 24–28 (CA:ED, 52).

[44]For a discussion of Clare's sense of transcendence, see Mueller, *The Privilege of Poverty*, 82ff.

[45]Clare of Assisi, *The Fourth Letter to Agnes of Prague* 1 (CA:ED, 54). Later in the letter, Clare states that she holds Agnes "dearer than all others" (Clare of Assisi, *The Fourth Letter to Agnes of Prague* 34 (CA:ED, 57).

[46]Ibid., 18-23 (CA:ED, 55–56).

[47]Saint Clare of Assisi, *The Form of Life of Saint Clare* 4.1–4 (CA:ED, 117–18). See also Mueller, *The Privilege of Poverty*, 116.

[48]Saint Clare of Assisi, *The Form of Life of Saint Clare* 6.7–9 (CA:ED, 118).

[49]Ibid., 6.11 (CA:ED, 118).

[50]Ibid., 6.12–13 (CA:ED, 118–19). In discussing the role of labor in the life

of her community, Clare does note that all temporal matters are to promote prayer (Saint Clare of Assisi, *The Form of Life of Saint Clare* 7.7.2 [CA:ED, 119]).

[51]Mueller views the commitment to absolute poverty as Clare's one absolute as she faced a world of violence, an observation that is supported by the centrality of poverty in Clare's Rule (Mueller, *The Privilege of Poverty*, 116).

[52]Clare of Assisi, *The First Letter to Agnes of Prague* 25 (CA:ED, 46).

[53]Clare of Assisi, *The Third Letter to Agnes of Prague* 24–26 (CA:ED, 52).

[54]Mueller, *The Privilege of Poverty*, 92.

[55]Ibid.

Motherhood, Violence, and Peacemaking

A Practical-Theological Lesson from Liberia

Elizabeth O'Donnell Gandolfo

The opening scene in the documentary film *Pray the Devil Back to Hell* offers a compelling depiction of the horrific reality of Liberia's fourteen-year civil war and its particular impact on women. As images of armed combatants, frightened and hungry children, desperate parents, and destroyed homes and infrastructure flash before the viewer's eyes, peace activist Leymah Gbowee shares part of her story:

> I am five months pregnant. My son is three and my daughter is two. So under rains of bullets we leave the house and we walk for like seven hours to my parents' house. And it was hell on earth. My three-year-old is sitting down, sweat pouring off his body, and he says to me "Mama, I wish just for a piece of doughnut this morning. I am so hungry." I'm sitting there and thinking, where am I gonna get a piece of doughnut for this three-year-old? . . . Liberia had been at war for so long that my children had been hungry and afraid their entire lives. . . . There is nothing in my mind that should make people do what they did to the children of Liberia.[1]

The image of Gbowee's anguish here calls to mind the classic figure of the *mater dolorosa*, the long-suffering feminine victim whose sacred vocation is the peaceful reproduction and protection of life in the face of violent conflict and destruction. When it comes to thinking about the roles of women and men in violent conflict and peacebuilding, images of women like Gbowee with her children make it tempting to buy into stereotypes that categorize women as morally superior victims of masculine violence. When the role of women as mothers is taken into explicit consideration, especially when motherhood is constructed as a religious vocation, the dichotomy becomes even more pronounced.

While it is empirically true that most war-making has been done by men, and that women (and their children) suffer from wars that are not of their making, peacebuilding requires rejecting mindsets that cast women (especially mothers) as naturally peaceful. Such gender essentialism can serve to obscure, perpetuate, and even legitimate violence. At the same time, however, critiquing the ideology of women's "special nature" should not require eschewing the distinctiveness of women's lived experiences in the world. And while there are numerous theoretical and practical problems with the idea of women's vocation to motherhood, it is imperative to honor the unique knowledge and contribution to peacebuilding that real-world mothers can and do make.

In what follows, I will provide a critical analysis of "official" Roman Catholic conceptions of femininity and motherhood, and the need for a strategic subversion of gender essentialism in order for women to take active and effective part in peacebuilding. I will then shine the spotlight on a particular group of contemporary women—Liberia's women peacemakers—who have effected this strategic subversion in their work for peace, especially in their use of motherhood as a powerful resource. I will conclude that these women transform what it means to be a mother in and through their self-assertion, as women and mothers, in the struggle for peace in their country.

Femininity and Motherhood in Roman Catholic Anthropology

Over the course of the last several decades, the Roman Catholic Church has made great strides toward affirming the equal human dignity of women and supporting women's demands for respect, equality, and full participation in society. Affirming the equal dignity of the sexes is a significant advance over classical teachings on women's secondary anthropological status, to be sure. However, the magisterium continues to ascribe ontological significance to differences in biological sex, male and female. Recent teachings from Rome insist that women and men image God in different and complementary ways and thus have different roles to play in social, ecclesial, and family life. These complementary differences are said to be inscribed in the psycho-physical structures of our bodies and revealed in scripture. As such, women should take care that their feminine "originality" and "genius" not be compromised as they rightfully go about opposing the injustices of sexism.[2]

The feminine genius of women is revealed in the biblical relationship of the church as bride to Christ the bridegroom is fulfilled in Mary's motherhood and virginity, and is characterized by traits such as "listening, welcoming, humility, faithfulness, praise, . . . waiting,"[3] and receptivity to new life and to others. These passive and receptive qualities of femininity are to complement the active qualities of masculinity, which are never described in as much detail as those of femininity, but which clearly entail the capacity for executing the headship that Christ as the active bridegroom exercises over his patient and receptive bride, the church. The truth about woman as bride and the dignity of her dual vocation to motherhood and virginity are thus revealed.

In this anthropological vision, Mary provides a model for women to carry out their universal vocation to motherhood, a vocation that belongs even to women who are not mothers, women who are called to "spiritual motherhood." Pope John Paul II describes the Marian characteristics that ought to inspire women's emulation, especially in the face of violence and suffering:

> Women, by looking to Mary, find in her the secret of living their femininity with dignity and of achieving their own true advancement. In the light of Mary, the church sees in the face of women the reflection of a beauty which mirrors the loftiest sentiments of which the human heart is capable: the self-offering totality of love; the strength that is capable of bearing the greatest sorrows; limitless fidelity and tireless devotion to work; the ability to combine penetrating intuition with words of support and encouragement.[4]

Of particular importance for the present consideration of motherhood and peacebuilding is the image of the *mater dolorosa* embedded in the pope's comments. The strength with which Mary bears "the greatest sorrows" clearly refers to her sorrow at the foot of her son's cross, a sorrow that women living in the midst of violence know all too well. As the Congregation for the Doctrine of the Faith's letter, "On the Collaboration of Men and Women in the Church and in the World," points out, "It is women, in the end, who even in very desperate situations . . . possess a singular capacity to persevere in adversity, to keep life going, even in extreme situations, to hold tenaciously to the future, and finally to remember with tears the value of every human life."[5] Because women are physically structured to receive and give life, we are psychically structured to intuit the goodness of actions that elicit and protect life. And, due to this psycho-physical make-up, women are especially attuned to the sorrow with which each loss of life ought to be met. In a world so broken by violence, all women (as spiritual or actual mothers) are, or ought to be, sorrowful mothers who long for peace.

Problems with Gender Essentialism for Peacebuilding

Theoretical and practical problems abound when it comes to gender essentialism and the idealization of women's "special nature," especially when the essence of woman is reduced to motherhood. These issues have been at the forefront of feminist theory, feminist theology, and feminist activism for decades.[6] Here I will confine my analysis to a critical assessment of how the romantic myth of maternal peacefulness (and the gender essentialism that it entails) can serve to obscure, legitimate, and perpetuate violent conflict rather than abolish it.

First, the gendered myth of maternal peacefulness obscures the complexity of violent conflict. The idea that women are naturally more peaceful and open to life than men simply does not accurately reflect the lived reality of both men and women on the ground. Real flesh and blood women have not proven themselves to be more naturally inclined to peacefulness. As international peace advocate Sanam Anderlini observes, "Women, like men, can spread fear and mistrust, commit atrocities, and send armies of young men and women to kill and be killed. As politicians, they can be as hawkish as men."[7] Indeed, the leadership of the most prominent female politicians of recent times has been oriented toward making war, not peace.

Real women—even women who have truly been victimized in war—are not only victims of armed conflict: some also "play crucial roles in supporting and perpetuating violence. Women and girls assume greater roles in contemporary armed conflict, including as frontline combatants, spies, messengers, porters and 'wives.' "[8] The characterization of victimhood that comes along with the myth of maternal peacefulness reduces women to the status of victim and overlooks very real ways in which women exert agency in the midst of conflict, even violent agency.[9]

It is important to note here that the myth of maternal peacefulness also obscures the fact that mothers in particular, precisely in their role as mothers, can perpetuate violence in many ways, even if they do not take part in violence per se. Feminist philosopher Sara Ruddick asserts that, given the often parochial nature of mothering, mothers possess "passionate loyalties to [their] own children, kin and people. Mothering offers distinctive occasions for tribalism and for racism."[10] These passionate loyalties can fuel hatred and violence toward those who are perceived to threaten a mother's own. There is no such thing as a pure maternal peacefulness.

When women choose, advocate, or fan the flames of violence over peace, it may be for good or bad reasons. The moral legitimacy of violence and war is a topic that far exceeds the scope of this essay. Regardless of the moral status of their actions, however, women's choice of violence is not reflective of their "masculinization," contrary to what the tenor of church teaching on gender complementarity seems to imply. If this is what the magisterium intends to decry in its lament for the loss of women's feminine genius, then it is men who should be far more offended than feminist women by Roman theories of gender complementarity.

Empirically speaking, yes, men are more responsible for violent conflict than women. But as Ruddick points out, the masculinity of war is largely a myth: "If men were so eager to be fighters, we would not need drafts, training in misogyny, and macho heroes, nor would we have to entice the morally sensitive with myths of patriotic duty and just cause."[11] While it is true that wars have been waged mostly by men, it is not true that all men tend toward aggressiveness and violence. Indeed, many men have committed their lives to the pursuit of peace. Are such men more finely attuned to the "femininity" of their human calling to promote life and dignity? The concrete contributions of men to peace may differ significantly from those of women, but is there really an ontological difference?

Second, although the church's hierarchy certainly would not intend for this to be the case, the romanticization of femininity and maternal peacefulness can and often does serve to legitimate violent conflict. When women are cast as virtuous yet vulnerable victims, they naturally need protection; it follows that men are expected to protect "their" women from danger, even if it means using violent force to do so. According to development scholar Caroline Sweetman, when maternal peacefulness is thought to characterize women, "Soldiers are thus provided with an idealized picture of a family and community whose interests must be served and protected. Women are depicted as creatures of innocence, purity, and fidelity, who nurture, comfort, and command male protection."[12] Militarists the world over morally justify their "rational" masculine pursuits not in opposition to the "passionate" feminine cry of the *mater dolorosa*, but rather in a protective response to that cry.

Third and finally, the feminine genius extolled in Roman Catholic anthropology can unwittingly perpetuate violence by casting women/mothers as relatively passive in their tenderness and perseverance in the face of sorrow. "Listening, welcoming, humility, faithfulness, praise, waiting" are admirable dispositions to be sure, and persons with such qualities are certainly indispensable to the work of building peace. However, they are not traits that lend themselves to active, assertive, and—when need be—tough and even aggressive opposition to violence. In her study of Mary, Elizabeth Johnson points out that these sentiments are "habits of the helper, the auxiliary, the hand-maid, not that of the resister of oppression—let alone the self-actualizing, creative leader."[13]

Although the hierarchy applauds the increased involvement of women in public life, women's primary role is still understood to be within the private realm of the family. The idealization of feminine virtues presented here further limits mothers and other women to a relatively passive and apolitical peacefulness that is soft, caring and nurturing, but that does not encourage, much less empower, active involvement in or leadership of public and/or political work for peace.

The psychic well-being and physical survival of mothers themselves, their families, and entire communities no doubt depend on the perseverance of sorrowful mothers in the face of unspeakable suffering. Promotion of such well-being and survival are integral to any efforts at peacebuilding. However, the idealized *mater dolorosa* envisioned here does not acknowledge the very real rage that mothers feel in the face of their sorrows, in the face of violence that threatens their children. Nor does it provide the resources for mothers to transform their rage into bold and decisive action against violence and for peace.

Ruddick illuminates the gap between a romanticized vision of motherhood, which is typified by apolitical perseverance, and the active, intellectual, and authoritative involvement needed if mothers are to construct their own distinctive politics of peace: "It is good to persevere and right to admire those who do. But the peacemaking woman has to become as active, inventive, and angry as an ordinary, harassed, coping mother. Yet unlike that mother she must find a way to see and resist the organized violence that 'befalls' her and her people."[14] The idealization of maternal peacefulness does not promote peace. It perpetuates violent conflict by romanticizing women's apolitical perseverance rather than by empowering their active participation and leadership in the processes of peace.

Dismantling the paralyzing femininities imposed by patriarchal culture and religion is not simply an interesting academic exercise for feminist theorists and theologians. It is a practical dismantling that needs to take place in the lives of "ordinary, harassed, coping" women so that the real life experience of women can be brought to bear on peacebuilding. Indeed, the subversion of these stereotypes is already and has been taking place in the lives of women around the globe and throughout history. Women are making a distinctive contribution to peacebuilding, not because of some special gene or "genius" that makes them more peaceful, but because of their adamant refusal to tolerate threats to the well-being of themselves, their children, and children everywhere. This refusal does not come naturally, but rather is the result of a struggle and a choice.

However, many women and many mothers do make such a choice, and the work of mothering and even the rhetoric of motherhood, while by no means the sum total of a woman's identity, can and does offer distinctive contributions to peacebuilding. For women's experiences as mothers to have an impact, however, the *mater dolorosa* must take her sorrow and transform it into bold, assertive, and often public and political action for peace. The women peacemakers of Liberia provide a powerful example of women who do just that. It is to their stories that we now turn.

The Rhetorical and Practical Authority of Motherhood: Liberia's Iron Ladies

The excerpt of Leymah Gbowee's testimony that introduces this essay, though tragic in itself, only hints at the full extent of the horrors undergone by Liberian women during their country's fourteen-year civil war (1989-2003).[15] While written in the early stages of the conflict, the 1994 position statement of the Liberian Women's Initiative sums up the suffering and resistance of Liberian women throughout the duration of the war:

> For the past four years, we have been killed, raped, starved to death, misused and abused. We have witnessed the horror of having our children, our husbands, our fathers and other relatives killed and maimed before our very eyes. We have experienced starvation to the point of becoming walking skeletons. We have been stripped of our dignity as human beings. The women have borne all of this victimization with suffering and stoic silence. This silence is not to be construed as weakness or acquiescence.[16]

Indeed, the women of Liberia were neither weak nor acquiescent in the face of the violent conflict that ravaged their country, their communities, their families, their children, and their own bodies. Rather than continuing to persevere in "stoic silence," thousands of Liberian women became increasingly involved in peacebuilding at all levels—from the domestic to the grassroots to the political realms. While these women organized and mobilized themselves as women, not explicitly as mothers, motherhood has functioned in their peacebuilding efforts as a powerful tool. In the process, the women peacemakers of Liberia have transformed the myth of maternal peacefulness critiqued above so that their maternal experience and practice have become empowering and effective resources for peacebuilding.

The women peacemakers of Liberia have destabilized the idealization of motherhood not by explicitly rejecting it, but by strategically using motherhood as a subversive source of rhetorical and practical authority in their work for peace. Anderlini suggests that by employing this strategy, women peacebuilders "are simultaneously reaching out widely to women and directly challenging the moral authority of states that typically define themselves through social conservatism heavily dosed with militarism and traditional family values that uphold motherhood as the ultimate virtue."[17]

Although their rhetoric may at times sound very traditional, their action is rooted in their everyday struggles and experiences as mothers, thus subverting essentialism. Strategic use of the symbols of femininity and maternal peacefulness, according to Ruddick, "translate[s] the symbols of mothering into political speech. . . . They speak a 'women's language' of loyalty, love, and outrage; but they speak with a public anger in a public place in ways they were never meant to do."[18] The women peacemakers of Liberia embodied this strategy in countless ways, at all levels and stages of the peacebuilding process. The following are just a few examples from the arenas of grassroots advocacy, mid-level mediation, and state-level politics.

Liberian women drew on the rhetorical and practical authority of motherhood in their peacebuilding efforts at the grassroots level both as individuals and as collectives mobilized in women's organizations. For example, individual women were known to go personally to the leaders of armed factions and beg them to stop the fighting. When they did so, they approached the men as if the men were their children: "We talked to them [the faction leaders]. They are children to us, and we wanted this fighting to stop. We the women . . . bear that pain. So we begged them—Kromah, Boley, Taylor—at different times."[19] When it came time for disarmament in 2003, individual women also conducted one-on-one negotiations with combatants, begging them, as their "mothers," to disarm. Their strategy worked. Some of the combatants even disarmed directly to the women, saying "we appreciate them a lot and we are still there for them. They are our mothers."[20]

As a collective, the Liberian Women's Initiative issued a Position

Statement on the Liberian War in 1994, invoking their authority and responsibility as "mothers of the land" to demand that the government and the armed factions put an end to the violence.[21] Similarly, the centrality of motherhood to the women's strategy is once again clear in the Liberian Women in Peacebuilding Network's 2003 position statement to President Charles Taylor: "We are now taking this stand to secure the future of our children. Because we believe as custodians of society our children tomorrow will ask us, 'Mama what was your role during the crisis?'"[22] While the women's statement was most likely not the only reason Taylor finally agreed to go to the peace talks in Accra, it certainly appears to have been a factor.

Women also drew on the authority of motherhood in their efforts to bring together the warlords for mediation. For example, in 1995, it was the women who convened and facilitated a pivotal meeting of men from rival factions. All the factions were represented with four of their "best men" at the two-day meeting, which then extended into four days. The men indicated that they otherwise would not have come to the table with one another, but that "when your mother calls you, you must show up."[23] Although there is no guarantee of success, the authority of motherhood, when exercised wisely, nonviolently, and in the interests of peace, can be capable of bringing even the most recalcitrant warlords to the table.

The examples cited above represent fairly generalized invocations of the authority of motherhood, appeals that could cross many cultural boundaries with relative ease. The following anecdote illustrates the way in which maternal power and authority can be very culturally specific.[24] During the peace talks in Accra in 2003, Liberian women sat outside the peace hall in an attempt to keep the men's prolonged negotiations on track. Meanwhile, back in the Liberian capital of Monrovia, all hell had broken loose. Upon receiving the news that a missile had landed in the American Embassy compound in Monrovia where internally displaced persons had sought refuge, WIPNET leader Leymah Gbowee remarked, "I just thought of my own children and I was just raging inside." She and her sister peacemakers blocked the entrance to the peace hall, and demanded that the men not leave the negotiating table until a peace agreement was signed.

When security guards attempted to remove the women, Gbowee stood up, began to remove her headdress, and threatened to strip naked. Gbowee's fellow peace activist, Etweda "Sugars" Cooper, explains: "It's a curse in Africa to see the naked body of your mother. Especially if she does it deliberately." Within two weeks, the peace agreement was signed and the fighting began to subside in Monrovia. Perhaps there were other factors that brought the talks to a close, but one wonders how much longer the talks would have continued, and how many more lives would have been lost, if Leymah Gbowee and the women of Liberia had not stepped out and done what they call "the unimaginable."

The power of motherhood has been used not only by "ordinary" women at the grassroots level, but also by women holding the highest political office in Liberia. Both Ruth Perry, the interim head of state from 1996 to 1997, and Ellen Johnson Sirleaf, the current president of Liberia, are politically powerful women who have been regarded as "National Mothers." Both have used the authority of motherhood in the service of peace through a combination of patience, tolerance, discipline, and toughness.

While preparing the country for democratic elections, Ruth Perry told Taylor and other warlords that she would "treat them like a mother and, if necessary that means discipline." She expected other members of the Council of State, "whether they agreed with her or not, to 'give her the respect they would give their mothers.'"[25] Perry's power and authority as head of state were limited, but she managed to hold the tenuous peace together until democratic elections were held in 1997.

In her presidency, Ellen Johnson Sirleaf, popularly known as Mama Ellen, has also taken what she calls the "Old Ma" approach. In the documentary film, *Iron Ladies of Liberia*, she explains that to take this approach, she "must listen in a way that says I want to hear you, I understand your plight. That's the Old Ma approach and it usually brings a positive reaction because I am coming as a mother to listen to them." On the other hand, she points out that the Old Ma approach also means that "when people act out of order, I can have an effective response that will keep them in order."[26]

Sirleaf's use of the rhetorical and practical authority of motherhood, then, includes both nurturing and, when necessary, aggressive (though nonviolent) confrontation. In her persona, and in the personas of thousands of other Liberian women peacemakers, the ideal of maternal peacefulness is subverted, transformed, and put to good use in and through its appropriation as a resource for active and assertive peacebuilding.

Conclusion: *Mater Dolorosa* Revisited

To conclude, let us come full circle and recall Leymah Gbowee's testimony, quoted at the beginning of this essay. Call to mind this image of the *mater dolorosa* with which we began and which I set out to problematize. It is true that, like Gbowee, most mothers are implacably sorrowful in the face of violence that threatens their children, that forces them to flee from their homes under rains of bullets, that renders them powerless to feed young hungry mouths. Women, especially women who are mothers, tend to know what white South African novelist, feminist, and critic Olive Schreiner calls the "history of human flesh" in a way that most men do not.[27] Mothers tend to know the cost of human lives because they have put their hearts, souls, and bodies into the service of birthing, preserving, and protecting those lives. This knowledge comes not from the possession of a uterus, a special gene, or a special "genius," but from the lived experience of doing the work that mothers empirically do: protecting, nurturing, and training the young.[28] The Liberian women sang their songs of protest—"We want peace, no more war, our children are dying"—not because it is in the nature of true womanhood or maternal peacefulness to do so, but because the work that they did as mothers was threatened.

All of this said, recognizing the sorrowing mother's privileged stand still carries with it all of the dangers mentioned in the above critique of gender essentialism, including the dangers of passivity and parochialism. What the testimony of the Liberian women peacemakers teaches us is that a mother's sorrow is a powerful motivator and an authoritative resource for involvement in peacebuilding, but only when that sorrow is accompanied by at least two additional dispositions: a commitment to nonviolent action, including assertive and public action, and an extension of maternal concern beyond one's own children to the children of other mothers (and children with no mother).

The "Iron Ladies" of Liberia embodied both of these dispositions in their work for peace. Recall that when Leymah Gbowee
was inspired to seize the peace hall in Accra and then threatened
to strip naked, she was motivated by the thought of her own
children suffering in Monrovia. But she transformed her sorrow
into rage and her rage into nonviolent, but authoritative, aggressive, and confrontational action for peace. She and her fellow
women peacemakers also came together across religious and
ethnic boundaries, extending their own personal sorrow and rage
beyond a parochial concern for their own children to a sense of
collective responsibility for all of Liberia's children.

While not without theoretical and practical dangers, the experience of motherhood and the work that ordinary mothers do can
offer powerful resources for peacebuilding in our world today.
"Insofar as they become publicly visible *as mothers* who are resisting violence and inventing peace, . . . [women peacemakers like the
Iron Ladies of Liberia,] transform the meaning of 'motherhood.' "[29]
Their bold and assertive example destabilizes the Roman Catholic
magisterium's idealization of the "feminine genius" because their
powerful, public, and authoritative action for peace subverts re-
ligiously endorsed gender stereotypes that confine women to the
status of passive victim or sorrowful mother.

In light of their stories, we can glimpse the beginnings of an
alternative theology of motherhood—a theology that is grounded
in the diverse contexts of women's lived experiences and that looks
to women in general and mothers in particular not only for symbolic representations of human receptivity, but also for concrete
embodiments of divine power and authority for healing in a broken
world. In short, the Liberian women peacemakers reinvent what
it means to be a mother, what it means to be a woman, and what
it takes to build peace.

The final scenes of *Pray the Devil Back to Hell* reflect this
transformation beautifully. The setting is the 2007 Mother's Day
Service at St. Peter's Lutheran Church in Monrovia. The music
being performed is a sentimental song thanking God for mothers, who are there to hold us close when we cry, who wipe our
tears, pick us up when we fall: "I thank God, thank God, for
my Ma." The song expresses traditional, even cliché sentiments
about motherhood, but these sentiments and the very meaning

of motherhood are transformed when coupled with the powerful images of a beaming Leymah Gbowee who received a Women's Guild certificate in her honor, and the hands of dozens of women holding their Women's Peace Initiative ID badges. Their weathered hands and hardened faces reflect the true meaning of motherhood—not an eternal, ontological understanding of motherhood, but rather the meaning that they had created in their bold and assertive struggle to bring an end to the violence that plagued their lives. In the women peacemakers of Liberia, the mythically passive and solitary *mater dolorosa* has been transformed into the Iron Ladies of Liberia, ordinary mothers in solidarity with other mothers committed to extraordinary action for peace.

Notes

[1]*Pray the Devil Back to Hell*, DVD, directed by Gini Reticker (New York: Fork Films, 2009). Shortly after this article went to press, Leymah Gbowee was named as one of three women peacemakers awarded the 2011 Nobel Peace Prize. Her sister Liberian, Ellen Johnson Sirleaf, the current president of Liberia featured later in this article, was also awarded the prize.

[2]See John Paul II, Apostolic Letter *Mulieris Dignitatem* (On the Dignity and Vocation of Women), August 15, 1988, 10, www.vatican.va.

[3]Congregation for the Doctrine of the Faith, "Letter to the Bishops of the Catholic Church on the Collaboration of Men and Women in the Church and in the World," May 31, 2004, 16, www.vatican.va.

[4]John Paul II, Encyclical *Redemptoris Mater* (Mother of the Redeemer), March 25, 1987, 46, www.vatican.va.

[5]Congregation for the Doctrine of the Faith, "Collaboration of Men and Women," 13.

[6]For an excellent selection of theological reflections on this topic, see Ann Carr and Elisabeth Schüssler Fiorenza, eds., *The Special Nature of Women?* (Philadelphia: Trinity Press International, 1991).

[7]Sanam Naraghi Anderlini, *Women Building Peace: What They Do, Why It Matters* (Boulder, CO: Lynne Rienner Publishers, 2002), 4.

[8]Dyan Mazurana et al., eds., *Gender, Conflict and Peacekeeping* (Lanham, MD: Rowman & Littlefield, 2005), 2.

[9]See, for example, Mats Utas, "Victimcy, Girlfriending, Soldiering: Tacit Agency in a Young Woman's Social Navigation of the Liberian War Zone," *Anthropological Quarterly* 78, no. 2 (2005), 403-30.

[10]Sara Ruddick, *Maternal Thinking: Towards a Politics of Peace* (New York: Ballantine, 1989), 57.

[11]Ibid., 152.

[12]Caroline Sweetman, ed., *Gender, Peacebuilding and Reconstruction* (Oxford: Oxfam Press, 2005), 3.

[13]Elizabeth A. Johnson, *Truly Our Sister: A Theology of Mary in the Communion of Saints* (New York: Continuum, 2004), 63.

[14]Ruddick, *Maternal Thinking*, 157.

[15]An overview of Liberian history and the Liberian civil war(s) exceeds the scope of this essay. For in-depth history and analysis, see Mary H. Moran, *Liberia: The Violence of Democracy* (Philadelphia: University of Pennsylvania Press, 2008), and Gabriel I. H. Williams, *Liberia: The Heart of Darkness* (Victoria, BC: Trafford Publishing, 2002).

[16]African Women and Peace Support Group, *Liberian Women Peacemakers: Fighting for the Right to Be Seen, Heard and Counted* (Trenton, NJ: Africa World, 2004), 8.

[17]Anderlini, *Women Building Peace*, 38.

[18]Ruddick, *Maternal Thinking*, 229.

[19]African Women and Peace Support Group, *Liberian Women Peacemakers*, 13.

[20]*Pray the Devil Back to Hell.*

[21]African Women and Peace Support Group, *Liberian Women Peacemakers*, 8.

[22]*Pray the Devil Back to Hell.*

[23]African Women and Peace Support Group, *Liberian Women Peacemakers*, 27.

[24]This entire scenario is portrayed in *Pray the Devil Back to Hell.*

[25]Colleen E. Kelley, "A National 'Mother' Scolds for Peace: Liberia's Ruth Perry," in *Women Who Speak for Peace*, ed. Colleen E. Kelley and Anna L. Eblen (Lanham, MD: Rowman & Littlefield, 2002), 171.

[26]*Iron Ladies of Liberia*, DVD, directed by Daniel Junge (Denver, CO: Just Media, 2008).

[27]Cited in Ruddick, *Maternal Thinking*, 186.

[28]See ibid.

[29]Ruddick, *Maternal Thinking*, 241.

Just Peacemaking Theory and the Promotion of Dignified Subsistence

Daniel P. Scheid

Just peacemaking theory (JPT) is a recent development within Christian ethical reflection that offers a new way of approaching the perennial problem of war. Of the ten practices that constitute JPT, one is the call to "foster just and sustainable economic development."[1] JPT makes the case that promoting just and sustainable economic development, in conjunction with the other principles, can dramatically decrease the potential for violent conflicts. I wish to strengthen the pursuit of peace via justice and sustainability by offering a caveat to the principle of promoting just and sustainable economic development. It is my belief that those who formulated JPT do not sufficiently appreciate the ways in which participating in the global economy on the one hand, and preserving the sustainable use of the Earth's resources on the other, are not just in tension but may be directly at odds.

Following a summary of this principle in JPT, I will draw on the work of Leonardo Boff to critique modern liberal notions of development. For Boff, the patterns of global industrial economies are unresponsive to the signals of ecological collapse. Similarly, advocating "sustainable development" is prone to feeding the same myth of progress and the control and the conversion of nature into human goods that drives the current form of unsustainable development. Instead of focusing on sustainable development, which connotes an environmentally friendly tweak of economic development, I propose that JPT promote "dignified subsistence"[2] and ecological subsidiarity.

Subsistence connotes sustainable sufficiency rather than a constant search for material progress, and it recognizes what is enough for human beings to live in dignity and to flourish. Subsistence encourages us to empower those in abject poverty to find local and ecologically appropriate ways to provide for their needs. This is something JPT intends to say, but I maintain that its language of "development" is problematic for encouraging subsistence and, in turn, an economy that contributes to a just peace.

Before I begin, a brief clarification. In no way do I intend to minimize the conditions of poverty that affect millions. I also appreciate that, at least for the foreseeable future, participation in the global economic system is for many the only hope of improving their well-being. Moreover, I recognize that such participation has the potential to reduce the immediate likelihood of violence, and so peacemakers are prudent to promote it. As Christian ethicists committed to justice and sustainability as well as peace, however, I think we must acknowledge that such economic development is not the final destination but is rather a temporary measure on the way to subsistence. In other words, I propose a challenge to JPT that must be borne, as Augustine might say, "in readiness of mind" as globalization continues to intensify and millions yearn for a better future.

Just Peacemaking Theory
and Just, Sustainable, Economic Development

JPT represents a third theory that reflects on the Christian call to be a peacemaker. A collaborative effort by twenty-three scholars, JPT expands on and appeals to both pacifism and just war theory and aims to supplement the weaknesses of both of these without, however, replacing either one. JPT strives to be "realist" in its aims, and rather than a "theory" *per se*, it is really ten practices, or concrete activities, drawn inductively from historical and empirical examples, that have proven effective in staving off conflict. In short, these principles have worked in the past and have the real potential to limit war and therefore deserve the support of every Christian called to be a peacemaker.

In their chapter in Glen Stassen's edited volume, *Just Peacemaking: Ten Practices for Abolishing War*, David Bronkema, David Lumsdaine, and Rodger Payne focus and expand on one of the ten practices of JPT, namely, the practice of just and sustainable economic development. They define development as "a process of material and social progress [that] usually leads to wider involvement in the world economy, and cultural adaptation to modern world customs."[3] While reminiscent of Catholic social thought and Benedict XVI's advocacy of "integral human development,"[4] the authors envision development incorporating more than just material well-being. Development is not simply about creating more wealth but ultimately aims at the flourishing of the whole human person.[5] They acknowledge that the phrase "sustainable development" is an attractive one that "[conjures] up a picture of continual, yet environmentally friendly, increases in material welfare that are locally generated and controlled."

The reality on the ground, however, is much more complex.[6] The poor frequently clamor for development projects, they note, but these often do not produce the intended results, and at times even useless or harmful projects are chosen despite protests by the local population.[7] The World Bank, for example, has funded many large capital projects that "have proven environmentally destructive, socially irresponsible, and economically unproductive."[8] Nevertheless, supporting just and sustainable development is a recognition that people in circumstances of abject poverty "consistently try to become more economically prosperous"[9] and many people in developed countries want to assist them. Development is not therefore merely an imposition of Western ideals, Bronkema and his colleagues argue, but represents an opportunity to participate to a greater degree in the world economy and produce the wealth that the poor themselves desire.

JPT argues that development must be just and sustainable in order to reduce war, and the authors do recognize the imbroglio surrounding economic development, justice, ecological integrity, and war. First, economic injustices, such as a chronic lack of jobs, often lead to social unrest, which is fertile ground for escalations of violence. In their introduction to the book *Just Peacemaking*, editors John Langan, Duane Friesen, and Glen Stassen single out the principle of sustainable development as particularly helpful in addressing the conditions that often fuel terrorism. For example, they note that Russia has struggled for years to defeat Muslim Chechen separatists, and yet their massive military interventions have yielded meager results. By contrast, Turkey altered its response to terrorist attacks by Kurdish rebels. Turkey focused less on military options and instead initiated health and education reforms for the Kurds, pouring billions of dollars into local economic initiatives. In combination with other approaches identified in JPT, economic development enabled Turkey to effectively end Kurdish terrorism within four years.[10] If terrorism is a major source of violence, it seems peacemakers should learn from the lesson of Turkey and support economic development.

Similarly, JPT recognizes there are multiple ways in which unsustainable economic development contributes to violent conflicts. First, "economic development that is not ecologically sustainable will cause unexpectedly worsening patterns of human life which may well lead to violence in the long run."[11] Ecological degradation threatens a community's ability to satisfy basic needs, so the poor theoretically would also seek ecologically sustainable economic development over less "green" development.[12] Moreover, while some ecological degradation may not be crippling in absolute terms, "resources scarcity, ecological deterioration, and relative deprivation" can also lead to violence.[13] Second, states may lack resources because of unsustainable economic development, and they may then use violence to get to raw materials, as demonstrated in the 1991 Persian Gulf War when Saddam Hussein invaded Kuwait to gain access to oil fields. In addition, development may not be able to keep up with population and the demands for finite resources such as water and fuel.[14] The 1967 Six Day War was partly due to struggles over water, which remains a contentious, vital, and scarce resource in the Middle East.[15] Finally, the economic injustice of severe poverty itself can be a cause of environmental deterioration. When the land is controlled by a wealthy minority, peasants compelled by desperation often move into ecologically fragile areas, which intensifies the depletion of natural resources and escalates environmental destruction.[16] Thus, any economic development that harms the Earth and in turn degrades social life cannot be considered sustainable.

JPT offers a robust understanding of sustainability and encourages a very different sort of development than what the word usually entails. Bronkema and colleagues acknowledge that the hasty consumption of resources has led to some losses, and that we must take care of creation in order to maintain development. "Infinite physical consumption" is not realistic, and we must learn to understand development and the improvement of life without constantly growing consumption. In this way, simple living is a part of sustainable development.[17]

They also acknowledge the downsides to economic development: the possibility (1) that it may occur in ways that threaten ecological well-being and hence lead to war; (2) that, empirically, free trade reduces wars, but it also sets back millions of poor people; and (3) that there remains a substantive question of how the global market can be reformed to make international corporations ethically responsible for conditions in countries where they can simply withdraw if challenged.[18]

Yet, in the end—and perhaps because of the enormity of global poverty and the importance of minimizing potential conflicts in the near future –advocates of JPT uphold that economic development is necessary. In a footnote, Bronkema and colleagues criticize those who might claim that development is not clearly a good objective: "The stark human need of poor people in poor countries is an obvious rationale for development aid. Further, the suggestion that development may not be a good or ought to be subordinated to ecological or spiritual concerns is often offensive to people from those countries because richer or 'more developed' countries evidently seek further wealth for themselves."[19]

The goal of lifting millions out of poverty and staving off cycles of violence is laudatory. However, my critique of this principle is not that it is not worth pursuing, but rather that it contains a fundamental contradiction. As Bronkema and colleagues have pointed out, "wider involvement in the world economy" is a process that militates against the kind of just, sustainable, and holistic development they desire. Clearly there is no nation in the world that does not have some measure of economic injustice; similarly there is no developed or developing economy in the world that is truly sustainable. Developed nations rely heavily on developing nations for access to cheap labor and cheap resources, as JPT recognizes.[20]

Development as currently configured and practiced presumes the use of renewable and non-renewable resources with little concern for the potential needs of future generations. For example, Bronkema and colleagues praise Taiwan and South Korea for their land reform and rapid industrialization, lamenting the "serious problems of environmental destruction and pollution" as an "unexpected consequence."[21] I argue that this should not be unexpected but instead anticipated. JPT asks ethicists to focus on empirical evidence of what is really happening and not focus on merely possible futures.[22]

Given the dynamic of ecological degradation and war, the prospects for truly sustainable development warrant further examination. Moreover, even the use of renewable resources can outstrip their renewability, as is true, for example, of water in the Middle East. Combined with growing populations, rising consumption, and the continual desire for material wealth, the engines of economic development will tend to exacerbate wars, not reduce them. From this, it is unclear why economic development will lead to sustainability, and in turn to justice or peace.

Unjust and Unsustainable Economic Development

I now focus on the work of Brazilian liberation theologian Leonardo Boff to explain why in its origins and its present dynamics the world economy may not be compatible with the kind of just, sustainable future that can truly limit wars. While many theologians critique the mentality of development and question its capacity to be sustainable, Boff provides a good resource for refuting the idea of sustainable development. Writing from the perspective of a firsthand witness to what economic development means in the developing world, Boff provides an authentic witness for ethicists and theologians from the North who also criticize the endless pursuit of economic development.[23] In *Cry of the Earth, Cry of the Poor*, Boff explains that ecology has moved beyond being merely a movement to save particular species and "has become a radical critique of the kind of civilization that we are building, which is energy-devouring and tends to demolish all ecosystems."[24]

Ultimately, Boff affirms what JPT seeks in just and sustainable development: greater justice and participation for the poor along with balanced ecosystems. More so than Bronkema's group, Boff recognizes a fundamental and perhaps irreconcilable tension within the search for sustainable development. For over four hundred years the world has been "held hostage to a myth, the myth of progress and of uninterrupted and unlimited growth."[25] Boff likens the achievements of the Industrial Revolution and the capitalist drive for constant profits to a kind of war waged on all fronts, producing victims of all kinds.[26]

Under the guise of development, the economy no longer produces just enough to sustain human needs, or even enough for a surplus to provide some additional security and enjoyment, but instead seeks to maximize production and lower costs in all possible ways. The ideal of sustainable development offers a nod in the direction of ecological concern, but at its root "it remains captive of the development-and-growth paradigm . . . it never gets away from its economic origins, namely, rising productivity, accumulation, and technological innovation."[27]

While it is true that conditions of poverty can be environmentally damaging, Boff disagrees that the solution is to speed the rate of development. For Boff, the real cause of poverty and ecological degradation is exactly the kind of development that has already been pursued. Whenever there is a conflict between development and sustainability, "development is usually chosen and the cost paid in environmental deterioration."[28] Boff therefore sees a potential clash between the logic of the market, which seeks continual growth, and ecological sustainability.[29] In this sense, Boff concludes, "*sustainable development* is an oxymoron. . . . [It] is nothing but rhetoric and illusion."[30]

The Amazon provides a helpful case study in this tension between ecology and economy because of its rich biodiversity and because it is the locus of intense efforts at development. In the Amazon, Boff contends, development itself is experienced as a form of war that kills not only nonhuman plants and animals but also those who stand in the way of economic development, including various indigenous peoples and the murder of Chico Mendes in 1988,[31] and I would add that of Sr. Dorothy Stang in 2005.

Capitalist endeavors deny the central truths of ecology, such as the interrelatedness and interdependence of all creatures.[32] Instead, nature itself has no internal norms; it is simply inert matter waiting to be shaped and reshaped according to the desires of the elites. For example, Boff describes the development project spearheaded by American billionaire Daniel Ludwig in 1967. Ludwig bought nine million acres of land to produce wood and agricultural exports such as beef, rice, and soybeans. "He cleared the native forest and on half a million acres he planted a hundred million plants of *Gmelina arborea* (brought in from Africa). . . . The trees were outside their own ecosystems, however, and they were attacked by a fungus . . . and devastated. The project had to be abandoned."[33] For Boff, the legacy of many megaprojects conducted in the Amazon and their impact on the poor, the indigenous, and the immense biodiversity within the Amazon shows that "the Amazon is the place that refutes modernity's development paradigm—unsustainable development full of capital sins (that is, sins of capital) and sins against ecology."[34]

Based on contemporary experience and historical memory, Boff discerns a clear clash between the forces of economic development and sustainability. To add a prefix like "eco" or the word "sustainable" to development projects "simply masks the inherent perversity of capitalism and its development paradigm."[35] However, Boff cannot simply be accused of being an elite Western environmentalist who privileges concerns for endangered species over that of the poor, and who subordinates development "to ecological or spiritual concerns," as Bronkema and colleagues fear. On the contrary, he is a liberation theologian whose primary concern is not wildlife or pristine wilderness but the poor. Boff thereby levies a poignant rebuttal to those who maintain that economic development must be pursued and can be adjusted to become sustainable and just. I do not suggest that all development projects promoted by international organizations are in fact just destructive capitalism under another name.[36] Instead, following Boff, I argue that greater participation in the global economic system contributes to an economic model that is, at its heart, unsustainable. The drive for more is an integral part of development, both in its origins and in practice. This should render the rhetoric of adding "sustainable" or "integral human" to "development" even more suspect.

Instead, Boff counsels that we must start from nature and its sustainability in order to find an alternative to the logic of capitalism.[37] Similarly, the starting point for addressing economic injustice and for resolving violent conflicts over scarce resources should be ecology, which is the study of the interconnectedness and relationships among myriad creatures within interacting ecosystems. The economy must be subservient to subsistence and sustainability in ways that pursuits of economic development have not been, and perhaps can never be.

Dignified Subsistence

Instead of promoting sustainable development, with all its internal contradictions, I propose that peacemakers should promote the search for "dignified subsistence." Despite the emendations of just peacemaking theorists, "development" continues to imply continual growth that makes resources more available and usable; Bronkema and colleagues implicitly acknowledge this when they remark that even "richer or 'more developed' countries evidently seek further wealth for themselves."[38] This sense of development does not have any *telos* or end and so will never come to completion.

As Boff warns, affixing the phrase "sustainable" to development is not a sufficient correction to the logic of capitalism. Similarly, Benedict XVI and perhaps the wider body of Catholic social teaching would do better to offer a new understanding of human flourishing rather than to ameliorate development by endorsing "integral human development." The concrete realities of economic development suggest that adding qualitative corrections such as "sustainable" or "integral human" to development is insufficient without a further, post-development goal.

In contrast, subsistence implies sufficiency and the maintenance of a healthy and truly sustainable material existence. Since "subsistence" has historically had the connotation of a bare and meager existence,[39] I qualify it with "dignified." Poverty, even if not fatal, is not compatible with human dignity. Dignified subsistence does not seek mere survival, but a satisfying and sufficient amount of material goods that enable the possibilities for human flourishing. At the same time, the pursuit of dignified subsistence implicitly rebukes the undignified lifestyle of many in the rich and developed world who purchase goods that stretch far beyond what is needed for a healthy and flourishing life, and this is to the detriment of the poor and of the Earth.

Dignified subsistence represents at least a partial rejection of the free market and its focus on endless opportunities for acquisition.

The model of subsistence also unmasks the injustice of the vast discrepancies in wealth between North and South and rich and poor. Conditions of abject poverty for millions in the so-called "developing world" are not simply evidence that more economic development is necessary. Instead, subsistence points to the origins of this poverty in colonialism and the Industrial Revolution and their legacies that led to the current patterns of the global market and resulted in a rich developed North and a poor and indebted developing South.

A corollary to the promotion of dignified subsistence is the promotion of ecological subsidiarity and political subsidiarity. Subsidiarity is integral to an ecological ethic of dignified subsistence because it stresses control and decision-making at the local level. Development projects imposed from without are often unsustainable in two senses: they lack local support, and they can cause serious pollution and environmental degradation. Ecological subsidiarity contends that sustainability is best achieved locally, without regard to the global forces of the market economy.

Ecological subsidiarity resonates with Rosemary Radford Ruether's call for "the rebuilding of primary and regional communities,"[40] with Robert Grant's "rural ecoregionalism,"[41] and with Michael Northcott's description of "parochial ecology."[42] I am sympathetic with Kevin O'Brien's proposal for "multiscalar ethics,"[43] which advocates addressing ecological concerns, such as preserving biodiversity, with action at local, regional, and global levels. Because development tends to be such a radically global and anti-local phenomenon, Christians ought to privilege local subsistence as a counterweight.

Similarly, ecological subsidiarity balances political subsidiarity—people working within political boundaries, at times arbitrarily drawn—with subsidiarity determined by the place on Earth where one happens to live. In order for people to take responsibility for the ecosystems on which they depend, decision-making powers should be afforded to those who would be affected within that ecosystem, not just within a particular political border. As Langan and his colleagues observe, there remains the pressing question of how to make transnational corporations responsible for their behavior when they are not beholden to the local population.[44] Dignified subsistence challenges that dimension of the global market, which is seemingly an inextricable part of development, and instead calls us to take responsibility for the part of Earth that sustains us.

Ecological subsidiarity thus points to a flaw in political realism, which does not take sufficient account of ecosystems and their influence on political decisions. Bronkema and colleagues acknowledge that the degradation of ecological systems can lead to even greater competition for scarce resources, and that the likely outcome would be war. They cite evidence of this in tensions in the Middle East over water, but it is unclear how they see wider involvement in the world economy not exacerbating this trend. As Thomas Homer Dixon explains, realists focus on international politics as an anarchic system in which nation states are "rational maximizers of power," and so they limit their discussion of how power is balanced between states. By limiting their focus to political distinctions, realists overlook shared environmental regions and problems, and thus do an inadequate job of connecting environmental differences and conflict:

> Realism thus encourages scholars to deemphasize transboundary environmental problems, because such problems often cannot be linked to a particular country, and do not have any easily conceptualized impact on the structure of economic and military power relations between states. Realism induces scholars to squeeze environmental issues into a structure of concepts including "state," "sovereignty," "territory," "national interest," and "balance of power." The fit is bad, which may lead theorists to ignore, distort, and misunderstand important aspects of global environmental problems.[45]

Dixon's analysis also suggests the viability of thinking in terms of ecological subsidiarity and subsistence within various bioregions, rather than focusing solely on political entities and the status of their domestic economies. Sustainability reminds us to return to that which sustains our life, namely the land. JPT should support ecological subsidiarity so that peacemakers will encourage and empower bioregional communities to create sustainable economies without necessarily succumbing to the demands of the global economy. While sustainable economic development may be necessary in the short term, JPT should promote a diversity of subsistent communities as a final goal, in order that just peacemaking may be truly sustainable.

The formulators of JPT stress that these are not theoretical principles but actual practices, something that an outsider can observe and document. Similarly, dignified subsistence and ecological subsidiarity entail practices, many of which have been thoroughly described.[46] We might consider these practices not only as minimizing our "carbon footprint" or our attempts to "reduce, reuse, recycle," but also as practices constitutive of a dignified subsistent life. As Boff suggests, ecology has moved beyond being a campaign to save a species or ecosystem: it has become "a radical critique of the kind of civilization that we are building."[47] Ecologically motivated practices become just peacemaking practices as they move to shape a new culture and new civilization leading toward subsistence.

Subsistence *practices* in the long term are more likely to prevent war than development practices even if the development is termed "sustainable." As Boff contends, sustainable development participates in a logic of control that in the end is unsustainable and both entails and leads to conflict. If JPT wants to advocate practices that prevent war, then it should incorporate the language of subsistence and critique the language of development. This is not to abandon the poor to a state of irremediable suffering but rather to say that the poor deserve what we all deserve—enough. Human dignity is served best by sufficiency, not development. Promoting dignified subsistence calls on all Christians to help and enable the poor to improve their conditions of life, but not through conscription into a global system that helped to create those conditions.

Conclusion

JPT aims to be an effective moral theory that is realistic, pragmatic, and rooted in historical examples. The practices it outlines have helped to stop or limit wars. It is realistic, therefore, to accept the short-term persistence of the global free market and to advance the poor's desire for economic development. For the near future, peacemakers must work within this system. Yet, to be realistic also means to challenge this system and to reject its ideological underpinnings. If it is to be pursued, sustainable development must be an interim palliative on the way to dignified subsistence.

One could say that the call for dignified subsistence is only a caveat to be "borne in readiness of mind" as we continue to support ventures of development that improve the lives of millions living in poverty. On the other hand, perhaps it is a caveat that serves as a foundational critique of the entire conceptual structure of "development." While working to improve the lives of the poor, perhaps Christian peacemakers should also be working to counteract the thrust of the globalizing market—which is the motive force of development—both conceptually and practically.

I do not intend my argument to be merely semantic. Although dignified subsistence sounds much like what Bronkema and colleagues describe as sustainable development, it is quite a different concept altogether. Recall Leonardo Boff's critique that the dynamics of development entail limitless desire for material growth, which will prove to be unsustainable and thus a cause of violence. JPT, as a part of its commitment to realism, ought to challenge and resist these endemic patterns of development.

Notes

[1] See Glen Stassen, ed., *Just Peacemaking: Ten Practices for Abolishing War*, 2nd ed. (Cleveland: Pilgrim Press, 2004).

[2] I thank my wife and colleague Anna Floerke Scheid for suggesting this term, and for her helpful comments on the entire paper.

[3] David Bronkema, David Lumsdaine, and Rodger Payne, "Foster Just and Sustainable Economic Development," in Glen Stassen, ed., *Just Peacemaking: Ten Practices for Abolishing War*, 2nd ed. (Cleveland: Pilgrim Press, 2004), 120.

[4] Benedict XVI, *Caritas in Veritate* (On Integral Development in Charity and Truth), *http://www.vatican.va*. See esp. 11, 18, 29-30.

[5] Bronkema et al., "Foster Just and Sustainable Economic Development," 121.

[6] Ibid., 119.

[7] Ibid., 120.

[8] Ibid., 126. For more, see Bruce Rich, *Mortgaging the Earth: The World Bank, Environmental Impoverishment, and the Crisis of Development* (Boston: Beacon Press, 1994).

[9] Bronkema et al., "Foster Just and Sustainable Economic Development," 120.

[10]John Langan, Duane Friesen, and Glen Stassen, "Introduction: Just Peacemaking as the New Ethic for Peace and War," in Glen Stassen, ed., *Just Peacemaking: Ten Practices for Abolishing War*, 2nd ed. (Cleveland: Pilgrim Press, 2004), 2-4.

[11]Bronkema et al., "Foster Just and Sustainable Economic Development," 122.

[12]Ibid., 121-23.

[13]Ibid., 123.

[14]For a detailed analysis of this from the perspective of a social scientist, see Michael T. Klare, *Resource Wars: The New Landscape of Global Conflict* (New York: Metropolitan Books, 2001) and *Rising Powers, Shrinking Planet: How Scarce Energy Is Creating a New World Order* (Oxford: OneWorld, 2008).

[15]Bronkema et al., "Foster Just and Sustainable Economic Development," 128.

[16]Ibid., 128. See also 137.

[17]Ibid., 134.

[18]Langan et al., "Introduction: Just Peacemaking as the New Ethic for Peace and War," 35.

[19]Bronkema et al., "Foster Just and Sustainable Economic Development," 209.

[20]Ibid., 127. See also 133.

[21]Ibid., 124-27.

[22]Glen Stassen, "The Unity, Realism, and Obligatoriness of Just Peacemaking," *Journal of the Society of Christian Ethics* 23, no. 1 (2003): 173.

[23]Among others, see for example Rosemary Radford Ruether, *Gaia and God: An Ecofeminist Theology of Earth Healing* (New York: Harper Collins Publishers, 1992); Larry Rasmussen, *Earth Community, Earth Ethics* (Maryknoll, NY: Orbis Books, 1996); and Michael Northcott, *The Environment and Christian Ethics* (New York: Cambridge University Press, 1996).

[24]Leonardo Boff, *Cry of the Earth, Cry of the Poor* (Maryknoll, NY: Orbis Books, 1997), 4.

[25]Ibid., 65.

[26]Ibid.

[27]Ibid., 66.

[28]Ibid., 5.

[29]Ibid., 8-9.

[30]Ibid., 67.

[31]Ibid., 98-103.

[32]Ibid., 86.

[33]Ibid., 91-92.

[34]Ibid., 103.

[35]Ibid., 86.

[36]I am grateful to an anonymous reviewer for this language.

[37]Boff, *Cry of the Earth, Cry of the Poor*, 101.

[38]Bronkema et al., "Foster Just and Sustainable Economic Development," 209.

[39] Webster's Dictionary defines "subsistence" as: "a: the minimum (as of food and shelter) necessary to support life; b: a source or means of obtaining the necessities of life." It also offers two definitions of "subsistence farming," tracing its first use to 1937: "1. farming or a system of farming that provides all or almost all goods required by the family usu. without any significant surplus for sale; 2. farming or a system of farming that produces a minimum and often inadequate return to the farmer" (*Webster's Ninth New Collegiate Dictionary* [Springfield, MA: Merriam Webster, 1991], 1176. Interestingly, the notion that having all the goods one needs without a surplus to sell could be labeled as providing "inadequate return" is a similar mentality to that of economic development and the constant need for more. I intend the promotion of dignified subsistence to counter such a mentality—it indicates having what one needs and as befits human dignity, without needing to seek a surplus to sell.

[40] Ruether, *Gaia and God*, 201.

[41] Robert L. Grant, *A Case Study in Thomistic Environmental Ethics: The Ecological Crisis in the Loess Hills of Iowa* (Lewiston, NY: Edward Mellen Press, 2007), 281.

[42] Northcott, *The Environment and Christian Ethics*, 308-27.

[43] Kevin J. O'Brien, *An Ethics of Biodiversity* (Washington, DC: Georgetown University Press, 2010), 79-108.

[44] Langan et al., "Introduction: Just Peacemaking as the New Ethic for Peace and War," 35.

[45] Thomas F. Homer-Dixon, "Environmental Changes as Causes of Acute Conflict," *International Security* 16, no. 2 (Autumn 1991): 84-85.

[46] In addition to the practices described by theologians like Boff, Ruether, and Northcott, see for example John Javna, *50 Simple Things You Can Do to Save the Earth* (New York: Hyperion, 2008).

[47] Boff, *Cry of the Earth, Cry of the Poor*, 4.

PART IV

THE VOCATION OF THE THEOLOGIAN IN THE TRANSFORMATION OF VIOLENCE

Bridging Jesus' Missions to the Poor and the Wicked

Contributions from Attention to Culture

Todd David Whitmore

There is a fissure—perhaps a crevasse—that splits current research regarding the "historical Jesus." The fault line, a long-standing one in theology, runs along the question of who Jesus is *for*. On whose behalf did he live and die? Liberation theology has brought this rift to public attention by emphasizing God's "preferential option for the poor." Critics counter that Jesus lived and died not specifically for the poor, but for sinners, even the wicked, an argument made most pointedly, perhaps, by John Meier in his 1988 plenary to Catholic Theological Society of America. Meier analyzes the work of Jon Sobrino and finds it lacking in academic rigor and therefore seriousness in its appeal to the historical Jesus: "At times, the historical Jesus seems to be Jesus insofar as he fits into Sobrino's program of liberation theology. For all the talk of a new approach, we are not all that far from the proof-text use of Scripture in the old Catholic manuals of dogmatic theology." Sobrino's Jesus, according to Meier, looks a lot like Sobrino.

Substantively, Meier criticizes Sobrino's emphasis on the "option for the poor." Closer examination of scripture, Meier says, reveals that what is really at stake is that Jesus forgives sinners: "There is no proof that Jesus' concern for economically poor or uneducated people caused a major scandal or persecution, or was the major reason for his execution. Matters may have been different with his free offer of forgiveness to public sinners," including "economic oppressors." He goes on, "The damaging charge against [Jesus] was not that he associated with the poor, but that he associated with the wicked. It is a mistake to think that the Pharisees were upset because Jesus ministered to the ordinarily pious common people and the economically impoverished."[1]

In what follows, I attend to this fissure in current understandings of the historical Jesus, and show how careful ethnographic attention to culture is necessary for theology. I first provide an overview of the socio-cultural presuppositions that underpin modern quests for the historical Jesus and lead to the option-for-the-poor versus option-for-the-wicked split. Such an overview allows us to investigate in more detail the fissure between what I call the liberationist and dispensationist types in Jesus studies. This analysis will lead into a treatment of the cosmological presuppositions that informed the cultural context within which Jesus witnessed, without contradiction, to both the poor and the wicked.

The next question that arises is that of how we in the present world can appropriate enough of Jesus the Nazarene's cultural presuppositions so that we, too, might witness to (as we are given witness by) both the poor and the wicked. The key here, I suggest, is attention to what I call "bridge cultures," that is, present-day cultures, often more oral than literate, that already share some of the cosmological presuppositions of first-century Palestine. Here, my exemplar is the culture of northern Uganda and the Acholi people who blend in multiple syncretistic ways a particular strand of Catholicism—what I call "magical Catholicism"—with traditional African practices that share key beliefs with the people of Jesus' culture. My overarching argument is that, for reasons that relate to conceptions of time and space that will become clearer, what enables Jesus to witness to both the poor and the wicked is his immersion in and presupposition of a particular culture's cosmology, one that, in John Pilch's words, involves a "densely populated spirit world and ready interference of those spirits in human life."[2]

Rationalization and Disenchantment: The Context of Modern Historical Jesus Studies

There is perhaps no greater sociologist of modernity than Max Weber, and it has often been argued that the core concept in his analyses of the modern era is that of "rationalization."[3] In most instances, Weber is referring to the rise and spread of instrumental means-end reasoning, whereby once one's desired end, whatever it may be, is chosen, the highest value is given to the predictable calculability of the means. Weber takes an earlier argument offered by Werner Sombart that calculability is the defining characteristic of the capitalist economy and applies it to all social spheres—the value of predictable calculability is definitive of modernity as such.[4]

The premium on calculability has led to the division of time and space into discrete, uninterrupted units. Although, as Weber makes clear in *The Protestant Ethic and the Spirit of Capitalism*, full-blown rationalization of religion did not come about until the Reformation, his book also highlights medieval precursors: the cloistered monk, with his ascetic life rationally—that is, instrumentally—ordered to achieve the end of salvation, was "the first human being" in the medieval West "to live according to a time schedule."[5] Later Weber scholars will further argue that the medieval cloister, with its methodical time regimentation, efficient labor, and technological advances was a nascent capitalist factory.[6] While the full-fledged division of labor, and thus the compartmentalization of not only time but also space into discrete units, does not come until later, it does come, and with it the eclipse of any cosmology that allows a blurring or, worse, rupturing of the discrete units of three-dimensional space and strict linear time.

The cosmological and theological implications of this compartmentalization of space and time did not go unnoticed by Weber. In his revised version of *The Protestant Ethic* he introduces the concept of "disenchantment." The modern world is such that, in Weber's words, "there are no mysterious incalculable forces that come into play, but rather . . . one can, in principle, master all things by calculation. This means that the world is disenchanted." The entire world has been "transformed into a causal mechanism."[7] Theologically, disenchantment is characterized by a remote God, one who does not interfere with our parsed time and space. It is not incidental that the two theologians most influenced by Weber and his colleague Ernst Troeltsch, H. Richard Niebuhr, and James Gustafson, would write of "radical monotheism" in Niebuhr's case and claim that "Jesus is not God" in Gustafson's.[8] This is a God who, in the end, will not bend down through the universe even for the incarnation.

The Disenchantment of Jesus: Biblical Studies

The use of methods of calculability in the search for the historical Jesus grew out of the disenchanted world that Weber describes, such that even scholars with other theological commitments are profoundly shaped by it. The result is a Jesus whose sense of time and space is parsed into discrete units: Jesus is either a reformer who calls for social change in the here and now *or* he is an "eschatological prophet" who points toward a future, if immanent, world that, at present, is elsewhere. To affirm both would constitute a contradiction, a violation of the laws of time and space. The consequence on the normative level is another parsing: Jesus is either for justice for the poor (in the here and now) or for forgiveness of sinners (in the hopes for a world that is not here, but is yet to come).

John Meier is right that both Jesus' deeds and his words convey a foregrounded message of forgiveness of the wicked. Concerning his deeds, Matthew and Luke depict, without rebuttal, Pharisees and scribes criticizing Jesus for welcoming, befriending, and eating with sinners (Mt 11:16-19; Lk 15:2). With regard to his words, the centerpiece is the Sermon on the Mount/Plain. We are told to love our enemies (Mt 5:43-48; Lk 6:27-36) and to forgive the debts or sins of others (Mt 6:12; Lk 11:4). Luke follows the call to love one's enemies immediately with the specific command not to judge or condemn, but to forgive (Lk 6:37). Jesus' words on forgiveness extend to the parables. Both Matthew (18:12-14) and Luke (15:1-6) tell the parable of the lost sheep, and Luke, once again, spells out its implications: "Just as, I tell you, there will be more joy in heaven over one sinner who repents than over ninety-nine righteous persons who need no repentance" (15: 7). Luke takes the message of forgiveness all the way to the cross: "Father, forgive them; for they know not what they are doing" (23:34).

It seems that Meier has a crucial point, then, regarding what may fairly be called Jesus' "option for the wicked," a point that Sobrino, at least, reads out of the gospel. Liberation theology so reads the gospel in terms of justice as a response to the oppressor/oppressed dynamic that it leaves little room for forgiveness of the wicked. The task of mercy here is not foremost to forgive the oppressors who, according to Sobrino, are the "sinners par excellence," but rather, again in Sobrino's words, to "take the crucified people from the cross." Yes, God is "essentially inclined to forgiveness," but there are differences between kinds of sinners, and the "presence of the greater sin" lies with "the oppressor."[9]

We should not let Meier off the hook, however. He works hard to minimize any option for the poor in the gospels. Although Meier indicates a special mission to those considered truly wicked,[10] over the course of his five-tome work, *A Marginal Jew*, he stresses less Jesus' positive mission to the wicked than the *absence* of a meaningful mission to the poor. Most references to a mission to the poor are only in passing.[11] The case against any "option for the poor" becomes explicit when he argues that because there were so many poor at the time of Jesus, the claim that he went *specifically* to the poor is all but empty of import. When Meier mentions that "Jesus reached out to Jews of all stripes, the respectable and (especially) the sinful, the rich and (especially) the poor," he adds the important qualifier: "to say that Jesus was concerned about the poor does not in the end say very much. About 90 percent of Galilean Jews would probably have qualified as 'poor' in some sense of the word."[12]

Why this bifurcation of Jesus' mission? Why can Jesus not have special missions to both the poor and the wicked? The impediment, I suggest, is a modern sense of time and space that places justice on behalf of the poor in the present world, and interprets forgiveness of the wicked as an act of anticipation of another world, one that has yet to come. This is all the more evident in the purer examples of what we might call the liberationist and dispensationalist ideal types of historical Jesus interpretation. Richard Horsley is closer to the ideal type of the liberationist than Sobrino. Like liberationists generally, he wants to offer a "people's history" of the gospels, a view from below, and foregrounds the oppressor/oppressed axis of interpretation.[13] What makes him a purer instance of a liberationist ideal type is his outright rejection of any future, otherworldly references in Jesus' teaching and mission. Claims in the gospel of a kingdom of God coming in the future functioned simply as a kind of "magic charm" that some peasants believed was "capable by itself, of transforming the world." This constituted a "mystification of the imperial situation." Any other-worldly cosmic struggle between God and Satan "was simply a symbolization of the violent social-political-religious conflict in which the people were caught individually and collectively."[14] It is not surprising that Horsley doubts the historicity of Jesus' forgiveness of the wicked.[15]

E. P. Sanders is a purer instance of the dispensationalist type than Meier.[16] He writes that if "Jesus expected *God* to change history in a decisive way in the immediate future, it seems unlikely that he was a social reformer" (emphasis in original). Yes, Jesus preached the kingdom of God, and the concept of "kingdom" is a political one, but, Sanders claims, it "refers only to supernatural society." To the extent that it is here and now, it can only be, in his words, "invisible."[17] Despite Sanders' insistence that Jesus was theological, his is a God who is not here, not yet.

Something is off about both the Sobrino-Horsley and Meier-Sanders readings of the gospel. Jesus clearly has a preferential option for the poor *and* for those deemed particularly wicked.[18] If we are to imitate *this* Jesus Christ, then we need to discern how he joins the two missions into a single one in announcing the reign of God. Sobrino's and Meier's shared mistake is that they trade one off for the other. The result, if their countercharges are correct, is that each ends with up a Jesus who looks much like the author. To counteract this common tendency, we need to engage not simply the historical Jesus, but the *cultural* historical Jesus as limned by anthropology.

The Nazarene: Toward a Cultural Historical Jesus

Anthropology has long been interested in the different, even the exotic. As a corrective for present tendencies in Jesus research to make Jesus mirror the author, it can be of particular service. The collection of scholars that is most dedicated to situating the historical Jesus in his cultural context calls itself the Context Group.[19] Bruce Malina, a member of the group, stresses that the culture in which Jesus lived is strikingly unlike our own. "Trying to understand the writings of the New Testament in an adult, scholarly way," he writes, "is much like trying to understand a group of foreigners somehow dropped into our midst."[20] Cultural anthropology seeks not just Jesus, but Jesus the *Nazarene*, the person in his collective cultural context.

John Pilch, also a member of the Context Group, has attended specifically to the phenomenon of spirit presence and spirit possession in ancient Mediterranean culture. Pilch notes that spirit experiences "are usually dismissed by [our] contemporaries as unscientific and uncritical." However, he adds that even today, let alone in the first-century Mediterranean world, over 90 percent of the people in the world have what social science describes as "altered states of consciousness" or "experiences of alternate reality." To dismiss these experiences is, in Pilch's words, "neither sufficiently historical nor critical." He writes, "Historical-critical biblical scholars concerned with determining factual, historical events in Jesus' life never attend to his *Mediterranean culture's consensus reality*, which is quite different from *Western culture's consensus reality*."[21] Pilch examines Jesus' baptism, the testing in the desert, the walking on the sea, the transfiguration, and the resurrection experiences, and finds in each case a "real experience of a real event in alternate reality."[22] One of the effects of engagement with the spirits is what anthropologist Paul Stoller, in his study of witchcraft among the Songhay people of Niger, calls the "fusion of the worlds": engagement with and possession by spirits overcomes the modern separation between the here and the there, the present and the past or future, the physical and the trans-physical worlds.[23] It is precisely this fusion that allows Jesus the Nazarene to understand his missions to the poor and wicked as not a contradiction between the here/now and the there/future.

I suggest that there are two possible avenues for the practice of what we might call the "reenchantment" of our own culture: first, engagement with what I will call "bridge cultures" and, second, retrieval of what I will term "magical Catholicism."

Bridge Cultures

Because our culture is so different from that of Jesus, it can be helpful to participate in and observe other cultures, contemporary to yet different from our own, to provide us with clues as to what it might mean to re-enact Jesus the Nazarene the Christ. We need exemplar persons and communities from cultures that share more with first-century Palestine than our own culture does. This approach raises the ante on liberation theology's claim that "the poor" have an epistemological advantage in reading the Bible because they are socially located in a way similar to the protagonists of the gospel. The liberationist claim holds, as far as it goes, but it needs to be taken further. There is insufficient cultural (as distinct from political and economic) analysis in the classic Latin American liberationist texts.[24] If we can identify bridge cultures—ones that share significant beliefs and practices with Jesus' Palestine—then we have a much better chance of locating exemplar people and practices that can show us how to reenact Jesus the Nazarene the Christ. One such bridge culture is in northern Uganda.[25]

The Acholi practice of communion with and even possession by spirits cuts across the modern strict demarcations of time and space that separate God acting here and now from God acting in a different place and time. Spirits—called *jogi*—of the dead continue to interact with the people who remain on earth. The dead are buried in family compounds where they can continue to dwell where they always have. Families keep ancestral shrines, called *abila*, where interaction with spirits is intensified. When a person dies from unnatural means or is not given a proper burial, he returns as *cen*, a vengeful spirit. The *ajwaka* or spirit medium regularly confers with her *jogi*—often the spirits of people long dead or even not yet born and geographically distant from the medium. When necessary, the *jogi* speak and act quite literally in and through her. Similar practices run throughout much of sub-Saharan Africa.[26]

The Acholi practice that bears most directly on joining justice for the wronged and forgiveness for wrongdoers is that of *mato oput*, which is a traditional cultural practice of reconciliation, typically called upon when there has been a murder. The clan of the killer pays remuneration to the clan of the victim, usually an agreed upon number of livestock (thus the justice aspect to the practice). A lamb is slaughtered and there is a feast. At the center of the process is the ritual—no less literal for being so—of drinking the mashed and liquefied root of the *oput* tree, which tastes very bitter. *Mato oput* translates, "drinking of the bitter root." The killer and a clan member representing—that is, re-enacting the spirit of—the victim kneel facing each other with their hands behind their backs and drink simultaneously from an *oput*-filled calabash.[27] They literally and figuratively swallow the bitterness.

All Acholi gather, the dead, the living, and the not-yet-born, in a justice that forgives and a forgiveness that is just.

Post-conflict Uganda has seen a revival of *mato oput*, along with an expansion of the applicability of the practice to include the possibility of reconciliation with people who have committed crimes—rape, incest, and cannibalism—previously considered unforgivable. Perpetrators of such crimes are traditionally called *obibi*, literally "ogres," to connote their nonhuman status, which would exclude many LRA from participation in *mato oput* because they have abducted and used girls as sex slaves and commanded abductees to eat human flesh. However, advocates of *mato oput* stress the need, in this situation, to extend the ritual to people previously considered *obibi*. With God's grace, extended partici-pant observation in such a culture with, as anthropologist and social theorist Pierre Bourdieu puts it, a "total availability" to the culture and "submission" to its "particular life history," can initiate a process of reenchantment.[28]

The role of traditional African culture in Christian reenchant-ment may seem scandalous to some, but the reality on the ground is more mixed. One of the reasons that the pre-Vatican II Catholicism of the Comboni missionaries became widespread and continues to flourish through such devotions as Eucharistic adoration and prayers to the saints is that both this Catholicism and the Acholi tradition affirm in their practice communion with the spirits. For many people in the region, affirmation of the traditional Acholi spirits dovetails seamlessly with lively interaction with the com-munion of saints. One of the *ajwagi* I interviewed received one of her most important *jogi* through a dream in which the *jok* took her to Bethlehem.[29] Even where Christian Acholi continue to consider practices of the *ajwaka* to be heathen, they do so as direct, almost mirror image competitors with the traditional healer.

On the last full day of my first extended stay in Lokung In-ternally Displaced Persons camp, the Christian community there put on a series of morality plays for me. This, they seemed to be saying, is who we are and how we want you to remember us. The plays were about how someone acting authentically in the name of Jesus Christ in the Holy Spirit can heal sicknesses and cast out demons better than the *ajwaka*. Evident here is a crucial way in which common interaction with spirits in the Acholi tradition has changed Catholic Christian practice. It is no longer the case that re-enacting Jesus the Nazarene the Christ is limited to the priest or bishop. The result has been an explosion of Charismatic Catholicism, not only in northern Uganda, but throughout sub-Saharan Africa. I suggest that what we see here, despite the violence and the consequent desire for revenge that is also present among the Acholi, a desire enabled through spirit engagement in curses, is a bridge culture that provides us with more than mere glimpses of the witness of Jesus Christ.

Magical Catholicism

As the syncretistic blends of traditional Acholi culture and Catholicism suggest, there are also bridges to Jesus the Nazarene the Christ through certain strands of Catholicism, and the effort to reenchant the world would do well to turn to them. I call these strands "magical Catholicism" not to discount their practices, but to affirm and appropriate them by taking the term "magical" out of the hands of those who would use it pejoratively. Some translators prefer to render *Entzauberung*, usually translated as "disenchantment," as "demagnification," because Weber identified modern religion as not just a move toward rationalization, but also a move away from what he considered magic.

Cosmologically (for Weber), while religion worships the one (true) God, magic appeals to lesser spirits, attempting to manipulate them for human benefit. Ethically, religion is systematically ascetic while magic is lax: it lets the believer off the hook by substituting incantation and ritual for moral reform. Sacramentality, for Weber, is the enemy of ethics. Weber claims that magic is a neutral term, but it is clear both in his writing and in common parlance that it functions pejoratively: those who practice magic are *not us*. In keeping with the tradition of those left on the outside, and appropriating the pejorative terms being applied to them, I wish to advocate a retrieval of magical Catholicism. What are the prospects?

Historically, there is precedent for reenchantment. While Weber and those who follow in his tradition understand Catholic syncretism as a "concession"—their word—to paganism,[30] I interpret it as the one thing that has kept Christianity true to the cultural historical Jesus. Weber writes that in the effort to win and hold converts, priests had "to compromise with the traditional views of the laity in formulating patterns of doctrine and behavior." Such compromise meant that priests were unable to release "the faith of the masses from its bondage to traditions based upon magic."[31] Yet if the gospels are even roughly accurate depictions of who Jesus was, then it is precisely through such miracles, and particularly the physical healings, that Jesus the Nazarene leveraged his authority, especially early on in his ministry. The building of shrines, prayers to intercessory agents, and the use of relics are all practices that Weberians identify with bondage. I interpret the practices to be part of a theological cosmology that breaks down the boundaries between the here and the there, the present and the future, ourselves and God's Spirit, a cosmology that facilitates our reenactment of Jesus Christ.

Given the affinities between bridge cultures and magical Catholicism, it serves us well to look to bridge cultures in our appropriation of such Catholicism. This would lead us to a truly post-Weberian Christianity. Weber counterposed ethics with magic. This opposition is a false one, however, and it is indebted to Weber's identification of ethics with a particular understanding of strict ascesis. Jesus the Nazarene was not an ascetic in the manner of John the Baptist. He was accused by his critics, and probably not all that inaccurately, of being at least a sometime winer and diner. His disciplines of itinerancy with specific rules about what to take on the road were, like his suffering and death on the cross, not ends in themselves, but practices in service to his mission. Yet that mission is deeply ethically oriented: solidarity with the poor, and forgiveness of the wicked. The opposition between ethics and magic ("sacramentality" is a less loaded term than magic) is a false one. This is abundantly evident in the witness of Archbishop John Baptist Odama of Gulu.

Exemplar Christianity:
An Invitation to Imitation Rather Than a Conclusion

The Weberian scholar Lutz Kaelber indicates that during the late medieval period adoration of the Eucharist began to take precedence over the use of relics as a source of "supernatural power."[32] Eucharistic adoration, and the cosmology it presupposes, is at the center not only of Archbishop Odama's devotional life but also his political life. Head of the Gulu Archdiocese since 1999, he is from an ethnic group that borders Acholiland and shares many of its cosmological presuppositions. A "thick description" culled from my interview with him offers a window to the witness I encountered in his bridge culture.

Archbishop Odama has offended everyone: the LRA rebels have threatened to kill him, and the Ugandan government has labeled him a collaborator with the rebels. His outward appearance gives no indication as to why this is. His outer clothes are the only ones I've ever seen him wear: a white episcopal cassock with red piping and buttons, with a two-inch silver cross hanging down by his abdomen. Short, bald, and very dark-skinned, he chuckle-giggles often. His voice and comportment are light, with an absence of sudden gesture. Nothing betrays the things he has seen or endured except the fact that many priests and the bishop before him could not stand the weight of war and had to leave.

After having known Archbishop Odama for five years, I decided to interview him formally, because the interviews by journalists inquire about his political role but not his devotional life, in which he participates in Eucharistic adoration for twelve hours every Thursday. He told me,

> Especially when I'm before the Blessed Sacrament, words of the Bible come spontaneously. Yeah, they come spontaneously. "Be not afraid. I am with you." Then, "Abide in me as I abide in you." These words come when I'm there before the Blessed Sacrament. They come in and they kind of reinforce, yes, they reinforce, my faith and also my commitment and outlook on the real life. I've ever been hopeful, always, even in the most desperate situations, I tell people, "Don't lose hope. Don't lose hope. Let us keep going. The Lord is there."

It is 2005. Attacks by the LRA and forced displacement of the Acholi on the part of the government have created a situation where over 90 percent of the population in northern Uganda, almost 1.8 million people, live in squalid camps for Internally Displaced Persons. Villagers who resist official displacement are, by policy, treated as rebels and attacked by government soldiers.

Raids on the remaining villages by the LRA have prompted a practice called "night commuting," whereby rural youth walk to the relative safety of the market centers, particularly the town of Gulu, to sleep for the night. In Gulu, many night commuters sleep on the tin-visored porches surrounding the bus park. In June 2003, Archbishop Odama and other members of the Acholi Religious Leaders Peace Initiative slept four nights in the bus park. Unlike in Meier's account of Jesus, the Archbishop makes no argument that because there are so many poor he has no special mission to them.

When he was asked, "Archbishop, are you ready, really, to go and sleep in the street there with the children?" he said, "We go." Archbishop Odama told me that this reply "really came just spontaneously and with very strong force," which he attributed to his devotional practice: "So, this visit to the Eucharist, for me, it gave me a lot of courage and a lot of determination. So, going there to sleep on the street was something very . . . for me, it was just a very simple thing." When the children saw him lie down, "like them," he said, "that thing, I saw it struck them. . . . But, later, they began to be, they began to *see*, because we went there four times, you know. They began to see it was something of our concern for them. And, they began to call us, you know, colleagues."

As the children "felt close to us," Archbishop Odama realized, too, that the religious leaders "felt very close to them," and he again pointed out that he "felt also the Adoration helped me to see more. . . . You see, as I told you, I was beginning to feel now, more and more, in a relation with people, with any group. Compassion and sympathy for the people's conditions began to grow more and more in me. . . . And even to the extent that I didn't bother about my security." His identification with "any group," which was the part of the "many fruits" of his devotional life, included, moreover, "even the ones growing in the bush. . . ."

The Archbishop's phrase, "the ones growing in the bush," refers to the top LRA rebel commanders in the bush country, with whom he has been involved in multiple negotiations. These are not your ordinary sinners, as evident in a testimony I received from a woman who lived in the Atiak IDP camp:

> The rebels came, picked my child and me up from the house, and walked us outside the trading center with many people—

women, men, old people, students, and young people who did not go to school. The rebels walked all of us across a river. There, at some point, we were made to sit down. At that point they started telling us, "If you know you are pregnant, if you know you have a baby, if you are below twelve years of age, go this way; and the rest of the people go the other way." I saw at one side a group of young people, mainly technical-school students and women without babies. The rebels ordered them to lie down on their stomach. They then called the young rebels and they told them to shoot them. I heard shots. All these people were killed. A few other people that were seen alive were chopped to death with a machete. Having killed all these young people and the women who were with them, they turned to us. "Do you see this lesson? Go tell your people this is what will happen to them." When they finished their job, they asked us to clap our hands in thankfulness to them. They asked us to laugh at what they had done. We laughed. We followed all of the instructions they gave us for fear they would kill us also.

The "ones growing in the bush" are, as Sobrino would say, "sinners par excellence." Yet, unlike Sobrino, Odama witnesses to these ones "in the bush," as well as to those whom they victimize. To use Sobrino's phrase, the ones in the bush also need to be "taken down from the cross."

The Archbishop then commented on the importance of a passage from Ezekiel: "I take no pleasure in the death of the wicked, but, rather, in the conversion of the wicked" (33:11). In a talk to some seminarians he said,

Look, to be honest, Jesus could have asked his father to send the angels, to wipe [out] all those who killed him, I mean, who fixed him on the Cross. But, now, you hear what he says. He says fundamental points. One, he says, "You, God, you are our common father. My father, and the father to these others." Two, he says, "Forgive them. Don't do the wrong they did to me back to them. No, no, no, no. Forgive them." He added, "Because they don't know what they are doing."

Archbishop Odama noted that he's "said this even about those of Kony," the rebel leader. When Odama meets with Kony and the other rebel commander, Kony "very often he recognizes my presence immediately." It is as if Kony asks, "Can you do something to change my condition?" The Archbishop remarked, "This is a kind of feeling I draw from him, and also from the others." Odama continues, "God's love is beyond the sin. His love cannot be prevented by sin, no. He loves the sinner as he or she is. What he desires for the sinner is: 'I love you so much, can you respond to me? Can you respond?'"

Conclusion

In sum, then, for Archbishop Odama, whose traditional African upbringing involving the engagement with spirits melds well with his Catholicism, to follow Christ is to have missions both to the poor in the bus park and to the wicked in the bush. Attention to the cultural contexts of both Jesus of Nazareth and northern Uganda provides ample evidence that such a twin mission does not involve a contradiction, but rather is the very heart of the gospel.

Notes

[1] John P. Meier, "The Bible as a Source for Theology," in The Catholic Theological Society of America, *Proceedings of the Forty-Third Annual Convention* 43 (Louisville/Chicago: The Catholic Theological Society of America, 1988), 1-14.

[2] John J. Pilch, *Flights of the Soul: Visions, Heavenly Journeys, and Peak Experiences in the Biblical World* (Grand Rapids: William B. Eerdmans Publishing Company, 2011), 134.

[3] Karl Mannheim, *Man and Society in an Age of Reconstruction* (London: Routledge, Kegan & Paul, 1948), 52.

[4] On this point, see Lutz Kaelber, *Schools of Asceticism: Ideology and Organization in Medieval Religious Communities* (University Park: The Pennsylvania State University Press, 1998), 14.

[5] Max Weber, *The Protestant Ethic and the Spirit of Capitalism* (New York/London: Penguin Classics, 2002), 78, n. 11.

[6] See, for instance, Eviatar Zerubavel, "The Benedictine Ethic and the Modern Spirit of Scheduling: On Schedules and Social Organization," *Sociological Inquiry* 50 (1980): 157-69; Lewis Mumford, *The Myth of the Machine* (New York: Harcourt Brace Jovanovich, 1967); and Randall Collins, *Weberian Sociological Theory* (Cambridge: Cambridge University Press, 1986).

[7]Max Weber, *From Max Weber: Essays in Sociology*, ed. H. H. Gerth and C. Wright Mills (Oxford: Oxford University Press), 139, 350.

[8]H. Richard Niebuhr, *Radical Monotheism and Western Culture* (Louisville: Westminster John Knox Press, 1993); and James M. Gustafson, "The Sectarian Temptation: Reflections on Theology, the Church, and the University," *Proceedings of the Fortieth Annual Convention: The Catholic Theological Society of America* 40 (1985): 93.

[9]Jon Sobrino, *The Principle of Mercy: Taking the Crucified People from the Cross* (Maryknoll, NY: Orbis Books, 1994), esp. 87-90.

[10]Sinners here are those who "intentionally rejected the commandments of the God of Israel." They are "Jews who, for all practical purposes, had thumbed their noses at the covenant and the commandments of God" (John P. Meier, *A Marginal Jew: Rethinking the Historical Jesus*, vol. II: *Mentor, Message, and Miracles* (New York and London: Doubleday, 1994), 149.

[11]See, for instance, Meier, *A Marginal* Jew, vol. II, 127, 134, 154, 169, 176, 202 n. 102, 400, 401, 436, 1042, 1043; vol. IV, 481.

[12]Ibid., 1042 and 1048, n. 2. See also vol. III, 246 and 620. Meier's repetition of this argument indicates that it is not simply an anomaly occurring in one passage.

[13]Richard A. Horsley, *Jesus in Context: Power, People, and Performance* (Minneapolis: Fortress Press, 2008), 128. See also 3, 11, 225, and 227.

[14]Ibid., 222, citing James C. Scott, "Protest and Profanation: Agrarian Revolt and the Little Tradition," *Theory and Society* 4 (1977): 220; Richard A. Horsley, *Jesus and the Spiral of Violence: Popular Jewish Resistance in Roman Palestine* (San Francisco: Harper and Row, 1987), 186-87; and Horsley, *Jesus in Context*, 158-60.

[15]Horsley, *Jesus and the Spiral of Violence*, 213-18.

[16]Sanders returns repeatedly to the point that Jesus was in fact not a moral or social reformer – there is no special social mission to the poor – and Meier follows him on this point. See, for instance, E. P. Sanders, *The Figure of the Historical Jesus* (London/New York: Penguin Books, 1993), 178-80, 183, 188, 230, 236, 255, 257, and 260-61. Meier explicitly cites Sanders over against Richard Horsley. See Meier, *A Marginal Jew*, II, 644-45, nn. 37 and 38. Where they diverge is in Sander's insistence that Jesus offers mercy – love and forgiveness – to sinners *without the need of their repentance*. Rather, Meier writes, "It may be that Jesus reformulated repentance in terms of accepting his message and himself" (Meier, *A Marginal Jew*, II, 485, n. 152, and 212, n. 154).

[17]E. P. Sanders, *The Figure of the Historical Jesus*, 178 and 170-71.

[18]To say that Jesus had particular missions to the poor and the wicked is not to say that he would not make the offer to join him if the wealthy approached him. The exchange with the "rich young man" is a case in point. My point is that (1) Jesus had a theologically driven specific and special mission to the marginalized, both poor and wicked; and (2) Jesus recognized from a practical standpoint that those who are not so marginalized tend to turn away from (in the case of the rich young man) or even attack the message (and messenger) when they hear it.

[19]See http://www.contextgroup.org.

[20]Bruce J. Malina, *The New Testament World: Insights from Cultural Anthropology*, 3rd ed. (Louisville: Westminster/John Knox Press, 2001), 24.

[21]John J. Pilch, "Altered States of Consciousness in the Synoptics," in Wolfgang Stegemann, Bruce J. Malina, and Gerd Theissen, *The Social Setting of Jesus and the Gospels* (Minneapolis: Fortress, 2002), 103, 112, and 105.

[22]Ibid., 110; see also 112. Interestingly, Meier insists on the reality of Jesus' miracles and thus the crossing of transcendent/immanent boundaries, but the modern understanding of discrete time and space that he inherits from the presuppositions of historical critical method, does not allow him to affirm in any forceful way a mission to both the poor and the wicked.

[23]Paul Stoller, *Fusion of the Worlds: An Ethnography of Possession among the Songhay of Niger* (Chicago and London: The University of Chicago Press, 1989).

[24]I am aware of the practice of living among the poor for liberation theologians. By and large, however, their mode of representation of the poor is highly abstract. A notable work among the exceptions is Ernesto Cardenal, *The Gospel in Solentiname*, 4 vols. (Maryknoll, NY: Orbis Books, 2010).

[25]It is important to be clear here about what I am *not* claiming. First, I am not claiming that the Acholi people are somehow inherently better people than people of other cultures. This claim would involve a romanticization of the Acholi that does not meet the empirical evidence (Acholi are, after all, leaders in the LRA) and would amount to simply being the inverse of the essentialism found in other parts of Uganda that views the Acholi as naturally ignorant and brutish. Second, I am not claiming that cultures are pneumatically sealed wholes. Again, such a presupposition is not only empirically unsustainable – cultures are always, to greater or lesser degrees, hybrid – but also would make our re-enactment of Jesus the Nazarene the Christ impossible.

[26]For instance, Peter Geschiere, *The Modernity of Witchcraft: Politics and the Occult in Post-Colonial Africa* (Charlottesville and London: The University Press of Virginia, 1997), and Bettina E. Schmidt and Lucy Huskinson, eds., *Spirit Possession and Trance: New Interdisciplinary Perspectives* (London and New York: Continuum, 2010).

[27]For an excellent treatment of *mato oput*, see Thomas Harlacher, et al., *Traditional Ways of Coping in Acholi: Cultural Provisions for Reconciliation and Healing from War* (Kampala: Caritas Gulu Archdiocese, 2006), 74-90.

[28]Pierre Bourdieu, et al., *The Weight of the World: Social Suffering in Contemporary Society* (Stanford: Stanford University Press, 1999), 609.

[29]Three of the four *ajwagi* I interviewed in depth are Roman Catholic. (This fits regional demographics. Almost all northern Ugandans are at least nominally Christian; almost three-quarters are Roman Catholic; most that I have met practice some degree of syncretism.)

[30]Kaelber, *Schools of Asceticism*, 105.

[31]Quoted in ibid.

[32]Ibid., 110.

Transformative Contemplation

Teaching Prayer in the Shadow of the "Violent Sacred"

William A. Clark

An Encounter with Sacred Violence

On May 1, 2011, while most of their professors were at home preparing for bed or already asleep, students at the small Catholic college where I teach participated in a dramatic demonstration of what must be called "sacred violence." That night, Al Qaida leader Osama bin Laden, for ten years the embodiment of "The Enemy" in the War on Terror, had been killed by U.S. commandos in Pakistan. Many students had just heard President Barack Obama declare to the nation: "We will be relentless in defense of our citizens and our friends and allies. We will be true to the values that make us who we are. And on nights like this one, we can say to those families who have lost loved ones to al Qaeda's terror: Justice has been done."[1]

As word of the event spread, two groups gathered on a broad brick plaza to offer their reactions to the campus community. The location, a quadrangle surrounded on three sides by ivy-covered academic buildings—the newest of which was dedicated only days after September 11, 2001—is called Memorial Plaza and it is graced by two plaques invoking the memory and providing the short roll of alumni/ae killed in the 9/11 attacks. The first group of students to arrive there on May 1 stood in silence with signs that read "Is This Justice?" Their quiet vigil was soon interrupted by the arrival of another group spilling over from the nearby library, where a spontaneous and raucous celebration of bin Laden's death had erupted earlier. Many of the celebrants carried, or wore, American flags and—accompanied by at least one bullhorn and a number of emergent cheerleaders—laughed, cheered, pumped their fists, recited the Pledge of Allegiance, and chanted, "Hey, hey, hey, goodbye!"

Before long, their unfavorable notice of the peace protestors took on belligerent tones, and they voiced objections about what they perceived as the peace protestors' disrespect for the victims of terror who are honored by the plaza on which the demonstrators were assembled. As reported by students at a later campus forum, the protestors were barraged with a string of vulgar epithets, among which "Faggots!" and "Communists!" were two of the more publishable. Eventually, at least some of the "Is This Justice?" signs were wrested away from their creators and torn to shreds.

At the beginning of my class session for Religious Studies 219, "Christian Prayer in Theory and Practice," three days later, I began my usual brief demonstration of some particular Christian prayer style by reading from the Sermon on the Mount and praying *ad libitum* ("free style," without a script) for the nation, for ourselves in the midst of a very emotional time, for the healing of all those whose deep hurt had inspired vengeful hatred, and for the soul of Osama bin Laden. I varied my ordinary practice by offering no time for reactions, and continued on with the planned class on the contributions of non-European cultures to the Christian prayer tradition. I knew the students' reactions would come, after a bit of time for gathering their thoughts, via the course's online discussion forum.

And come they did, in comments running the full gamut from indignant patriotism, through confusion and doubt, to awe at newly discovered depths of Christian faith; from the bluntest prose to soaring poetry. Analysis of the comments could easily fill the remainder of this brief article, and probably an entire book on the uneasy relationship between students' patriotism and their faith. Let me share a small sample:[2]

> "I believe what those Navy SEALS did was the right thing to do and I am honored to live in a country that is served by such brave men and women."
>
> "I mean this with the utmost respect for everything holy—

but Osama Bin Laden deserves to rest in hell for all eternity."

"[The] 'prayer' today was an eye opening experience for me. . . . I felt like I was being ridiculed."

"I do not believe that I am less of a Catholic based on the fact that I have not prayed for Osama, but I do believe that I am more of a human."

And then, just when I might have begun to despair of my action having any of its intended effect:

"I suppose today I've learned how faith can be both comforting and challenging."

"Part of the process is learning to know when God is telling us 'no' to something that we *so* strongly, and often *so* sincerely want. We have to learn to bow our will and accept that perhaps the one who created us knows better the tune and melody our life should sing."

"[Here] is a really shocking statement. Jesus loved Osama and continues to love him wherever he is."

"In order to remain committed to Christ, I must realize that ultimately I must view this event as an opportunity to promote peace and love as the solution to end the cycle of violence that only begets more violence in the world and leads us all further away from God's will for us."

Recognizing Sacred Violence: The Theory of René Girard

The discomfort and amazement of these students arose from their being forced, as one of them put it, to choose "between my country and my faith." That is to say, both patriotism and religion were making claims to the same ground, so that if the claims proved incompatible one or the other might have to yield. The students, then, were being forced to recognize their own participation in a national phenomenon: the violent death of one particular individual, Osama bin Laden, which, although occurring under rather obscure circumstances and on the other side of the globe, had been almost instantly interpreted as an event not only beneficial but in a certain way *sacred*. "For God and country," began the message that announced bin Laden's death,[3] and one reveler at New York's Ground Zero summed up his reaction with "just one word"—"Redemption!"[4]

"Healing" and "hope" were other words used again and again in response to the news[5]—the language of spirituality and ultimate meaning being applied freely and unselfconsciously to connect a single death, resulting from a military and policy decision, with the honor and remembrance due the 9/11 dead, with the bonds of family and friendship, with love of country, and even with trust in the divine. It was bound, then, to be jarring at best for some of my students to encounter evidence that the Christian tradition—still the primary cultural arbiter of the sacred in the understanding of nearly all of them—might not necessarily and unambiguously endorse such interpretations.

None of this, however, could have been much of a surprise for those acquainted with the work of French social theorist René Girard or of his avid student, British theologian James Alison. Now a defining presence in the study of the relationship between religion and violence, Girard's theory arises from his initial work in literary analysis and is, as one interpreter, Michael Kirwan, has described it, "tripartite" (both logically and, as it turns out, more or less chronologically in terms of Girard's writing career).[6] It deals in turn with themes that could be abbreviated as "mimetic desire," "the scapegoat mechanism," and "redemption through revelation."

In the first theme, Girard demonstrates that human desire (and so also subsequent values and ethical judgments based on that desire) is *mimetic*. That is to say, we learn what to consider good and desirable by observing and imitating others. Unlike instinctual *appetites*, more or less dictated by biology, *desire* is seen by Girard as a specifically human, social reality for which the notion of an "autonomous self" is insufficient to account.[7] Its imitative character means that with great frequency the very models from whom we learn desire (whether its object is a commodity, a person, a status, or something more subtle) will quickly become our rivals for fulfilling that desire. The resulting conflict can be seen in perhaps its simplest form in the familiar vignette of two children fighting over the same toy in a room filled with other playthings.[8] Girard's work, however, explores striking patterns of adult desire, rivalry, and conflict, through literature, psychology, anthropology, and the whole range of human studies.[9]

Girard ultimately comes to the conclusion that virtually all of human cultural production is in some manner shaped by the forces of mimetic rivalry, and our attempts to avoid its potentially disastrous consequences.[10] In particular, his second theme presents the notion that human societies create internal scapegoats—usually marginal persons or groups who are used as symbols for all social ills and are treated accordingly. External enemies, real or imagined, fulfill a similar purpose. By making use of the mimetic impulse itself to focus a society's own violence on a common victim, this mechanism functions to relieve the internal tensions associated with mimetic rivalry.[11]

So long as its underlying meaning is kept hidden from view, the attention given to the choice and destruction (either symbolic or actual) of the victim replaces fractious rivalry with a social cohesion that had been entirely elusive before. The transformation is so remarkable that the victims themselves inspire a kind of awe and take on a certain sacred quality.[12] Girard's cultural critique now brings him to the realization that constant mundane examples of this behavior are summarized and embodied ritually in the sacrificial cults of religions throughout history and around the world, which come to be understood as vital to the identity and the very survival of the society. Thus Girard can declare, "Violence is the heart and secret soul of the sacred."[13]

This startling conclusion leads by way of a surprising paradox to the third and perhaps most controversial theme of Girard. In contrast to other cults, says Girard, Christian revelation and the sacrificial language it contains represent a distinct departure from these violent social mechanisms and a potentially transformative moment in human history. Girard finds that while the kind of sacred story to which he reserves the term *myth* strives to hide the truth of the scapegoat mechanism and to uphold the righteousness of the victimizers, what he refers to as the *gospel* perspective does the reverse.[14] Taken as a whole, across both the Hebrew Bible and the New Testament (but particularly in the prophetic tradition within which the teaching of Jesus stands), the biblical approach *unmasks* sacred violence, condemns it as hypocrisy, and takes the part of the victim rather than the dominant group. As Kirwan puts it, "Biblical history is the history of one true, loving God urging us to cast aside false idols and to live in the truth—and the most important of the untruths which must be rejected is the false transcendence which issues from our conflictive desires and our negotiation of them through sacred violence."[15] Understood in this way, the story of the sacrificial death of Jesus, who otherwise might seem the very paradigm of the "sacred victim," can be seen as the undoing of the violent sacred.

Teaching Prayer in the Shadow of the Violent Sacred

Much can and has been said by way of complicating and critiquing the Girardian approach. To many, it has seemed unduly pessimistic, and its appreciation of the biblical tradition suspect in the historical shadow of so much "Christian" violence.[16] It is not my purpose here to give a full exposition and defense of the theory. However, considering Girard's ideas in the context of my recent teaching experiences, it is impossible to ignore the very helpful light his thinking and its theological implications cast upon the tensions and challenges inherent in teaching the Christian prayer tradition with integrity. The tensions arise in ways both overt and hidden, and they deal not only with international politics and great historical events, but also with the subtleties of pedagogical motivation and the banal workings of institutional bureaucracy.

I taught my first iteration of "Christian Prayer in Theory and Practice" as the war in Iraq—which not infrequently nor coincidentally invited the use of both the terms "crusade" and "jihad"—was being prepared and launched. Although in these circumstances the surrounding presence of the violent sacred seemed to grow stronger with each passing year, its effect on the course itself has never been as clearly visible as it was at the beginning of May 2011. Returning for a moment to those events, it is easy to recognize that the Girardian themes and their corollaries were all on display: the scapegoat mechanism itself (as one student put it, "Since I was nine, bin Laden has been the boogeyman, and now he's dead"); the vindication of righteous anger (which James Alison describes as, "The need . . . for there to be bad guys by battling with whom I become good"[17]); the greater meaning and purpose given to very personal tragedies and wounds (in light of which some students sensed "disrespect" toward them in my prayer for their enemy); the social unanimity expected in the wake of the sacrifice of a sacred victim (and the outrage when unanimity is denied); even, for some, the realization that Christ's life and teaching and the manner of his death break the cycle and invite us to see the world in a profoundly different way.

Clearly, there was already a deep connection between the students' orientation toward the place and significance of Christian prayer, and their understanding of the world around them (and its violence). It was unavoidably necessary to account for this mutual influence within the course itself, never more so than at that crucial moment following the death of bin Laden. As I stood before the class with my Bible open to Matthew 5, feeling a bit the way I had as a child just before diving into a deep swimming pool for the first time, I could see that I could approach this accounting in one of three ways. I could accept the sacred reinterpretation of violence and use the Christian prayer tradition to reinforce it. I could remain silent about what we all knew had just happened in the world, thus tacitly accepting the prevailing interpretation while also allowing Christian prayer to appear aloof from, perhaps even irrelevant to, some of the most charged moments of my students' lives. Finally, instead of either of those choices, I could run the risks of polarization, reject the sacralizing of violence, and provide a forceful reminder that Christian prayer, whatever else it might be, is at least an *invitation* to radical transformation. My choice of this third option was not at all a foregone conclusion, but having actually taken it I now see nothing so clearly as the incompatibility of the other two choices with my deepest desires for my students.

Transformative Contemplation

James Alison, whose distinctive position as a gay man and former Dominican priest lends a deep poignancy to his theology, dwells lovingly on the profound difference between the violence of the world and the invitation of Christ. He describes that invitation as "being called into being."[18] In keeping with Girard's mimetic theory, he takes it as a universal phenomenon that human beings learn their desires by imitating others, and believes that so it is with Christians who, as he puts it, "learn to desire according to the eyes" of Christ.[19]

Unlike any other model upon whom one might fix, however,

Jesus "although he was in the form of God, did not deem equality with God something to be grasped" (Phil 2:6). Unlike any other mimetic model, Jesus "*empties* himself" (2:8). In him, says Alison, we find "a human heart and eyes so utterly held by the Creator that they speak the Creator's heart about this world."[20] There is no righteous anger, no resentment here; rather, by becoming the willing victim of just such resentment, Jesus breaks the cycle of imitation, rivalry, and violence. To see the world with the eyes of Christ, says Alison, is to find oneself "being *in on* the centre of things without *being* the centre,"[21] that is, without having to fight one's way into and lay claim to what is most desired by a violent act of possession.

Paradoxically, Alison continues, this experience leads also to "a sense of being on the periphery,"[22] in that one may "relax into being loved"[23] and "discover one's being in being known by God."[24] This permission to lose the anxiety of endlessly striving to *please* God—by knowing and fulfilling (and inevitably resenting) all the "right formulas"—is what Alison refers to in the title of one of his books, *On Being Liked*. In this way, he builds on Girard's foundation by showing us what "faith beyond resentment" (another Alison book title) might actually look like in practice.

Alison's aspiration "to see as Christ sees"—to desire, indeed to love, as Christ loves—is surely a valid description of a basic goal in Christian prayer. The possibility of transformation that Alison attributes to it is, then, near the heart of the many things that a teacher of the prayer tradition could hope for students to encounter. The difficulty, of course, is that the teacher, the teacher's colleagues, and the institution within which the teaching takes place, are as fully enmeshed in the mimetic system as the students are.

In my own case, to whatever extent these ideas might have been vaguely in my mind at the time, my original inspiration for designing a course on prayer was ambiguous enough. I had discovered, by the end of my first year of teaching introductory theology to undergraduates, how foreign the idea (not to mention the experience) of a "relationship with Christ" was to many of my students—a perceived lack that seemed greatly to affect their understanding of the doctrine and practice of the church that I was trying to convey to them.

It was quite a while later that I began to reflect on the ambiguity of relying on this lacuna as a motivation for a course on prayer.

It seems to me now that this one notion actually provided several rather incompatible motivations. On the one hand, there was a simple pedagogical problem and a proposed solution: a concept was missing; I needed to supply it. Yet there was also a measure of fear of the future—of my own loss of familiarity, identity, and control, at the hands of a generation bereft of knowledge that I, obviously (as I thought at the time), possessed. On still another level dwelt the motivation that I now see as more worthy of Alison's insight: the desire to share "relationship with Christ" not as an attempt at indoctrination, but rather as a potential spiritual seedbed for the intellectual openness, courage, passion, and *compassion* that I value and seek both personally and as an integral aspect of the Catholic and Jesuit educational tradition.

The negation of these values could easily have developed into the major agent in my design of the course, had the "fear of the future" motive prevailed (which is, in the sense I have described it, a variety of the "us against them" thinking that Alison rejects). The need to stress religious identity *over against* others, which leads quickly to an emphasis on correctness of doctrine and practice at all costs, in my experience also brings a sense of distance, formality, and "foreignness" for many students—which would, of course, have been an ironic end to my concern for a "relationship with Christ." Further, if the course were then centered on a survey of the historical development of approaches to prayer, or on the orthodox doctrine expressed in various traditional prayer forms, or even on formation in a particular prayer practice and its expected results, the question "*Whose* history, *whose* orthodoxy, *whose* practice?" would remain. Fortunately, both my own "mixed motives" and the expectations of my colleagues allowed me to see the necessity of a far more contextual and practical approach, which has broadened further with each iteration of the course and has allowed my own experience and understanding of Christian prayer to grow along with that of my students.

The first lesson in context, however, came with negotiating the course's initial approval through the college's standard curriculum procedures. The school's own history and culture are, as Girard and Alison would expect of any such institution, fraught with many embattled identities, "sacred spaces," and associated scapegoats. Perhaps the first and most obvious is an ingrained and not entirely unjustified fear of the very sort of indoctrination that I might have been proposing, and the specter of ecclesiastical control and limitation of academic freedom that is often assumed to be waiting in the wings. For some of my colleagues, the danger is understood to be doctrine itself, and the challenge it seems to issue to a particular understanding of Reason (which, lest we forget, was also once given a sacred, quasi-divine status—in the shadow of the guillotine). The heritage of several decades of negotiation for shared power in the college—sometimes friendly, sometimes less so—between lay faculty and Jesuits has also left many carefully guarding their spheres of influence (despite the fact that the steady diminishment of the active Jesuit presence on campus has significantly altered the political situation over the years).

Unfortunately, the mere mention of "prayer" seemed enough to set off one or more of these alarm bells for some colleagues. At one point, after the appearance on the college website of a photo of my class in the midst of a few moments of centering meditation, I was asked what sort of "voodoo teaching" I was engaged in. Most other critical questions were more substantive and ultimately more helpful: the word "Christian" in the course title drew some skepticism; didn't I actually mean "Catholic," and wasn't that too exclusive? The practical component in the course was an obvious target; what was to prevent the whole project from becoming a catechetical, rather than an academic, exercise?

It seemed ironic to me that such reactions would occur in a milieu in which the growing commoditization of education is frequently lamented, its increasingly brutal time-and-task demands on students decried, and interest in "contemplative practice" often professed as a response. Undoubtedly, an understanding like Alison's—of Christ as an opening toward a call "into being," rather than into the confines of indoctrination—is still counterintuitive to many. Yet, although the reactions were not always sympathetic nor fully understanding of my aims for the course, in the end learning to take collegial caution seriously proved very helpful for setting the course on a path that has increasingly allowed it to reflect the true breadth of the Christian prayer tradition.

As is surely evident enough even in this brief description, it has not always proven easy to resist entering the fray with my own colors flying—not easy to choose instead the "looking away" from resentful competition, to which Alison insists we are invited by Christ himself.[25] If not for the presence of the Girardian critique, the temptation to use the course as an instrument of my own *ressentiment*[26] would probably be utterly irresistible, primarily because I would not even recognize it as a temptation. What could be wrong with acknowledging these colleagues as my opponents in the "culture wars," and exposing the weaknesses of their position as I defend Christian practice at a Catholic institution? How could one object if my most responsive students began to experience themselves as something of an embattled minority, struggling to keep an aspect of the truth from being completely overwhelmed by heedlessness of it? And would it not be simply jealousy if others found it problematic for me to grow into the role of a sort of "spiritual master" to such students? All that, of course, is the direct road not only to verifying the objections raised by my colleagues, but also to accepting a notion of Christian prayer that makes it dependent on an opposing force over which to triumph—dependent, that is to say, on implied (and even actual) sacred violence.

The students themselves, as we have seen amply demonstrated, are also accustomed to the "us-against-them" approach to life. Consequently, despite the energy that they typically bring to the course, some of their attitudes and actions in the classroom—even apart from dramatic moments such as the death of bin Laden—constitute yet another challenge to the critique of sacred violence. Students' approaches to themselves, to authority, to tradition, frequently display this embattled view of the world. They are dutifully and self-consciously "good" or gleefully "bad" in response to expectation; they defer to "whatever Father says" or they insist on their own inviolate opinion in the face of all argument; they stand defiantly with a fundamentalist chip on their shoulder, or they speak haltingly of faith while searching in desperation for some authoritative signal, or they turn away with studied indifference. The common need to label themselves and others as "right" or "wrong" requires definite answers and clear procedures, leaving many students deeply uncomfortable with ambiguity or multi-valence in the study of the Christian tradition, even as they are steeped in a "pluralist" worldview. Indeed, when they detect the presence of a standard by which to measure, it is possible for them to quickly achieve self-righteousness, and to become positively Corinthian in their enthusiasm for "amazing" or even "miraculous" spiritual experiences that assist them, subtly or otherwise, in establishing their own superiority.[27]

In all such ways, the students act out—in company, let me quickly add, with *all* their teachers—their very human resistance to both terms of some key Christian paradoxes: the self as *loved by* God, the self as *surrendered to* God; tradition as *challenged*, tradition as *embraced*; prayer as *discipline*, prayer as *gift*. The possibility in such impossible pairs—as well as their explanatory power—becomes evident and compelling only in an *experience* of Christian prayer that moves beyond "sacred meanings" held as a kind of exclusive *gnosis*, and beyond "religious identity" wielded as a defensive weapon. In such paradoxes can be found an expression of the transformative potential of Christian prayer, because in them mimetic acquisitiveness becomes openness to gift, embattled identity becomes dynamic engagement, and resentful subservience becomes radical love.

The pedagogical method that opens in the direction of this transformation is one that I must still say I "aspire" to perfect. For now, between fits of pseudo-sacred imposition, I move with my students from practice to theory, rather than the reverse—we participate, we reflect, we study. Our participation covers a broad range of practices, from the simple, contemplative "Jesus Prayer" to exuberant Pentecostal services. It includes some experiences that are outside of my own comfort zones, in the hope that students will observe some of my own ongoing struggle with growth in prayer (indeed, the prayer for bin Laden was one of these). In both spoken and written forms, we offer reflections on these experiences that are broad and open and allow amply for enthusiasm about what seems positive, but also for puzzlement, complaint, and examination even of what might seem "failed experiments" on the students' part or mine. It is then possible to require serious intellectual consideration, through analysis of texts, history, and criticism, of very diverse corners of the tradition, with their interconnections, oppositions, accomplishments, and failures, without seeming to elicit a particular set of "approved" insights and conclusions.

The method thus moves, in imitation of some of the very prayer forms it considers, from the *outside* to the *inside*. The inner stillness of Byzantine *hesychasm* (from the Greek for "silence"), for example, although prepared for by the repetition of the "Jesus Prayer" specifically as a means of self-emptying, is in itself a gift of the Holy Spirit who comes in his own time. The *Suscipe* ("Take and Receive") at the end of the *Spiritual Exercises* of St. Ignatius Loyola is indeed a prayer of self-offering, but it comes only in response to the recognition of the endlessly active love of God, unfolded throughout the whole four-week course of the *Exercises*. Even the far-from-silent Pentecostal and charismatic experience of glossolalia is invariably called "the *gift* of tongues" and is frequently described, with reference to Romans 8:26, as "the Spirit groaning within us."

The fundamental movement in all these forms of prayer is not from an internal choice toward an external action, but rather the reverse. In this way, the tradition itself recommends to the student of prayer a receptive and transformative stillness, which is the negation of sacred violence. "As we learn to desire through the eyes of another," writes Alison, "so we are given the heart of another, and what we learn is the extraordinarily benign, peaceful power of one holding everything in being, liking and delighting in us, without distinction."[28]

In many ways, it is a frightening approach for both students and teacher. At its most intense it does indeed eventually set aside, or at least radically relativize, the expected academic emphasis on a student's "grasp" of material, and substitute instead the opportunity for the student to "be grasped." Ultimately, in work for which the course itself can only begin to prepare, it goes even further, pressing toward another *outward* move: the transformation of our action in the world that would come with the setting aside of sacred violence. In prayer approached in this way, what was "other" does not remain perpetually external and alien, like the hated bin Laden consigned to "rest in hell forever." On the contrary, "it" comes to be seen through the eyes of the One who *possesses* us, and alters from the inside our way of seeing and our very way of being.

We may even find ourselves praying for the enemy.

Notes

[1]Barack Obama, "Remarks by the President on Osama bin Laden," The White House Blog, May 2, 2011, http://www.whitehouse.gov/blog/2011/05/02/osama-bin-laden-dead (accessed June 30, 2011).

[2]Student quotations presented here anonymously to preserve privacy are excerpted from signed contributions to "Christian Prayer Discussion Forum," RELS 219 "Moodle" course page, College of the Holy Cross, Worcester, Massachusetts.

[3]"How the US Tracked Couriers to Elaborate bin Laden Compound," MSNBC.com, http://www.msnbc.msn.com/id/42853221/ns/world_news-death_of_bin_laden/t/how-us-tracked-couriers-elaborate-bin-laden-compound/ (accessed September 8, 2011).

[4]"Huffington Post: The People at Ground Zero," Huffingtonpost.com, http://www.huffingtonpost.com/2011/05/02/osama-bin-laden-dead-ground-zero_n_856145.html (accessed September 8, 2011).

[5]For examples, see "Huffington Post: The People at Ground Zero," "Huffington Post at Ground Zero," and "Students React to Osama bin Laden's Death," Huffingtonpost.com http://www.huffingtonpost.com/2011/05/02/osama-bin-laden-dead-ground-zero_n_856145.html (accessed September 8, 2011).

[6]Michael Kirwan, *Girard and Theology* (London: T & T Clark, 2009), 21. See also Kirwan, *Discovering Girard* (London: Darton, Longman, and Todd, 2004), 5. For Girard's own summary, see René Girard, "Mimesis and Violence: Perspectives in Cultural Criticism," *Berkshire Review* 14 (1979): 9-19, appearing also as Chapter 1 in James G. Williams, ed., *The Girard Reader* (New York: Crossroad, 1996).

[7]See René Girard, *Violence and the Sacred* (Baltimore: Johns Hopkins, 1977), 146, and Kirwan, *Discovering Girard*, 15-23.

[8]Kirwan, *Discovering Girard*, 21. René Girard, *Things Hidden since the Foundation of the World* (Stanford: Stanford University Press, 1987), 9, uses a version of this scenario.

[9]René Girard, *Deceit, Desire, and the Novel: Self and Other in Literary Structure* (Baltimore: Johns Hopkins, 1965) uses literary analysis; Girard, *Violence and the Sacred*, makes use of ancient literature and contemporary psychology and sociology; Girard, *Things Hidden since the Foundation of the World* considers ethnology, biblical studies, theories of human sexuality, and other areas.

[10]Girard, *Things Hidden*, 27.

[11]Kirwan, *Discovering Girard*, 38-39.

[12]Girard, *Things Hidden*, 28.

[13]Quoted from Girard, *Violence and the Sacred*, in Kirwan, *Discovering Girard*, 39, 41.

[14]Kirwan, *Discovering Girard*, 68-69; this distinction is generically the same as another that Girard makes between "the romantic lie" and "novelistic truth."

[15]Ibid., 71.

[16]Kirwan, *Girard and Theology*, 132-42, summarizes major theological critiques of Girard.

[17]James Alison, *On Being Liked* (London: Darton, Longman, and Todd, 2003), 72-73.

[18]Ibid., xvi.

[19]Ibid., 13.

[20]Ibid., 14.

[21]Ibid., 72.

[22]Ibid., 73.

[23]Ibid., 76.

[24]Ibid.

[25]Ibid., 14.

[26]Used by both Girard and Alison, *ressentiment* refers to the bitter, unfulfilled desire for vengeance, turned toward self-hatred, which Friedrich Nietzsche insisted is the root of "Christian love." Girard calls it "the interiorization of weakened vengeance," and philosopher Max Scheler describes it as including "revenge, hatred, malice, envy, the impulse to detract, and spite" (see Kirwan, *Discovering Girard,* 34-37.)

[27]In 1 Corinthians 11-14, St. Paul dwells on the Corinthians' tendency to split into rival factions and to prefer extraordinary "charisms," such as speaking in tongues, to the far more demanding and fundamental gift of love.

[28]Alison, *On Being Liked,* 16.

Treating Nature Nonviolently

Developing Catholic Social Teaching on the Environment through Nonviolence[1]

J. Milburn Thompson

Both John Paul II and Benedict XVI have tried to link the environment and peace by focusing one of their annual World Day of Peace messages on the environment.[2] Neither of them, however, convincingly connects peace with the environment: they assert the connection more than demonstrate it. Furthermore, some in the peace movement have tended to see ecological concerns as peripheral.[3] Nonviolent activists often lead a simple lifestyle that happens to be environmentally friendly, but environmental activism can seem something of a distraction when people are oppressed and violence is raging. Peacemaking tends to focus attention on the human community and the community of nations.

I wish to develop a direct connection between peacemaking and the environment by raising and unpacking the metaphor "treating nature nonviolently." I apply a philosophy and practice of nonviolence to the way humans should treat the Earth. In the process of doing so, I hope to fruitfully transcend the environmental ethic articulated by Catholic social teaching. First, I will outline the church's contemporary environmental ethic, as expressed by Pope Benedict XVI. Second, I will suggest that the church's anthropocentric position might be even more helpful if it moved to a creatiocentric vision toward nature. Finally, I will explore "treating nature nonviolently" as a way to move toward a creation-centered vision, which recognizes the intrinsic, but not absolute, value of creation.

A Catholic Environmental Ethic

Pope Benedict XVI is being called "the Green Pope."[4] In two recent statements—his 2009 social encyclical, *Charity in Truth* (48-51), and his 2010 World Day of Peace Message, "If You Want to Cultivate Peace, Protect Creation"—he has developed a distinctively Catholic voice on the environment by expanding on the use of the principles of Catholic social teaching to articulate an environmental ethic for the contemporary church.[5] Its foundation is the belief that creation is a gift of God entrusted to humanity to care for and cultivate. According to Benedict: "Human beings legitimately exercise a *responsible stewardship over nature*, in order to protect it, to enjoy its fruits and to cultivate it in new ways, with the assistance of advanced technologies, so that it can worthily accommodate and feed the world's population" (*Charity in Truth*, 50). Humans, made in God's image, are to be co-creators with God and stewards of Earth and its resources. Thus the church's environmental ethic is clearly and consciously human-centered or anthropocentric.

In this way, Benedict steers a middle course between the extremes of an Earth-centered approach (biocentrism or ecocentrism espoused by deep ecologists and others) and the total human domination of the Earth that has characterized the Christian West.[6] "Nature cannot be seen as more important than the human person, nor is nature simply raw material to be exploited at humanity's whim. Rather nature is the wondrous work of the Creator, containing a 'grammar' that dictates its 'wise use, not its reckless exploitation' " (*Charity in Truth*, 48).

Benedict develops the church's environmental ethic by drawing on and expanding the principles that form the core of Catholic social teaching (CST). He places concern for the environment in the context of "integral human development," which is the general theme of his encyclical *Charity in Truth* and a consistent concern of CST. By expanding the principles of the option for the poor, the universal destiny of created goods, and the common good to future generations, Benedict extends the virtue of solidarity to the environment: "The environment must be seen as God's gift to all people, and the use we make of it entails a shared responsibility for all humanity, especially for the poor and future generations" ("If You Want to Cultivate Peace, Protect Creation," 2; *Charity in Truth*, 48).

Benedict also creatively links human ecology with environmental ecology, in effect extending the American church's concept of the consistent ethic of life to include a healthy environment (*Charity in Truth*, 51). He asserts that the same attitude that demeans human life also results in environmental degradation. Human dignity and the sacredness of human life cannot be safeguarded without protecting the environment. Thus the sanctity of life could be a link between peacemaking and protecting creation, but, again, Benedict assumes this connection, rather than demonstrates it.[7]

John Paul II advocated adding a "right to a safe environment" to an updated U.N. Charter of Human Rights ("The Ecological Crisis," 9). Benedict XVI also links environmental responsibility with human rights. Benedict catalogs the elements of the ecological crisis: climate change, desertification, deterioration of vast agricultural areas, pollution of rivers and aquifers, the loss of biodiversity, the increase of natural catastrophes, deforestation, the phenomenon of environmental refugees, and conflicts over natural resources. Then he points out that all of these issues have a "profound impact on the exercise of human rights, such as the right to life, food, health, and development" ("If You Want to Cultivate Peace, Protect Creation," 4).

Finally, the church calls both for a change in lifestyle (toward sobriety, solidarity, and sacrifice) and for structural change (such as an economy directed toward sufficiency, community, and the common good). Both personal conversion and social transformation are necessary to meet the needs of the poor and of future generations and to exercise a responsible stewardship toward the Earth. Greed, selfishness, and the exploitation of a consumerist mentality have resulted in environmental and economic crises and in human suffering and inequity. Simplicity, sacrifice, and justice are the ways forward.[8]

This environmental ethic of human stewardship for the natural world is theologically defensible and environmentally helpful. Genesis is clear that God created the world and remains in charge of it. "Everything that exists belongs to God, who has entrusted it to man, albeit not for his arbitrary use. . . . Man thus has a duty to exercise responsible stewardship over creation, to care for it and to cultivate it" ("If You Want to Cultivate Peace, Protect Creation," 6). The "dominion" given to human beings, who are created in the image of God, can be understood in terms of responsibility rather than authority. Humans are to care for and cultivate the Earth so that humanity can flourish. Pollution and the over-consumption of natural resources harm humans, and especially the poor. Both practices threaten the future of humankind. Wise environmental practices are in the enlightened self-interest of humanity. Benedict's stewardship ethic can justify and motivate important changes in human behavior and significant social transformations.

Toward a Creation-Centered Vision of Nature

The church has made great strides in its attitude toward nature. It has gone from an attitude of disregard and domination to an ethic of responsible stewardship and care for creation. Many commentators, however, think that the church needs to move from an anthropocentric approach to the environment to a creation-centered vision of nature.

An anthropocentric ethic does not *logically* give intrinsic value to the Earth or to other creatures. Nature has only the instrumental value of being used for and by humanity. What difference does this make? One of the issues Benedict lists as part of the environmental crisis is the loss of biodiversity—the depletion of species of plants, insects, and animals. Species become endangered or extinct when their habitats are altered or destroyed through, for example, human encroachment or global warming. Species naturally come and go, but human activity is accelerating the pace of extinctions at a rate thousands of times faster than the natural pace of evolution. This reduction of the genetic heritage of Earth may well be harming human interests (perhaps the cure for cancer has vanished in the Amazon forest), but it may also be true that humans can flourish without the polar bear or the spotted owl or the timber rattlesnake. Unless flora and fauna are seen as fellows and the web of life is valued in itself, humanity has little incentive to protect it.

Moreover, this anthropocentric view does not adequately account for the whole scientific or theological truth, and thus it may be incapable of effecting the change in the human-nature relationship required to respond to the ecological crisis. Scientifically, humans are not so much above nature as part of, derivative from, and dependent on it. The human species has become prolific and powerful, but humans were not present for most of the Earth's 4.6 billion years, and should humanity go the way of the dinosaurs, the Earth will continue on for some time. Humans are more dependent on the Earth than the Earth is on humans.[9] Human consciousness gives us a special role and responsibility in the web of life, but it is not only about us.

Theology reinforces this case for human humility and interdependence in regard to nature. Scripture is neither anthropocentric, nor ecocentic, but theocentric. Thus many theologians have moved toward a creation-centered view, what theologian John Hart calls a creatiocentric consciousness.[10] The focus on creation acknowledges that God created the universe, that all of creation is "very good," and that humans are in *relationship* with God, each other, and all of creation. Both anthropocentrism and ecocentrism place humanity and nature at odds with each other. A creation-centered approach gives the world a sacred quality that can be perceived by a sacramental vision, and it puts nature and humanity in relationship with each other. The companionship between humankind and the natural world implies an interdependence and mutuality, a respectful I-Thou relationship. Theologians have recovered the roots of this attitude in the Christian tradition—in the Noahic covenant in Genesis 9:10, the mystical visions of Augustine of Hippo and Hildegard of Bingen, and in the life of Francis of Assisi.[11] St. Francis realized the kinship that characterizes the web of life; thus, he treated all of creation—sun and wind, birds and wolves, lepers and popes—as companions, as a Thou, not an It. Francis provides a model for a creation-centered re-thinking of the human-nature relationship, and he also exercised an option for the poor and a call to peacemaking.[12]

A creatiocentric consciousness does not yield easy answers, but it does change the nature of the questions and of the conversation. It would be a more fruitful foundation for the church's environmental ethic. The next step, then, is to forge a link between peacemaking and protecting creation by considering the contribution that "treating nature nonviolently" might make to forming a creatiocentric consciousness.

Treating Nature Nonviolently and the Development of a Creatiocentric Consciousness

It is difficult to move from an anthropocentric to a creatiocentric view of nature. If we have been formed in an anthropocentric view, we do not habitually give intrinsic value to Earth and to fellow creatures. One way of moving toward making peace with Earth might be to "treat nature nonviolently." This is first of all a metaphor or image that can help instill in us a consciousness of the intrinsic value of all creation. Treating nature nonviolently also means applying the fundamental assumptions and the practices of a nonviolent theology to our relationship with nature. Of course, living nonviolently is also very challenging. Nonviolence is a spirituality, a way of life, a practice, and not merely a technique. It is at least compatible with Christian discipleship, if not required by it. I hope the thought experiment of applying a nonviolent spirituality to nature might help us understand the change and development that humankind needs to undergo in adopting a creatiocentric consciousness. There are, I think, three dimensions or aspects of the theology and practice of nonviolence that could be extended to include nature: fundamental values, principles that guide the practice of nonviolence, and elements in the formation of a nonviolent spirituality.

Foundational Values for Nonviolent Living

There are three basic values or fundamental assumptions that give a foundation to a theology of nonviolence:

1. Each and every person has dignity and value because we are created in the image and likeness of God. Thus we are to respect human dignity and love one another.

2. Persons are created to live in harmony and community with one another. Thus we are to treat one another with fairness and justice and build a healthy community.

3. God works in history on the side of human dignity and just community, which gives us hope in our struggle for just community.

Violence is counter to human dignity and just community. Conflict can be resolved reasonably, justly, and in a manner that strengthens relationships and community, that is, nonviolently. To extend this theology of nonviolence to nature would be:

- to affirm the intrinsic value of the natural world because it, too, is created by God,
- to recognize that humans are meant for relationship and community with Earth and our fellow creatures, and
- to understand that God calls humanity into a healthy relationship with nature.

As we are to treat one another nonviolently, we are to treat nature nonviolently.[13]

These fundamental values of a nonviolent perspective stand in contrast to a domination worldview. A domination worldview manifests itself in patriarchy that oppresses women,[14] white supremacy that discriminates against people of color,[15] a capitalism that exploits the poor and reduces humanity to consumers, and a technological imperative that bestows idolatrous power on science and technology.[16] A Franciscan, creatiocentric worldview that recognizes the intrinsic value of all humanity and of the Earth community is a fundamental alternative to the domination worldview.[17] A nonviolent spirituality that includes treating nature nonviolently is a way of accomplishing the conversion from a domination perspective to a creatiocentric consciousness.

This is a fundamental transformation. The embrace of a creatiocentric consciousness is theologically grounded in the doctrine of creation and in Christ's redemption of all creation (Rom 8:18-23).[18] The transformation of one's attitude, perspective, and practice, however, is complicated and difficult.

Five Principles for the Practice of Nonviolence

In his interpretation of Gandhian nonviolence Martin Luther King, Jr., outlined five principles for the practice of nonviolence.[19] These principles that focus on resolving conflict are more difficult to apply to our relationship with nature.

The first principle is that nonviolence is *active*, not passive;

it is a way of resisting wrong and working for good. Pacifism is not passive, it is about making peace. Nonviolence seeks to build community, to resist injustice, and to accomplish reconciliation. Just so we need to actively build a relationship with nature, and we need to resist the assaults on Earth that characterize our past and present. Greenpeace is an organization known for its dramatic and courageous nonviolent direct action on behalf of nature, such as disrupting whale hunts or painting "Quit Coal" on the smokestacks of one of the most polluting coal plants in the United States. People for the Ethical Treatment of Animals (PETA) also engages in direct action campaigns on behalf of animal rights. PETA's actions, however, sometimes border on violence. Acts of sabotage against laboratories that experiment on animals, for example, are morally problematic. Nonviolent direct actions will often be controversial, they will usually be consciousness-raising, and sometimes they will be effective in bringing about change.

Second, nonviolence is *reconciling*: it tries to restore relationship and create community. Nonviolence seeks to convert enemies into friends. Humanity certainly needs to befriend and reconcile with nature. As St. Francis so clearly understood, humans are kin to Earth and sun, wolf and bird. Family, friendship, and fellowship are good metaphors for describing and building this relationship with nature. Enmity with creation is as unnatural as it is with fellow humans. God made us for community with one another and with creation. This principle of reconciliation can give guidance to our approach to fellow humans who do not share a creatiocentric consciousness, who might deny that there is an ecological crisis, who might tenaciously hold to a domination approach to nature. Respect for persons and a genuine search for truth are keys to reconciliation.

Third, nonviolence believes that *means are end-creating*, in other words, means and ends are related like the seed to the tree. There is no way to peace; peace itself is the way. Thus *how* we restore our relationship with Earth is as important as any particular goal, such as stopping mountaintop removal or maintaining biodiversity. This principle may lead us toward natural solutions that work with ecology. Thus alternative energy sources, such as solar and wind power, are preferable to nuclear power.

The fourth principle is that *suffering love can be redemptive und reconciling*; suffering love is the power or force behind nonviolence. The nonviolent resister is willing to sacrifice by absorbing the violent response of the opponent in the belief that such suffering out of love for the other will redeem the relationship.[20] We seem to want to repair our relationship with nature without any change in the lifestyle that has caused the rupture. A nonviolent perspective, based on the spirit of love, would recognize the need to sacrifice in order to restore the damage we have inflicted on the Earth community. Such a sacrifice will not only begin to reverse the damage to nature and repair our relationship with nature, it will likely build a more healthy human community and a more meaningful human life. Perhaps our next vehicle should be a bicycle rather than an SUV.

Fifth, nonviolence not only refuses to harm, it refuses to hate. Nonviolence develops a *spirituality of love*. In his sermon "The Three Dimensions of a Complete Life," King preached about the length, breadth, and height of love, that is, love of self, love of each other, and love of God.[21] The environment, love of creation, should be added to this triangle, producing a circle of love. Agape—understanding, universal, redemptive good will—must be applied to the whole Earth community, to nature.

Four Elements in Forming a Spirituality of Nonviolence

A nonviolent spirituality does not just happen; it is the result of practices that move the human heart to love. The religions of the world suggest similar practices for developing a spirituality of love. It seems to me that there are four elements of a nonviolent lifestyle that are common to those who have lived nonviolently. It would be natural, and is now necessary, to incorporate a relationship with nature into each of these four elements—contemplation, resistance, simplicity, and community.

Contemplation is the first element of a nonviolent lifestyle. God is found in stillness and silence, and God is found in creation. We should seek God in silence and in creation where we will find that God is already present. Then we begin to see that God is present throughout our life, we become aware. Union with God unites us with each other and with creation and opens us to suffering.[22] This seems to be the witness of mystics such as Francis of Assisi and Hildegard of Bingen. One result of our union with God, each other, and creation, is to come together in praise and celebration. In worship we join with nature to praise God. Thus, in the Eucharist we offer bread and wine, fruits of the Earth and work of human hands, to the Creator of all.[23]

To develop a creatiocentric consciousness, it is important to build a relationship with Earth, to befriend nature. This is not easily done in the concrete desert of modern cities or in fast paced, hi-tech lives. It takes a conscious effort to seek out green spaces in cities or to notice the beauty of the seasons. I have English friends who are keen gardeners, hikers, and bird watchers. On walks they not only notice wildflowers but identify them by name and talk about their characteristics. They take delight in seeing an unusual bird. Having a genuine relationship with nature; they can call flora and fauna by name.

From a Catholic perspective, my friends have cultivated a sacramental vision. Every creature and all of creation is a sacrament of the love of God that causes all things to be. A sacramental vision reverences creation and recognizes other creatures as companions with unearned, intrinsic value because they have been created by God.[24] Some of the psalms (for example, Pss 96, 97, 98, and 104) seem to be born of a sacramental vision, for they praise and thank God for the wonder of creation and portray the whole Earth community singing the praise of God who does justice.[25]

Contemplation does not lead to inertia or indifference. On the contrary, genuine contemplation inevitably leads to *service* and *resistance*.[26] It bears fruit in the corporal works of mercy: feeding the hungry, giving drink to the thirsty, sheltering the homeless, clothing the naked, welcoming the stranger, freeing the prisoner, and caring for the sick (Mt 25:31-46). To these traditional corporal works of mercy we can legitimately add, for example, cleaning the local stream, recycling our waste, and tending to wounded animals. From the perspective of a creatiocentric consciousness, endangered species, for example, are clearly among "the least of these" today.[27] Direct, hands-on service to the poor and to nature is an essential dimension of a nonviolent spirituality.

Action on behalf of the wounded in the Earth community, however, has to go beyond charity, beyond direct service; it should also include work for justice, that is, *advocacy and resistance*. Our relationships with creation are not only personal, but also communal, social, economic, political, structural. The social structures we establish can either promote the flourishing of creation, or they can be obstacles to it. Those committed to nonviolence must resist social structures that harm people and nature, and build social structures that enable all of creation to flourish. Social structures and ecological systems are complicated. Thus this work for justice and for community is ambiguous and controversial. It requires humility, solidarity, wisdom, prudence, and courage. It tackles poverty and oppression, pollution and habitat destruction using the strategies of nonviolent resistance. There are a number of organizations already dedicated to protecting nature and advocating for social structures that will allow the whole Earth community to flourish. This work for justice in the Earth community is the foundation for peace on Earth.

Creative simplicity of life is the third ingredient in a nonviolent spirituality. The Christian tradition has sometimes referred to this as gospel poverty. Francis, for example, not only embraced the poor, he became one of them by choice. Francis sought Lady Poverty with the passion of a lover. He pursued downward mobility. Francis discovered that once we realize that we and all of creation are utterly dependent on God, we can let go not only of things and security but also of self. Paradoxically, it is downward mobility or de-class-ification that results in joy.[28]

There are a variety of creative ways to embrace simplicity of life.[29] In a tight-fisted, bottom line, consumerist culture it means striving to live an open-handed, open-hearted, generous life. Simplicity of life expresses solidarity with the poor and makes a just economic order more possible. A simple lifestyle also expresses friendship with the Earth and fellow creatures, and it slows the depletion of natural resources and decreases the rate of pollution. Simplicity of life is a necessary step in resisting both poverty and pollution, in working for justice and fitting in to the web of life.

Finally, *community* is both the goal and the source of a nonviolent spirituality. The practice of nonviolence seeks reconciliation, which is dependent on repentance of wrongs done and on forgiveness. When our enemies become our friends they are enveloped in an enlarged community. Ultimately the whole of humanity is one family. Community is the goal of nonviolence. It is also the way to nonviolence. Jesus gathered disciples, Francis attracted what became the Friars Minor, Gandhi lived in an ashram. There are many ways to join with others, but a nonviolent lifestyle, and indeed Christian discipleship, require us to join with others to foster an emptying of self and a commitment to the common good.

A contemporary nonviolent spirituality will include the whole Earth community in its vision and practice. This is so because humans cannot flourish on a sick planet, but more so because it is the truth—we are in relationship with all of God's creation. Ultimately the unity and health of the whole Earth community is both the goal and the source of a nonviolent spirituality.

This essay has argued that a creatiocentric vision would be a more truthful and effective foundation for the church's environmental ethic than its current anthropocentric position. It has also explored "treating nature nonviolently" as a way to embrace a creatiocentric vision and to put it into practice. If you want peace on Earth, make peace with Earth.

Notes

[1] This essay is based on The Edwards Peacemaking Lecture, given on October 21, 2010 at Louisville Presbyterian Theological Seminary. I wish to thank the two anonymous reviewers and the editors of this volume for their helpful questions and suggestions.

[2] John Paul II, World Day of Peace Message, "The Ecological Crisis: A Common Responsibility" (1990); Benedict XVI, World Day of Peace Message, "If You Want to Cultivate Peace, Protect Creation" (2010). Vatican documents can be found on the Vatican web site, www.vatican.va.

[3] For example, *The Prophetic Call: Celebrating Community, Earth, Justice and Peace*, ed. Hugh Sanborn (St. Louis, MO: Chalice Press, 2004) has four sections on the themes in the book's subtitle, each with three chapters. Although direct connections are made between the other sections, none are made between Earth (environment or ecology) and peace.

[4] See Woodeene Koenig-Bricker, *Ten Commandments for the Environment: Pope Benedict XVI Speaks Out for Creation and Justice* (Notre Dame, IN: Ave Maria Press, 2009); and Catherine Pepinster, "The Green Pope," *The Tablet* (September 4, 2010): 10-11.

[5] J. Milburn Thompson, *Introducing Catholic Social Thought* (Maryknoll, NY: Orbis Books, 2010), 156-63 serves as a general outline for this section.

[6] The latter is the argument of Lynn White, Jr., "The Historical Roots of Our Ecologic Crisis," *Science* 155 (March 10, 1967): 1203-7.

[7] David P. Gushee develops the connection between the sanctity of life and the sacredness of all creation in "The Sacredness of God's Creation,"

Perspectives in Religious Studies 36 (Summer 2009): 187-97.

[8]"If You Want to Cultivate Peace, Protect Creation," 9. See also 5 and 11. See also John Paul II, "The Ecological Crisis," 13.

[9]See Christine Firer Hinze, "Catholic Social Teaching and Ecological Ethics," in *And God Saw That It Was Good*, ed. Drew Christiansen and Walter Grazer (Washington, DC: USCCB, 1996), 169.

[10]John Hart, *Sacramental Commons: Christian Ecological Ethics* (Lanham, MD: Rowman and Littlefield, 2006), 17-18, 117-21.

[11]Michael J. Himes and Kenneth R. Himes, *Fullness of Faith: the Public Significance of Theology* (New York: Paulist Press, 1993), 104-24; Dawn M. Nothwehr, "From Ontology, Ecology, and Normativity to Mutuality: The Attitude and Principle Grounding the Ethic of Life," in *The Consistent Ethic of Life*, ed. Thomas Nairn (Maryknoll, NY: Orbis Books, 2008), 132-51; and Thomas Finger, "An Anabaptist/Mennonite Theology of Creation," in *Creation and Environment: An Anabaptist Perspective on a Sustainable World*, ed. Calvin Redekop (Baltimore, MD: The Johns Hopkins University Press, 2000), 154-69, at 158-64. Hinze ("Catholic Social Teaching and Ecological Ethics," 172-73) suggests that Thomas Aquinas might be another source of this relational environmental ethic.

[12]Leonardo Boff, *Saint Francis: A Model for Human Liberation*, trans. John W. Dierckmeier (New York: Crossroad, 1982), 34-47.

[13]Two religious groups that have also developed a nonviolent environmental ethic are the Mennonites (Anabaptist) and the Jains. In "Toward a Mennonite Theology and Ethic of Creation," *The Mennonite Quarterly Review* 60 (July 1986): 387-403, at 400-2, Calvin Redekop, a Mennonite theologian, uses "shalom" as a metaphor for a constructive environmental ethics. Shalom, as practiced by Jesus, includes love of neighbor and care of creation, entailing conservation and protection of nature. See also Calvin Redekop, ed., *Creation and Environment*. On the basis of a more pantheistic theology, the Jains hold *ahimsa*, non-injury or nonviolence, as a basic principle for life, and they strive to apply *ahimsa* to all of life. See Christopher Key Chapple, ed., *Jainism and Ecology: Nonviolence in the Web of Life* (Cambridge: Harvard University Press, 2002); Vincent Sekhar, "Significance of Jain Philosophy for Preserving Life and Environment," *Journal of Dharma* 26 (January-March 2001): 47-59; and Michael Tobias, "Jainism and Ecology: Views of Nature, Nonviolence, and Vegetarianism," in *Worldview and Ecology*, ed. Mary Evelyn Tucker and John A. Grim (Maryknoll, NY: Orbis Books, 1994), 138-49.

[14]"The central insight of ecofeminism is that a historical, symbolic, and political relationship exists between the denigration of nature and the female in Western cultures" (Charlene Spretnak, "Critical and Constructive Contributions of Ecofeminism," in *Worldviews and Ecology*, ed. Tucker and Grim, 181-89, at 181).

[15]See James H. Cone, "Whose Earth Is It, Anyway," in *Earth Habitat: Eco-Justice and the Church's Response*, ed. Dieter Hessel and Larry Rasmussen (Minneapolis, MN: Fortress Press, 2001), 23-32.

[16]See James M. Harder and Karen Klassen Harder, "Economics, Development, and Creation," in *Creation and Environment: An Anabaptist Perspec-*

tive on a Sustainable World, ed. Calvin Redekop (Baltimore, MD: The Johns Hopkins University Press, 2000), 3-26; and Kenton K. Brubaker, "Science, Technology, and Creation," in *Creation and Environment: An Anabaptist Perspective on a Sustainable World*, ed. Calvin Redekop (Baltimore, MD: The Johns Hopkins University Press, 2000), 37-38; and Himes and Himes, *Fullness of Faith*, 118-24.

[17]See White, "The Historical Roots of Our Ecologic Crisis," 1203-7; and Boff, *Saint Francis*, 38-41.

[18]For a systematic, ecological theology see Denis Edwards, *Ecology at the Heart of Faith* (Maryknoll, NY: Orbis Books, 2006).

[19]Martin Luther King, Jr., *Stride Toward Freedom: The Montgomery Story* (New York: Harper and Row, 1958), 83-88. King includes a sixth conviction, that "the universe is on the side of justice." I have incorporated this in the foundational values of a theology of nonviolence.

[20]See Martin Luther King, Jr., *Strength to Love* (New York: Harper and Row, 1963), 40.

[21]Ibid., 67-77.

[22]Martin Laird, *Into the Silent Land: A Guide to the Christian Practice of Contemplation* (New York: Oxford University Press, 2006), 7-18.

[23]Denis Edwards, "Eucharist and Ecology: Keeping Memorial of Creation," *Worship* 82 (May 2008): 194-213.

[24]Himes and Himes, *Fullness of Faith*, 112-14.

[25]Walter Klassen, "Pacifism, Nonviolence, and the Peaceful Reign of God," in *Creation and Environment: An Anabaptist Perspective on a Sustainable World*, ed. Calvin Redekop (Baltimore, MD: The Johns Hopkins University Press, 2000), 139-53, at 152-53.

[26]James W. Douglass, *Resistance and Contemplation: The Way of Liberation* (New York: Dell Publishing Co., 1972).

[27]Klassen, "Pacifism, Nonviolence and the Peaceful Reign of God," 153; and Finger, "An Anabaptist/Mennonite Theology of Creation," 157.

[28]Boff, *Saint Francis*, 38-40, 64-80.

[29]See J. Milburn Thompson, *Justice and Peace: A Christian Primer* (Maryknoll, NY: Orbis Books, 2003), 206-12.

List of Contributors

Kevin J. Ahern, a doctoral candidate in theological ethics at Boston College, is concerned with the theological significance of Catholic NGOs. From 2003 to 2007 he served as the president of International Movement of Catholic Students-Pax Romana. In 2008, he published *The Radical Bible* with Orbis Books and has served as an adjunct professor at Blessed John XXIII National Seminary.

William T. Cavanaugh is Senior Research Professor at the Center for World Catholicism and Intercultural Theology at DePaul University. He is co-editor of *Modern Theology* and the author of five books, most recently *The Myth of Religious Violence* (Oxford, 2009) and *Migrations of the Holy* (Eerdmans, 2011).

William A. Clark, S.J., is an associate professor of religious studies at the College of the Holy Cross, Worcester, Massachusetts, where he teaches courses in Catholic life and doctrine, Christian prayer and spirituality, and local church community. He is the author of *A Voice of Their Own: The Authority of the Local Parish* (Liturgical Press, 2005).

M. Shawn Copeland, a former president of the Catholic Theological Society of America, is a professor of theology at Boston College. She also teaches systematic theology at the Institute for Black Catholic Studies at Xavier University in New Orleans. Her recent publications include *Enfleshing Freedom: Body, Race, and Being* (Fortress Press, 2010), and *Uncommon Faithfulness: The Black Catholic Experience* (Orbis, 2009), co-edited by LaReine-Marie Mosely and Albert J. Raboteau.

Elizabeth O'Donnell Gandolfo is a Ph.D. candidate in theological studies at Emory University, with a concentration in religious practices and practical theology. She holds a Masters' of Theological Studies from the University of Notre Dame. In her dissertation, she constructs a feminist practical theology of suffering and grace starting from maternal experiences of vulnerability and resilience.

Daniel P. Horan, OFM, a Franciscan friar of Holy Name Province, was a lecturer in the Department of Religious Studies at Siena College (New York) and currently serves on the Board of Directors of the International Thomas Merton Society. Some of his recent publications include "A Franciscan Millennial and the Memory of 9/11" (*Franciscan Voices on 9/11*, 2011); "How Original Was Scotus on the Incarnation? Reconsidering the History of the Absolute Predestination of Christ in Light of Robert Grosseteste" (*Heythrop Journal*, 2011); and the forthcoming book *Dating God: Franciscan Spirituality for the Next Generation* (2012).

John V. Kruse is a historical theologian with expertise in Franciscan spirituality and the office of the papacy. Dr. Kruse, a resident of Wilmington, Delaware, is an associate professor of theology at Neumann University in Aston, Pennsylvania. His publications include "The Changing Role of Hugolino dei Conti di Segni (Gregory IX): A Hermeneutical Tool for Understanding the Lives of Francis" (*Miscellanea Francescana*, 2008) and "Apostolic Visitations: Clare of Assisi's Insights from the Thirteenth Century" (*Review for Religious*, 2011).

James Logan was born in Harlem and raised in the South Bronx. He is an associate professor of religion and an associate professor and director of African and African American studies at Earlham College. Logan's current publications include "Liberalism, Race, and Stanley Hauerwas" (*CrossCurrents*, Winter 2006); *Good Punishment? Christian Moral Practice and U.S. Imprisonment* (2008); *Ethics That Matters: African, Caribbean, and African American Sources*, co-edited with Marcia Riggs

(Fall 2011); and "Immanuel Kant on Categorical Imperative," in *Beyond the Pale: Reading Christian Ethics From the Margins*, ed. Miguel De La Torre and Stacey Floyd-Thomas (Westminster John Knox, 2011). Logan's current manuscript in process is tentatively titled *The Limits of Perfection: Race, Nonviolence and Peace Church Assimilation into the American Social Order.*

Scott MacDougall received his Master of Arts in theology from the General Theological Seminary of the Episcopal Church in 2007. He is now a Ph.D. candidate and teaching fellow in the Department of Theology at Fordham University, where he is writing a dissertation on eschatological ecclesiology.

Gael Mooney, a painter who writes and lectures on the relationship between art and spirituality, is an adjunct professor of theological aesthetics at Dominican University in Illinois.

Margaret R. Pfeil is an assistant professor of moral theology at the University of Notre Dame and a faculty fellow of the Kroc Institute for International Peace Studies. Her research interests include Catholic social thought, racial justice, ecological ethics, and peace studies. With Gerald Schlabach, she is co-editor of *Sharing Peace: Mennonites and Catholics in Conversation* (forthcoming, Liturgical Press, 2012), and with Laurie Cassidy and Alex Mikulich she is co-author of *The Scandal of White Complicity in U.S. Hyper-incarceration: A Nonviolent Spirituality of White Resistance* (forthcoming, Palgrave, 2012). She is a founder and resident of the St. Peter Claver Catholic Worker Community in South Bend, Indiana.

Brian D. Robinette is an associate professor in the Department of Theological Studies at Saint Louis University. He teaches and researches in philosophical and systematic theology and is the author of *Grammars of Resurrection: A Christian Theology of Presence and Absence* (Crossroad/Herder, 2009). He is currently working in the area of theological anthropology with interdisciplinary interests in Christian ascetical and contemplative traditions.

Daniel P. Scheid is an assistant professor of theology at Duquesne University in Pittsburgh. His publications include "Expanding Catholic Ecological Ethics: Ecological Solidarity and Earth Rights," in *Religion, Economics, and Culture in Conflict and Conversation*; and "St. Thomas Aquinas and the Thomistic Tradition," in *Green Discipleship: Catholic Theological Ethics & the Environment*. His research interests are in ecological and comparative ethics.

J. Milburn Thompson is chair and professor of theology at Bellarmine University in Louisville. He is the author of *Introducing Catholic Social Thought* (Orbis Books, 2010) and *Justice and Peace: A Christian Primer* (Orbis Books, rev. ed., 2003).

Elisabeth T. Vasko is an assistant professor of theology at Duquesne University in Pittsburgh. Her research and teaching interests include christology, soteriology, theological anthropology, and feminist liberation theologies. Her present work analyzes the way in which theological constructions of sin and redemption frame attention to suffering in the context of gender-based violence.

Todd David Whitmore is an associate professor in the Department of Theology and faculty fellow at the Joan B. Kroc Institute for International Peace Studies at the University of Notre Dame. He has been doing fieldwork in northern Uganda and South Sudan since 2005. He is also co-founder and president of PeaceHarvest, a non-profit that combines agricultural training and peacebuilding in the region.

Tobias L. Winright is an associate professor of theological ethics at Saint Louis University. His research interests include just war theory, issues in criminal justice, nonviolence, and ecological theology. His recent publications include, with co-author Mark J. Allman, *After the Smoke Clears: The Just War Tradition & Post War Justice* (Orbis, 2010) and the edited volume *Green Discipleship: Catholic Theological Ethics and the Environment* (Anselm Academic, 2011).